SMITHSONIAN ANNALS OF FLIGHT · NUMBER 8

Wiley Post, His *Winnie Mae,* and the World's First Pressure Suit

Stanley R. Mohler
and
Bobby H. Johnson

SMITHSONIAN INSTITUTION PRESS
City of Washington
1971

SERIAL PUBLICATIONS OF THE SMITHSONIAN INSTITUTION

The emphasis upon publications as a means of diffusing knowledge was expressed by the first Secretary of the Smithsonian Institution. In his formal plan for the Institution, Joseph Henry articulated a program that included the following statement: "It is proposed to publish a series of reports, giving an account of the new discoveries in science, and of the changes made from year to year in all branches of knowledge." This keynote of basic research has been adhered to over the years in the issuance of thousands of titles in serial publications under the Smithsonian imprint, commencing with *Smithsonian Contributions to Knowledge* in 1848 and continuing with the following active series:

> *Smithsonian Annals of Flight*
> *Smithsonian Contributions to Anthropology*
> *Smithsonian Contributions to Astrophysics*
> *Smithsonian Contributions to Botany*
> *Smithsonian Contributions to the Earth Sciences*
> *Smithsonian Contributions to Paleobiology*
> *Smithsonian Contributions to Zoology*
> *Smithsonian Studies in History and Technology*

In these series, the Institution publishes original articles and monographs dealing with the research and collections of its several museums and offices and of professional colleagues at other institutions of learning. These papers report newly acquired facts, synoptic interpretations of data, or original theory in specialized fields. These publications are distributed by mailing lists to libraries, laboratories, and other interested institutions and specialists throughout the world. Individual copies may be obtained from the Smithsonian Institution Press as long as stocks are available.

S. DILLON RIPLEY
Secretary
Smithsonian Institution

Official publication date is handstamped in a limited number of initial copies and is recorded in the Institution's annual report, Smithsonian Year.

UNITED STATES GOVERNMENT PRINTING OFFICE
WASHINGTON : 1971

For sale by the Superintendent of Documents, U.S. Government Printing Office
Washington, D.C. 20402 - Price $1.50 (paper cover)
STOCK NUMBER 4705-0008

Foreword

Many rewarding and some unrewarding experiences evolve from being the brother of a world-renowned figure. All close relations are extremely proud of the accomplishments and contributions of near and dear kin. Yet, none desire to bask in reflected glory.

Wiley Post, in a short span of seven years, rose from a laborer in the Oklahoma oil fields to a person of world prominence. He was acclaimed world hero by presidents, the man on the street, and all who knew of his daring achievements in the field of aeronautical science.

Wiley was a barnstormer, speed flier, test pilot, globe conqueror, and a pioneer of pressurized flight. He was some twenty years ahead of the field in his thinking with regard to advancement of aviation. He envisioned the development of air transportation far beyond any dream of his contemporaries.

At an early age he flew into eternity, accompanied by a close friend—a man known throughout the world as a great humanitarian, the sage of Oklahoma, world citizen, one who had humble regard for the well-being of his fellow man—Will Rogers.

It is difficult for me to think of Wiley as a researcher, a pioneer in a field of science, explorer in the realm of space. Rather, I remember him best as a companion on hot summer nights when we fished and slept on the banks of the Washita; during the golden-leafed autumn days when we stalked the white-tailed deer in the Big Bend Country of Texas; and on the windy wintry days when we hunted ducks on Lake Kickapoo. This is the way I best remember him, for he was my brother.

GORDON POST

Statement of Appreciation

The authors extend appreciation to all of the persons referenced in the book who granted time, documents, and photographs to the accomplishment of this undertaking. Especially helpful were the immediate family of Post and his close friends. Among these were Mae Post, Gordon Post, Winnie Mae Fain, Will D. Parker, L. E. Gray, Carl Squier, George Brauer, J. Bart Scott, Jimmy Gerschler, Fay Gillis Wells, Ernest Shults, and Edwin O. Cooper. The authors also would like to recognize the many pilots and technical personnel from the era of the 1930s who provided comments and information on the flight environment and equipment of that period. Also, they recognize Mr. Herbert Brawley, who expertly drew the various figures. Special appreciation is given to the four typists who successively typed and edited eight consecutive emerging draft manuscripts during the ten years required to prepare the final manuscript. They are Aline "Corky" Koch, Adele C. Donovan, Sharon B. Morley, and Marian E. Davis. In addition, essential suggestions and technical editing were received from Dr. Richard K. Smith, Louis S. Casey, and David H. Scott. Also, appreciation is given to Mrs. Mary Frances Bell who provided editorial assistance and Boris N. Mandrovsky who assisted with certain Russian translations.

Introduction

He won the top awards in aviation. He was honored by two New York City ticker-tape parades and was given the keys to the city. He was received twice at the White House: by President Herbert Hoover in 1931 and by President Franklin D. Roosevelt in 1933. He became a recognized master aviator, noted for his flight conquests of time, distance, and altitude. These later achievements occurred primarily within a span of only five years, 1930–1935.

This narrative provides the story of Wiley Post, his beloved Lockheed Vega, the *Winnie Mae,* and his pressure suit, which was the world's first, practical flight-pressure suit. It also includes Post's studies of biological rhythms in relationship to flight, which were the world's first such studies, his discovery of the jet stream, and his other experiments. All known details of the rich and exciting life of Post cannot be presented. We have selected pertinent points from those we know, but many, of course, are unknown.

By mid-1935, Post had flown longer at ground speeds of 300 miles per hour than any other man and had more flight hours in the stratosphere than any other airplane pilot.

Let us journey through the exciting life of this most unusual individual, whose indomitable spirit and faith in tomorrow should inspire all who come to know him.

THE AUTHORS

The Golden Age of aviation produced a number of famous pilots and aircraft. None were better known than Wiley Post and his Lockheed Vega, the *Winnie Mae*.

The authors of this Annals of Flight monograph tell the story of the man and the machine as few persons could, for they have access to documents and the cooperation of persons most closely connected with this inseparable man-machine team.

The *Winnie Mae,* one of the historic specimens in the collection of the National Air and Space Museum, is a prime example of the most efficient aircraft of its day. It set the fashion and the pace influencing the design of later and larger transport aircraft.

This monograph, the result of several years' research and writing by Stanley R. Mohler, M.D., and Bobby H. Johnson, Ph.D., documents for the Smithsonian's National Air and Space Museum, Annals of Flight series, the historical, technical, and biographical details of this world-famous aviator and his airplane.

LOUIS S. CASEY, Curator
Assistant Director
Aeronautics
National Air and Space Museum

Contents

		Page
FOREWORD		iii
INTRODUCTION		v
CHAPTERS:		
1 /	Oklahoma Prologue	1
2 /	Globe Girdling with Gatty, 1931	17
3 /	Epic Solo Flight, 1933	39
4 /	The First Practical Pressure Suit	71
5 /	Stratosphere Flights, 1934–35	91
6 /	Point Barrow	107
APPENDIX:		
Post's Pilot Records		124
Post's Three Airplanes		124
Diagrams of the *Winnie Mae*		126

1 / Oklahoma Prologue

A COVERED WAGON crept across the treacherous Red River sand that separated Oklahoma from Texas. William Francis Post was coming back to Texas in the summer heat of 1898 after several hard months of itinerant farming in Oklahoma. With him were his pregnant wife Mae Quinlan and his young boys James, Arthur, and Joseph, oldest to youngest. In the hot summer air, William Post stopped at the Hardeman farm near Denison, Texas, where he took work for the rest of the summer, camping in the Hardeman's front yard.

At summer's end, the Post family proceeded slowly across the Texas prairie to their quarter-section (160-acre) farm near Grand Saline in Van Zandt County, 65 miles east of Dallas. Here Mae Quinlan delivered her fourth son in the modest farmhouse on November 22, 1898. The Posts named their new son Wiley Hardeman Post, his middle name a respectful remembrance of the elder Hardeman.[1]

In 1902, the year that the Wright brothers fully mastered the flight control of gliders, the Post family moved to another farm a few miles north of Abilene in central Texas. This was a one-half section of land that the elder Post purchased from a man who was heading north to Oklahoma to search for oil. After farming various areas around Abilene for five years, the family went to southwestern Oklahoma and settled six miles west of Rush Springs. In 1910, William Post again moved his family, this time four miles south to the community of Burns. Family members report that during this period Wiley began to dislike farm work and that he became more and more restless and dissatisfied with life on the soil.

Wiley never did take to farming. His oldest brother, James, tells that Wiley often hitched the mules on the wrong side, a circumstance very irritating to the mules. James also noted that school did not interest

Stanley R. Mohler, M.D., is Chief, Aeromedical Applications Division, Office of Aviation Medicine, Federal Aviation Administration, Department of Transportation, Washington, D.C. He formerly was Director of the Civil Aeromedical Research Institute, Oklahoma City, Oklahoma. He also holds an Airline Transport Pilot Rating.

Dr. Bobby H. Johnson holds a Ph.D. in history, and is an assistant professor at the Stephen F. Austin University, Nacogdoches, Texas.

Wiley. Reports on his early life indicate that Wiley had developed an intense dislike for school from the very beginning. His childhood schoolmate, now Mrs. G. R. Ingram of Rush Springs, reports that Wiley was considerably more interested in playing than learning; "He was a lively, talkative and mischievous boy," she recalls. Wiley, himself, stated that he had completely lost interest in school by the age of eleven. About the only things Wiley really liked were mechanical devices, and during this period, he developed some local recognition as a youth who was handy at repairing machinery.

Then in 1913, one of those pivotal events in a personal life occurred: Wiley saw an airplane for the first time. He and James had gone to a county fair at Lawton, Oklahoma, where they saw a Curtiss Pusher flown by Art Smith, the early exhibition pilot who was a contemporary in fame to the great Lincoln Beachey. Smith spun, looped, made steep vertical dives and tight spirals; he attached roman candles to the aircraft and performed night aerobatics, which was the first such dramatic pyrotechnic display.[2] Post immediately decided that he would become a pilot. There is documented evidence that the young Post intuitively began to sense that he might be destined to do something significant in aviation. He wrote that even on his way home from the county fair on this day in 1913 he began to dream of "The Wiley Post Institute for Aeronautical Research."[3] Post also saw his first automobile at the fair and contrived to get a ride part way home in it.

Three years later, farm life became so distasteful for Wiley that he left home. The practical facts of the external world, however, sent Wiley back to the farm. He needed money. His father promised him the returns for working a ten-acre cotton field, so Wiley remained home for one year and made one crop. With his cotton money, he went to Kansas City and took a seven-month course at the Sweeney Auto School. Later, when James asked him if he intended to become an automobile mechanic, Wiley told his brother that he was going to use motors—not work on them.[4] This training gave Post a basic understanding of reciprocating engines that would prove invaluable to his future flying activities.

Figure 1.—William and Mae Post, expecting their four child, proceeded in the summer of 1898 by covered wagon (similar to the one illustrated) from Oklahoma across the Red River into Texas. Wiley Post was born November 22, 1898, on a farm near Grand Saline, Texas (65 miles east of Dallas). (Courtesy Oklahoma Historical Society.)

Following the entrance of the United States into World War I in April 1917, Wiley began to spend many hours of his days around the military airfield at Fort Sill near Lawton, hoping to find a way into flight training. The airport is known as Post Field, named after Lieutenant Henry B. Post, who was no relation to Wiley.[5] Meanwhile, Wiley was working at the airfield with the Chickasha and Lawton Construction Company.

Wiley's three older brothers joined the Army at Lawton, and he decided to enroll in the Students Army Training Corps at Norman, Oklahoma.[6] He studied radio in Section B of the Radio School, which provided him with a basic training in electrical communications that later proved very useful in the years ahead. In the European skies, meanwhile, pilots were demonstrating the capabilities of aircraft, and a thriving U.S. aviation industry was laying the basis for a post-war civil fleet of surplus aircraft. Section A of the Radio School was sent to Europe, but the war ended before Post's group completed its course. Shortly after the Armistice his Section B was disbanded and demobilized back into civil life.

In 1918, the elder Post bought a farm near Alex, a few miles each of Chickasha, but Wiley did not return to the farm; the Army had spoiled him for that. Immediately after the Armistice, he found a job as a "roughneck" in the oil fields near Walters, Oklahoma. This was Wiley's first association with the oil industry and he found it a good means of income. Nonetheless, Wiley's deep yearning to get into aviation continued unabated. In the summer of 1919, he paid twenty-five dollars to Captain Earl H. Zimmerman, a barnstorming pilot visiting Walters, for a flight in an open-cockpit biplane.[7]

Wiley asked if he could experience every maneuver that Zimmerman knew. During Zimmerman's acrobatics, Wiley did not feel the exhilaration he had hoped for; he subsequently remarked that with this flight he realized that pilots did not have "supernatural powers." This letdown was a major disappointment to him.

In 1920, William F. Post obtained a farm just north of Maysville, a town 45 miles south of Oklahoma City, and the family moved again. Wiley remained very restless but his own information of this period, as told in his book, *Around the World in Eight Days*, is very sketchy. During this unhappy period, Post deepened his commitment to a lifetime career in aviation.

In the fall of 1922, Wiley returned to the oil fields and worked near Wewoka, where oil had been discovered. The area around Wewoka, Holdenville, and Seminole began to throb with the excitement. The economically booming atmosphere of easy come, easy go was an ideal situation for barnstormers. Flying World War I biplanes, they began to arrive on weekends and to entertain oil-field workers with aerobatic maneuvers, parachute jumps, and "penny per pound" hops.

While working near Holdenville in the spring of 1924, Wiley noted that a flying circus was to appear ten miles away at Wewoka; Burrell Tibbs was bringing his "Texas Topnotch Fliers" to town. Wiley went to Wewoka and met several members of the crew, and when he learned that Pete Lewis, the group's regular parachute jumper, had been injured in a recent exhibition, he offered to jump in Lewis's place. Many times the "local yokels," as Tibbs called them, would agree to jump, only to refuse to leave the plane once it was airborne. Wiley persisted, however, and Tibbs agreed to give him the opportunity.

A Hardin exhibition parachute was used. It was packed in a bag that was tied to the strut of the right wing. Lewis showed Wiley how to don the harness and Wiley climbed into the Curtiss JN-4 with Tibbs. When they had reached a height of about 2,000 feet, Tibbs gave Wiley the ready signal and cut the throttle to diminish the propeller blast. Wiley climbed out of the front cockpit onto the wing, holding the struts tightly, and buckled the harness to the rings of the chute. "He then jumped as though he had done it all his life," Tibbs later reported.[8] The shroud lines of the parachute were fastened to an automobile steering wheel, which the chutist could hold. The wheel was supposed to help steer the descent, but it really didn't work very well. The people below looked like "so many ants" on "brown and green carpets," Wiley reported, adding that the jump gave him "one of the biggest thrills of my life."[9]

Wiley was subsequently given a job with the flying circus. He was assigned to the group's second plane, a Jenny piloted by a young pilot named "Tip" Schier. The airplanes fascinated Wiley, and he picked up snatches of flight instruction while the circus traveled from town to town. Eventually, Wiley decided that he could make more money jumping on his own. Enthusiastic boosters in various towns paid well for a

FIGURE 2.—Little Wiley Post (uncomfortably provided with a dress) and his older brothers, Joe, Arthur, and James (left to right), stand before a suspended rug on the grass outside of the Post farm, Grand Saline, Texas, in the summer of 1900. Their panting dog and their bare feet give testimony to the summer heat. (Courtesy Gordon Post.)

weekend exhibition. By arranging his own appearances, Wiley made as much as $200 a jump—a sizable figure considering the fact that he seldom paid more than $25 to hire a plane and pilot.

On one occasion, Wiley booked a jump over his hometown of Maysville. W. J. Showen, Editor of the *Maysville News*, had undertaken to promote the project as a means of creating community spirit. Because Wileys' parents lived at Maysville, the event was particularly interesting to the town. Just before the jump was to take place, Wiley discovered that his parachute, which had been left at his parents' farm home, was not where he left it. He searched frantically but could not find the chute. He then learned that his father did not like the idea of the jump and had hidden the parachute. Wiley never found it. He jumped the following week, from an OX Standard biplane flown by Virgil Turnbull of Pauls Valley, but used a borrowed parachute.

Wiley made 99 jumps in two years, and he was convinced that he would find a future in aviation. "I was studying crowd psychology—my desire to thwart the spectators' hope of witnessing my untimely end was so strong that I grew so reckless as to scare myself."[10] Wiley began doing delayed openings and jumps with two parachutes.

During this period of jumping, Wiley received some flight training from a man named Sam Bartel and in 1926 made his first solo in Bartel's Canuck, a Curtiss JN-4 Jenny built in Canada.[11] The airplane was worth $150 and Wiley had to provide a security of $200 prior to solo. He admitted later that he was not really ready to solo, and almost lost control two or three times during the flight. Following his 1926 solo, Wiley wanted an airplane of his own, so he returned to the lucrative oil fields. He needed his own plane so that he could build the necessary flight experience to get into commercial aviation.

Wiley was directing work on a drilling rig near Seminole on October 1, 1926, when an iron chip flew from a bolt struck by a roughneck's sledgehammer. The chip lodged in Wiley's left eye. When his physician observed that the left eye had become infected and the infection appeared to be affecting the other eye (this is called sympathetic ophthalmia), the left eye had to be removed.[12]

The loss of the eye was a severe blow to the young Oklahoman's dream of becoming a flier. Wiley was an ex-farm boy and laborer, nearly 28 years of age, with only an eighth-grade formal education. He had never traveled beyond the Midwest and had neither the benefit of military flight training nor formal civil flight training. Now he had only one eye. For Post, however, three factors were working: (1) his inherent genius for aeronautics, (2) his compelling urge to get into aviation, and (3) his steel-willed determination to accomplish an established objective.

Through the stressful and depressing days of treatment and convalescence, Wiley could easily have been tempted to sink into self-pity and overpowering depression. He could have let his handicap shatter the dream of a career in aviation. However, the spirit of a champion began to work within Wiley. He spent two months recuperating at the home of an uncle in the Davis Mountains in southwest Texas, where, by estimating the distance to a given object, often a tree, and then pacing off the distance to determine the accuracy of the estimate, Wiley trained the vision of his right eye.[13]

In spite of the temporary blow to his aviation dreams, Wiley managed to capitalize on the loss of the eye. Records of the Oklahoma State Industrial Court reveal that he was awarded $1,800 in workmen's compensation on October 30, 1926, and that he was given a lump sum of $1,698.25.[14] In the spring of 1927, he used part of the money to buy a damaged Canuck and had it repaired by Art Oakley at Ardmore. Wiley paid $200 for the plane and spent $340 on repairs. In effect, fate enabled Post to trade his left eye for an airplane. During this period, Post became acquainted with Luther E. Gray, a young red-haired Oklahoman, who became one of his best friends. "Red" Gray also owned a Canuck.[15] Also during this time, Wiley did not need to hold a pilot's license; the newly inaugurated Aeronautics Branch of the U.S. Department of Commerce had not yet begun to implement the airman licensure program. Wiley could legally hop passengers for a fee and even give flight instruction.

In addition to his airplane, Wiley had another major interest in the spring of 1927. Miss Mae Laine, a lovely girl from Sweetwater, Texas, was competing with the Canuck for Wiley's attentions. Wiley met Mae while hopping passengers on Sundays at Sweetwater, one of several towns on his barnstorming circuit. Her parents had known the Post family years before at Grand Saline, where Mae was born 11 years after Wiley. Although the pair now lived about 200 miles apart, Wiley's airplane covered the distance quickly by 1927 standards. Mr. and Mrs. Dave Laine, who operated a ranch, discouraged any thought of marriage, stating that at 17 Mae was too young to know for certain that it was Wiley whom she really wanted to marry. Her father also had some reservations about Wiley's vocational intentions and capabilities. In 1927, a career in aviation still appeared to most persons as similar to that of a juggler or

FIGURE 3.—Wiley Post patiently tolerates his little sister, Mary, at their Abilene, Texas, farm in 1902. Mary, somewhat petulant here, has just kicked Wiley's right foot. The willow chair was a popular item of outdoor furniture of the period. (Courtesy Gordon Post.)

acrobat; otherwise it seemed like a quick way to get killed.

Wiley and Mae secretly decided to get married and to use his airplane for travel. On June 27, 1927, Wiley and Mae eloped in the Canuck and headed toward Oklahoma from Sweetwater. Suddenly, the old Canuck's engine failed near Graham, Oklahoma, and Wiley made a forced landing in an open field, where he discovered that the distributor rotor had failed.[16] Wiley had previously put over 800 hours on the Canuck without engine failure. In Oklahoma, unlike Texas and many other states, there was no waiting period for persons deciding to get married, so the stranded couple found a preacher and got married. The first few hours of the "honeymoon" were spent by Wiley repairing the distributor; then they took off, no longer fearful of pursuit.

Wiley continued to barnstorm, but while on a hunting trip in Mexico that autumn, his income was jeopardized when the plane was seriously damaged in a ground roll. He managed to transport the Canuck back to Oakley's shop at Ardmore where it was repaired, but he could not raise the money to pay for the repairs. J. Bart Scott, another flying enthusiast, bought the airplane from Wiley for about $350. Wiley agreed to work for Scott as a barnstormer and instructor and moved with Mae to Purcell, a little town 32 air miles south of Oklahoma City, where Scott had a landing strip.[17]

The next few months were difficult for the young couple. While flying for Scott, Post gave rides at two and one-half dollars for a short flight, and instructed would-be pilots. Wiley's flight pay was $3.00 per hour, but there was no guarantee of an eight-hour day, and with no students, there were no "hours." James Hamilton Conger, a teacher in the Purcell schools, was one of Post's first students. Conger remembers Wiley as a natural pilot, who seemed to be a part of the airplane he piloted. "He didn't just fly an airplane," Conger observed, "he put it on." [18]

Captain Frank Hawks, in his book *Once to Every Pilot*, relates one of Post's barnstorming experiences of the 1927–1928 period. Wiley was flying an old Hispano-Standard in Wyoming and was using a plot of grazing land 6,000 feet above sea level as an airfield. Two ranchers approached and hired Wiley to fly them to Cheyenne, 200 miles away. Wiley tried four times to take off with the ranchers and their baggage. The hot thin noonday air provided inadequate support for his loaded craft at this altitude, because, even on the ground, his airplane was already 6,000 feet "in the air." Needing the money, Post began lightening the load by eliminating baggage, and, ultimately, some gasoline. On the last attempt of the afternoon, he made 100 feet of altitude, but despite a wide-open throttle the plane mushed back to earth within one mile. Wiley then knew that he would have to wait until evening, when the air would cool and increase in density. He successfully delivered his passengers that evening. Wiley was learning firsthand about the atmosphere and about the effects of temperature and altitude on flight performance.[19]

As the winter of 1927 approached, barnstorming became less lucrative and Wiley moved to other work at Duncan. This proved only temporary and he soon found himself job hunting. At this point, the unemployed flier met with good luck when he happened to call on two oilmen from Chickasha, Oklahoma, who were giving serious consideration to utilizing an airplane in their business. Powell Briscoe and F. C. Hall were partners in the oil business, and they had already learned the value of quick transportation in beating their competitors to prospective lease sites. Briscoe had known the Post family years earlier when Briscoe and his brothers operated a store in Marlow. Hall had missed making an oil-leasing deal he wanted because he arrived later than his competitor, and the possibility of obtaining an executive aircraft had a special appeal for him. The two oilmen were planning to buy a new 1928 three-place, open-cockpit Travel

FIGURE 4.—Wiley Post's original flight inspiration, Art Smith (right top), and two assistants, prepare a Curtiss Pusher for an exhibition flight. Post saw Smith perform all types of flight aerobatics at the 1913 Lawton, Oklahoma State Fair, and was immediately enthralled. The aircraft is powered by a Kirkham water-cooled engine. The fuel tank is to the top left and the two stopcocks are in the off position. (Courtesy James R. Greenwood.)

Figure 5.—This is the dynamic Art Smith preparing for an exhibition flight. The early Curtiss Pusher had certain novel control linkage features which differed from other aircraft of that time and from later aircraft. The shoulder straps are fastened to lateral arm supports that pivoted at the seat level. This mechanism was then connected with the ailerons (located between the wings) that were operated by leaning the torso to one side or the other for banking the aircraft. The wheel was connected to the rudder used for yaw. The fore and aft motion of the wheel worked the horizontal tail for pitch up or down. On the wheel yoke was a spark-advance and retard lever and on the wheel was an on-off ignition switch. The engine throttle worked with a foot attachment (for details see *U.S. Naval Institute Proceedings,* July 1971, pages 34–43, article by Thomas Ray). Smith wears corduroy trousers and high buckle shoes. (Courtesy Will D. Parker.)

Air biplane made in Wichita, Kansas, at the time Wiley asked for a flying job. Wiley camped in Hall's outer office for several days, until the oilman finally agreed to see him and to discuss the possibility of a job.[20]

Hall and Briscoe had sponsored some local endurance flights in airplanes made by the Ryan Company of San Diego, which had developed Lindbergh's *Spirit of St. Louis.* Briscoe had retired from the sponsorship of these flights, but Hall's interest continued unabated.

Despite Post's lack of one eye, Briscoe and Hall were favorably impressed with him, and they hired Wiley as their personal pilot at a salary of about $200 a month. At last Wiley Post had found a reasonably steady job in aviation. Briscoe later recalled that Wiley, whose hobby was hunting, bought a high-powered rifle with his first paycheck, even though his personal wardrobe was somewhat on the skimpy side. Wiley also doubled as a chauffeur for Briscoe and as a companion on hunting trips.

Prior to working for Briscoe and Hall, Wiley had flown without a pilot's license from the U.S. Department of Commerce Aeronautics Branch, which had been established in 1926 and had developed pilot-licensing standards. Now that the Civil Airman licensing program was being generally instituted, the one-eyed Wiley feared that he would fail the newly required physical examination, so he often landed in out-of-the-way places to avoid Government Aeronautics Branch inspectors. Because he was piloting a commercial craft, however, it was now mandatory that he obtain an advanced license.

The three types of federal pilot licenses that Post could have sought at this time were (1) private pilot, (2) industrial pilot, and (3) transport pilot. The medical standards for each of these licenses were as follows:

Figure 6.—Wiley Post at age 19, when the family lived in Alex, Oklahoma (near Chickasha). Wiley was enrolled in the Signal Corps Telegraphers school at Norman, Oklahoma, 1918. (Courtesy Gordon Post.)

FIGURE 7.—Young Wiley Post, less than two years after losing his left eye (Oklahoma oil field accident on October 1, 1926), was a barnstorming pilot with Burrell Tibbs' "Texas Top-notch Fliers." Post, fifth from left, is shown with (left to right) Jay Sadowsky, Burrell Tibbs, colleague French, Harold Parker, colleague Best, and Pete "Slim" Lewis. Lewis taught Post how to parachute in 1924. Post had soloed a Canuck in 1926, prior to losing his left eye. The photograph appeared in the *Daily Oklahoman*, January 30, 1927, volume 35, number 20, section 13. Five months later, Post eloped with Mae Laine of Sweetwater, Texas, in a Curtiss Canuck on June 27, 1927. (Courtesy Daily Oklahoman.)

Section 66 of Chapter 4, "Licensing of Pilots and Aircraft," of the new *U.S. Air Commerce Regulations*, effective December 31, 1926, required:

Private pilots to have an absence of organic disease or defect which would interfere with safe landing of an airplane under conditions of private flying; visual acuity of at least 20/40 in each eye; less than 20/40 may be accepted if the pilot wears a correction in his goggles and has normal judgment of distance; no diplopia (double vision) in any position; normal vision fields and color vision; no organic disease of eye or internal ear.

Industrial pilots were to have an absence of any organic disease or defect which would interfere with the safe handling of an airplane; visual acuity of not less than 20/30 in each eye, although in certain instances less than 20/30 may be accepted if the applicant wears a correction to 20/30 in his goggles and has good judgment of distance without correction; good judgment of distance; no diplopia in any field; normal visual fields and color vision; absence of organic disease of the eye, ear, nose or throat.

Transport pilots were to have a good past history; sound pulmonary, cardiovascular, gastrointestinal, central nervous and genito-urinary systems; freedom from material structural defects or limitations; freedom from diseases of the ductless glands; normal central, peripheral, and color vision, normal judgment of distance; any slight defect of ocular muscle balance; freedom from ocular disease; absence of obstructure or deseased conditions of the ear, nose and throat; no abnormalities of the equilibrium that would interfere with flying.

It was stated that "waivers" in the case of trained and experienced aviators were possible, and that the Secretary of Commerce could grant waivers for physical defects designated as disqualifying by the regulations when in his opinion the experience of the pilot compensated for the defect.

The Aeronautics Branch administered a written test that Wiley passed. He also was required to fly a probationary period of about 700 hours before the Branch would grant him a license. He reached this level of flight time within eight months and received air transport license number 3259 on September 16, 1928.[21]

Wiley's ability at pilotage (the art of flying from one place to another by ground reference) was particularly valuable to his employers. His years in the oil fields, where surveying and mapping activities are so vital, proved very useful; he knew Oklahoma's terrain so well that he seldom had to refer to maps.

"He apparently didn't have a nerve in his body," Briscoe recalls, with regard to Post's piloting demeanor; "when other people were scared, Wiley just grinned."

Once, when he was flying Briscoe and Hall in the Travel Air to Amarillo, Texas, Wiley had an opportunity to demonstrate both courage and skill. A sudden

Figure 8.—The Curtiss "Canuck," Canadian version of the famous Curtiss JN–4 "Jenny" military training airplane of World War I, became a popular barnstorming airplane in the 1920s. The Canuck was typically powered by a Curtiss OX–5 engine of 90 horsepower, which gave the airplane a 60-mile per hour cruising speed with a 45-mile per hour stalling speed. The Canuck had ailerons on both wings, which gave it a more rapid roll rate than the American Jenny. The OX–5 engine was a water-cooled, eight-cylinder engine that consumed nine gallons of fuel per hour. The fuel tank capacity was 20 gallons. (Courtesy Smithsonian Institution.)

Figure 9.—Wiley Post's youngest brother, Gordon, sits in Wiley's Curtiss Canuck (number 1767) in the late summer of 1927. This is the airplane in which Wiley Post and Mae Laine eloped on June 27, 1927, at Sweetwater, Texas. They were forced down by engine failure at Graham, Oklahoma, and got married. The airplane is on a stubbled corn field. The name Post is painted just below, and aft, of the rear cockpit. (Courtesy Mae Post.)

rainstorm near the Texas Panhandle town of Shamrock forced Wiley to look quickly for a place to land. While his passengers grew nervous, Wiley set the plane down in a rough field. The airplane received a broken strut but no one was injured. Later, Wiley made repairs with wire and a two-by-four timber and ferried the plane to an airport.

Meanwhile, a new cabin plane, the Lockheed Vega, became generally available, and one of the new Vegas had proved itself magnificently when Ben Eilson and Hubert Wilkins flew the machine from Point Barrow, Alaska, across the Arctic Circle to Spitzbergen. What is more, Erle Halliburten, Lockheed's Midwest distributor, had given an inspiring demonstration of the Vega's merits in the Ford Reliability Air Tour in the summer of 1928. Halliburten had a difficult time in not selling his demonstrator airplane to several eager buyers. This inspired Allan Loughhead and Norman S. Hall of Lockheed to make a 2,500-mile tour of Texas and Oklahoma in hopes of selling Vegas to wealthy oil men. One of the oilmen they encountered was F. C. Hall, who was weary of the rigors of open-cockpit flying. After a flight in a Vega, Hall was sold on this rugged but comfortable high-speed airplane, and within a few months Wiley found himself ferrying the old Travel Air out to the west coast, where it was turned in on a new Vega, fresh from the Lockheed factory at Burbank, California.

Designed and built by the Lockheed Aircraft Corporation, a division of the Detroit Aircraft Corporation, the Vega was a novel airplane when it appeared in aviation's cluttered world of struts, wires, and fabric-covered frames that prevailed in 1928. The Vega had a smooth but tough hull-like fuselage of carefully finished plywood that provided an aerodynamically clean surface; its wings and tailgroup were all internally braced, and thus dispensed with the struts and wires that were the hallmark of most airplanes of the 1920s; but the cylinders and cylinder heads of its air-cooled radial engine, along with the cylinder's hundreds of cooling fins, were not yet neatly streamlined by the deep cowling developed by the National Advisory Committee of Aeronautics (NACA, predecessor organization to NASA). A further reduced air drag, where the landing-gear struts were carefully streamlined and their wheels shrouded in streamlined cowls, generally known as "pants" had not yet been employed. The Vega's wing had a Clark Y-18 airfoil at its root and a Clark Y-9.5 near the tips, which provided excellent load carrying ability, good slow-flight characteristics, and gentle stall qualities. This model of the Vega did not have a U.S. Aeronautics Branch Type Certificate of Airworthiness.

The Vega, which was rolled out of the Lockheed factory to be turned over to Wiley Post, was the factory's serial number 24, and on its wings and fuselage was painted the airplane's federal registration number: NC 7954. Hall named the airplane, *Winnie Mae,* after his daughter, and it was the first of three Vegas that Hall would own, each carrying the same name (the third was purchased after the 1931 world flight and was piloted by Frank Hoover).

Wiley subsequently flew the oilmen on several business trips in this first *Winnie Mae,* but the stock-market crash of 1929 and the economic slump thereafter soon led Hall and Briscoe to sell the Vega. With the name of *Winnie Mae* deleted from its fuselage, this Vega was subsequently sold to Nevada Airlines and then to several other owners, including Roscoe Turner, Art Goebel, and Laura Ingalls; it was finally washed out in a crash at Albuquerque, New Mexico,

FIGURE 10.—J. Bart Scott's airport at Lexington, Oklahoma, and Scott's two Canucks, bask in the late summer sun of 1927. Scott purchased Canuck number 1767 from Post in the fall of 1927. The Canuck had been damaged when Post took it on a hunting trip to Mexico and the repairs at Arthur Oakley's shop, Ardmore, Oklahoma, exceeded Post's financial resources. Wiley barnstormed and instructed for Scott, earning $3.00 per flight hour. (Courtesy J. Bart Scott.)

FIGURE 11.—J. Bart Scott (rear seat) and Wiley Post (front seat) prepare to take a spin in one of Scott's Canucks, 1927. Behind them, a contemporary Model T Ford proceeds along a country road. Note that the tire-inflation valves are on the inside of the wheels. (Courtesy J. Bart Scott.)

August 11, 1941. Turner had the NACA cowling and the wheel pants installed.

After Wiley returned NC 7954 to the Lockheed factory in Burbank, he knew that he had no further employment with the now-planeless Hall and Briscoe, so he took a job at Lockheed as a sales representative and test pilot. Although his career with Lockheed was relatively brief, Post gained a great deal of technical knowledge about aircraft. At this time, Lockheed employed only 50 persons, so there was ample opportunity for many exchanges of viewpoints and knowledge by the engineers and pilots. Engineers at Lockheed included Jack Northrop, Gerald Vultee, Allan Loughhead (one of the "Lockheed" brothers)[22], and Richard Palmer, all of whom ranked among the world's best aeronautical engineers.

At this time, Lockheed was not only developing its famous Vegas series but was moving on toward its even more sensational Orians. Wiley was not only able to acquire invaluable knowledge of aircraft design and flight-test procedures, but also added a considerable number of hours to his pilot time by delivering Lockheed aircraft to Washington, Oregon, and other cities. He also flew for the airline operated by the Detroit Aircraft Corporation, piloting Vegas between El Paso and Brownsville, Texas, and Mazatlan, Mexico.[23] A matter of primary significance here is that Wiley was exposed to the comparatively recent development of blind-flight techniques, flight by reference to gyroscopic instruments when visual contact with the natural horizon is lost.

Using the Vega that Hall and Briscoe had just sold, Wiley flew as escort for the women pilots in the Santa-Monica-Cleveland Derby of 1929s National Air Races. In this competition Louise Thaden was first in a Travel Air, Gladys O'Donnell was second in a Waco biplane, Amelia Earhart was third in a Vega, and Blanche Noyes was fourth in a "Speedwing" Travel Air, an open-cockpit, three-place biplane. Amelia Earhart subsequently remarked in her book, *Last Flight*, that she met Wiley for the first time just prior to the race. Years later, during 1934 and early 1935, Amelia had occasion to consult Post concerning several of her planned long-distance flights.

During this time, Wiley's right eye had become very good, and, in addition, he had learned to judge distances by using familiar objects such as yardsticks. Today, this process of depth estimation is known by specialists in visual perception as the "adjacency principle." The following incident illustrates the acuity of Wiley's eye. One day at Burbank, Roscoe Turner, James Doolittle, Carl Squier, General Manager of

Lockheed, and Marshall Headle, Lockheed's chief test pilot, were with Wiley in Squier's office. The group got into a discussion concerning who had the best vision. They went to a window and Wiley could read signs at distances that no other person in the group could make out. Not believing that Wiley was really reading these signs, the group proceeded down to the street and, sure enough, Wiley had accurately read every sign.[24]

On June 5, 1930, Hall called Wiley. Hall had moved his office to the Commerce Exchange Building, Oklahoma City, and needed a personal pilot again. Wiley agreed to return to Hall and to supervise the construction of the new Lockheed Vega 5B that Hall had ordered. This was a seven-place cabin land monoplane, which cost $22,000 and was powered by a 420-horsepower Pratt & Whitney Wasp engine. Hall's airplane rolled out of the Lockheed plant in June 1930.

The detailed Aeronautics Branch records reveal the following sequence of events for the new Vega:

FIGURE 12.—A 1928 Travel Air Model 4000 with a Wright J-4 engine of 200 horsepower represents the type of three-place biplane purchased by F. C. Hall and Powell Briscoe, the Oklahoma oilmen who gave Wiley Post his first job as an executive pilot late in 1927. (Courtesy Beech Aircraft Co.)

FIGURE 13.—The original *Winnie Mae*, Lockheed Vega NC 7954, is shown in 1928 at Grand Central Airport, Glendale, California. NC 7954, completed on August 12, 1928, is at the far right. The second aircraft to the left is another Vega, with two Lockheed Air Express Aircraft as numbers three and four. The remaining aircraft are Vegas. Note that the N.A.C.A. engine cowlings were not used at this time. Wheel pants also were not used. The construction work that was progressing on the terminal building is clearly evident. (Courtesy Lockheed Aircraft Corporation.)

Figure 14.—In 1929 F. C. Hall sold the first *Winnie Mae* (NC 7954) back to Lockheed, who in turn sold the aircraft to Nevada Airlines. The Vega was equipped with a N.A.C.A. cowling and wheel pants, and was renamed "Sirius." "Captain" Roscoe Turner (later "Colonel") flew the aircraft in the 1929 air races, coming in third in the free-for-all speed contest, at an average speed of 163.44 miles-per-hour (mph), behind Doug Davis, first, (194.90 mph in a Travel Air) and R. G. Breen, second, (186.84 mph in a Curtiss P–3–A). (Courtesy Lockheed Aircraft Company.)

Figure 15.—The *Winnie Mae* in its original trim, Union Air Terminal, summer, 1930. The building behind is the old Lockheed hangar, which had once been a "glass factory," between Glendale and Burbank, California. The NC–105–W license was changed to NR–105–W on August 22, 1930, in preparation for the Los Angeles-to-Chicago Men's Air Derby, which Post won on August 27, 1930. (Courtesy Lockheed Aircraft Company.)

On March 27, 1930, an application for a commercial license was made for a Lockheed Vega 5B, manufacturer's serial number 122. The application was made by the Lockheed Aircraft Corporation, Burbank, California, and signed by Carl B. Squier, general manager. E. S. Evans was listed as company president, James Work was listed as vice-president, and Frank Blair was listed as chairman of the board. It

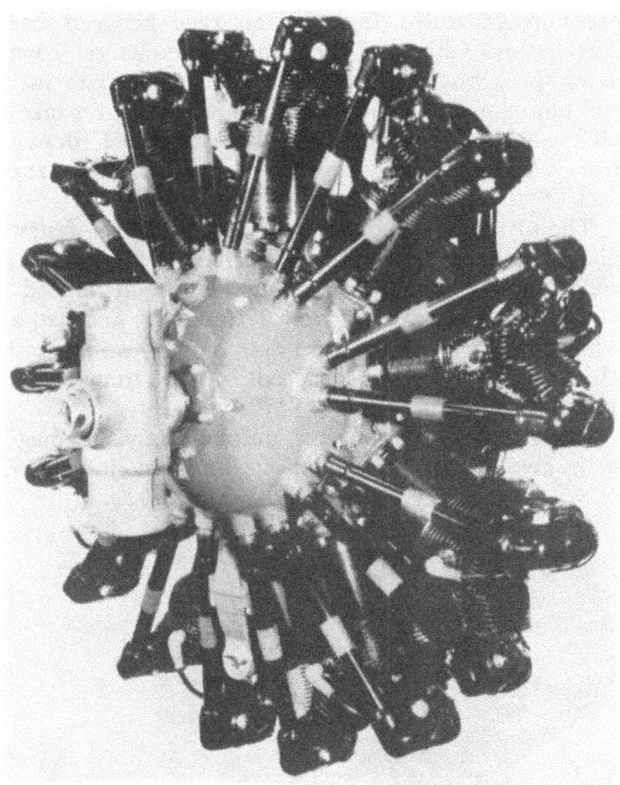

FIGURE 16.—This is the Pratt and Whitney Wasp engine used to power Lockheed Vegas such as the *Winnie Mae*. Engine serial number 3088 was used in NC 105 W (sometimes NR 105 W) and was delivered to the Lockheed Company by Pratt & Whitney on May 10, 1930. The engine is a Wasp Type C and had an approved type certificate, number 227. It originally was a 420-horsepower engine and had nine air-cooled cylinders. (Courtesy Smithsonian Institution.)

was stated that the airplane had a Pratt & Whitney Wasp Type C engine. The airplane was described as having been manufactured during March-April 1930, and was stated to be in compliance with approved type-certificate number 227.

An operation inspection report of June 20, 1930, was rendered by J. Nall, a representative of the Aeronautics Branch of the Department of Commerce, which reported that the aircraft had Wasp engine number 3088 (shipped to Lockheed by the Pratt & Whitney Company, East Hartford, Connecticut, on May 10, 1930), equipped with a steel Standard propeller; it had 150-gallons gasoline capacity, but with a full cabin load the airplane was placarded to read that only 67½ gallons of fuel could be carried. The airplane was then approved, and license number NC-105 was assigned to it.

On June 21, 1930, a bill of sale was drawn up and Lockheed Vega monoplane serial number 122, equipped with an electric inertia starter, was sold to F. C. Hall, Box 1442, Oklahoma City, Oklahoma.

Wiley encountered Red Gray at the Lockheed factory one day. Red had come in to take delivery of a Vega for the Julian Oil and Royalty Company. Gray's plane was number NC 106W, the next off the production line. Department of Commerce pilot records show that on March 19, 1930, Post's air transport license was renewed, with his age given as 31 years, his weight as 155 pounds, and his height as 5 feet, 5 inches. He was listed as having brown hair and brown eyes and as living at 706 West 29th Street, Oklahoma City, Oklahoma.

Hall named the new white and purple-trimmed Vega after his daughter, Winnie Mae, just as he had done with his first Vega. Wiley wished to see what he and the new *Winnie Mae* could do in a competitive flight, and the first test came when he got Hall's approval to enter the nonstop air derby that August between Los Angeles and Chicago. This was a special event of the 1930 National Air Races for aircraft capable of carrying 1,000 pounds or more payload. By removing the passenger seats and adding extra fuel tanks, Wiley knew that he could increase the Vega's nonstop flight range, and he wanted to continue on past Chicago to New York, in an effort to break the cross-country speed record. With the problems of his aircraft worked out to his satisfaction, he asked Harold Gatty, an Australian-born navigator who lived in California, to lay out a course. Post had been referred to Gatty by Commander P.V.H. Weems, U.S.

FIGURE 17.—This is a rear view of the Pratt and Whitney Wasp engine. The updraft, double-barrel, Bendix Stromberg carburetor is shown at the lower right. The two Scintilla magnetoes are seen just above the carburetor. The engine had a dual-ignition system to ensure reliability. (Courtesy Smithsonian Institution.)

Navy (Retired), who was already one of the world's authorities on the art of aerial navigation.

On August 22, 1930, Wiley Post applied, on behalf of F. C. Hall, for a restricted license for the airplane NC 105W, which was necessary in order to modify the *Winnie Mae* for the race. It was noted on the operation inspection report by L. J. Holoubek, who inspected the aircraft at the Lockheed Company on August 21, 1930, that the airplane now had five fuel tanks, having a total capacity of 500 gallons, and a total oil capacity of 25 gallons. The Wasp C engine had a special supercharger, engine geared, with a speed ratio of 10:1. It was popularly known as a "ten-to-one blower."[25] The standard ratio was 7:1, but for this race the 10:1 internal supercharger was felt necessary. Under "remarks," it was noted: "Extra gas tankage added for non-stop race between Los Angeles and Chicago." The 10:1 supercharger gave extra speed but also imposed a penalty of extra fuel consumption. Post could pull 500 horsepower for take-off for about five minutes with 87 octane fuel (drawn from a special tank); the other tanks had 80 octane fuel.

The plywood Lockheed Vega was one of the fastest planes then available, largely due to its aerodynamically "clean" design. It was an "internally braced" airplane that was a little over 27 feet long and had a wingspan of 41 feet. Depending upon loading and altitude, it could cruise at speeds ranging from 150 to 190 miles per hour.

The Air Derby began, but, unfortunately, the magnetic compass of the *Winnie Mae* stuck just after

FIGURE 18.—Leland "Lee" Schoenhair, Roscoe Turner, Art Goebel, Wiley Post, and Billy Brock pose in a pre-takeoff photo just before the August 27, 1930, Los Angeles-to-Chicago Air Derby, an event of that year's National Air Races. Post, a total unknown, beat all of these famous pilots and thus achieved his first, tentative, national prominence. Goebel came in second, Schoenhair third, Brock fourth, and Turner (with his lion Gilmore) fifth. (Courtesy Lockheed Aircraft Company.)

takeoff, which caused Post a navigation loss of 40 minutes. Continuing by pilotage (visual reference to terrain), Wiley flew the 1,760 miles in nine hours, nine minutes, and four seconds. Averaging 192 miles per hour, Wiley nevertheless beat his nearest rival by seconds to win the $7,500 prize. However, the faulty compass ruined his chances of setting a transcontinental speed record, so Wiley remained in Chicago instead of flying on to the east coast. Art Goebel, who had won the 1927 Dole Air Derby, finished the race with the second best time.[26] Interestingly enough, Goebel was flying NC 7954, the first *Winnie Mae*. Leland Schoenhair was third, and Billy Brock fourth, both flying Wasp-powered Vegas. Roscoe Turner and Gilmore were fifth (Gilmore was Turner's pet lion), flying a Hornet-powered Lockheed Air Express. It was races such as this that inspired a popular remark of the day: "It takes a Lockheed to beat a Lockheed!"

A 31-year-old, eighth-grade dropout now found himself a "more than average," steadily employed, executive pilot by the end of 1930. He and his employer now began to talk about doing something very unusual, and there was nothing more unusual than a flight around the world. It had only been done twice: first by the World Fliers of the U.S. Army Air Service in 1924 and then by the German airship *Graf Zeppelin* in 1929. This was nevertheless what Post had in mind for the *Winnie Mae* in 1931—to fly around the world, with all possible speed.

NOTES

1. Wiley Post was destined to have a sister (Mary), and two additional brothers (Byron and Gordon), in that order. His father was of Scotch and his mother of Irish descent.
2. LESTER MAITLAND, *Knights of the Air* (Garden City: Doubleday, 1929).
3. WILEY POST AND HAROLD GATTY, *Around the World in Eight Days* (London: John Hamilton, Ltd., circa 1931), 221 pp; also published in the United States by Rand McNally, 1931, 304 pp. Page references in this monograph will be to the British edition. Hereafter this book will be cited as Post and Gatty, *RW*.
4. James Post interview.
5. Lieutenant Post had been killed at San Diego, California, on February 9, 1914.
6. James Post interview.
7. Zimmerman later became an instructor for The Pikes Peak Flying School, Colorado Springs, Colorado. *Popular Aviation*, vol. 3, no. 3 (September 1928), p. 74.
8. Burrell Tibbs interview.
9. POST AND GATTY, *RW*, p. 188.
10. POST AND GATTY, *RW*, p. 195.
11. The Canuck had ailerons on both upper and lower wings, in contrast to the JN4, which had ailerons only on the upper wing. The Canuck was, accordingly, much more sensitive with respect to roll maneuvers.
12. Dr. T. G. Wails, one of the Oklahoma physicians who treated Post, later observed that had antibiotics been developed at that time, the eye would very likely have been saved.
13. In later years Post told of the problems he had adjusting to one eye. Wiley initially found it hard to determine the size and distance of different objects in the visual field. Slowly, however, he became accustomed to monocular vision, and he remarked to *The Los Angeles Times*, of March 10, 1934, that "one real good eye is better than two fairly good ones."
14. The Oklahoma Industrial Commission records show that Post was earning an average wage of $7.00 per day at the time of his injury. He was employed by Droppleman and Cuniff, who were insured by the Maryland Casualty Company. The facts published in the Commission's *Journal*, vol. 159, pp. 660–61, reveal that Wiley H. Post (claimant) "was in the employment of the respondent (Droppleman and Cuniff) and was engaged in a hazardous occupation covered by and subject to the provisions of the Workmen's Compensation Law and that while in the course of such employment and arising out of same the claimant sustained an accidental injury on the first day of October, 1926. That as a result of said accident the claimant sustained the loss of the left eye." It was ruled by the Commission in response to Post's claim number 91165 that Post was due compensation at the rate of $18.00 per week for 100 weeks, computed from October 6, 1926. Since Post wanted a lump sum, he got something less than $18.00 (he was given a check for $1,698.25, representing about 94 weeks compensation).
15. Gray later served as senior pilot for the Continental Oil Company.
16. A few years later, government regulations required a dual ignition system to help preclude such engine failures.
17. J. B. Scott interview.
18. J. H. Conger interview.
19. FRANK HAWKS, *Once to Every Pilot* (New York: Stackpole Sons, 1936), pp. 35–37.
20. Winnie Mae Fain interview.
21. FAA, Airman Certificate Branch Records. The original records are lost. This information came from the index card.
22. The spelling "Loughead" was changed for company purposes to "Lockheed" to simplify the phonetics. Victor Lougheed and his two half brothers, Allan and Malcolm Loughead, were pioneer airplane designers and aviators from the pre-World War I era. Victor used two "e's," while Allan and Malcolm used "ea" in their last name.
23. Post received Mexican pilot's license number 96.
24. Carl Squier interview.
25. The normal cylinder firing order was 1-3-5-7-9-2-4-6-8.
26. *New York Times*, August 27, 1930.

2 / Globe Girdling With Gatty (1931)

EARLY IN 1931, Post and Hall decided to postpone an attempt at the transcontinental record and to attempt the unique undertaking of an around-the-world speed flight. Post felt that "aviation needed something original to stimulate passenger business."[1] Also, the economic depression had reduced Hall's personal flying requirements, and Post desired more flight activity.

When it was made known that Wiley Post planned to fly from New York to Europe, and continue on around the world, with the termination at the New York origin, many considered the risks too high, especially in view of the technology of the time. Wiley's opinion was that adequate aviation progress had occurred and that a high-speed dash around the world could be accomplished with proven equipment that was already available. He savored the challenge of proving whether or not he had weighed and measured the difficulties and prepared accordingly.

In early January 1931, Wiley flew the *Winnie Mae* to Los Angeles, with his wife Mae in the rear cabin; he was taking the airplane to the Lockheed factory in order that certain "long range" modifications could be made. He visited Harold Gatty in San Diego at Lindbergh Field on January 17, 1931, discussed his intention to undertake a world flight, and made plans with the Australian navigator to enlist his assistance.

If Post could get off before various others planning to fly the Atlantic, he would accomplish the twenty-eighth transatlantic flight,[2] including nonstop flights and airship flights. If successful in flying around the world, his would be the fourth around-the-world flight. Only the U.S. Army's World Fliers in 1924, in two Douglas DWC World Cruisers, and the *Graf Zeppelin* had done it before. The Army's DWCs were large open-cockpit biplanes, each with a crew of two; they spent almost six months between April 6, 1924, and September 28, 1924, flying around the world from Seattle to Seattle.[3] The German airship *Graf Zeppelin* spent 21 days flying the circuit during August 1929.[4] Post planned to beat the *Graf Zeppelin's* record; he hoped to complete the around-the-world flight in ten days.

F. C. Hall has remarked that an around-the-world flight had become Post's life ambition. Hall told the Associated Press that Post finally sold him on the idea as a sporting proposition and later said that his late wife made the first actual suggestion for a global flight.[5] Powell Briscoe, although joining Hall in backing early endurance flights by other pilots, refused to take part in the planned world flight because he feared that Post would be killed. Hall looked about for financial contributions of support but could not raise significant donations. Consequently, Hall paid for most of the costs of the flight out of his own pocket. He wrote the editor of the *Chickasha Daily Express* a month before the flight began, bringing his financial role to the attention of the readers:

This flight will be the biggest flight in aviation's history, and as I told you in Chickasha we will return to Chickasha the first Oklahoma town. I want you to whoop them up there. Remember boy, your humble servant is putting the dough up in gobs and no one else is helping in any respect.[6]

Wiley began to concentrate on flight preparations. His experience in the 1930 race had proved the value of proper navigation preparations, and he and Harold Gatty began planning the flight in February 1931, Gatty working on the route and ground organization and Post on the aircraft.

Gatty was a man with a wealth of navigational experience. A native of Campbelltown, Tasmania, Gatty was three years younger than Post. He had spent three years at the Royal Australian Naval College preparing for a career as a ship's navigator and then served on merchant vessels before immigrating to the United States in 1927.[7] Gatty had established a navigation school for aviators in California and already had trained many fliers, including Anne Morrow Lindbergh and Art Goebel.[8] The kind of training he offered was considered vitally important in a day when radio-beacon air routes were virtually nonexistent, weather information was often sketchy, and the quality of aircraft radio was still poor.

17

FIGURE 19.—F. C. Hall is flanked by Post on his left and Gatty on his right, as the *Winnie Mae* is ready to fly from Oklahoma City to New York City, May 1931, for the around-the-world record attempt. For ease of ramp handling, the swivel tailskid rests upon a small-wheeled dolly. A late-model contemporary car is parked at the rear of the *Winnie Mae* just off the ramp. (Courtesy Winnie Mae Fain.)

FIGURE 20.—Post and Gatty pose with the *Winnie Mae* just prior to the 1931 around-the-world flight. The aircraft sports the Pathé News emblem, and the on-board radio transmitter and receiver can be seen through the fuselage windows. On the tripod to the right is a contemporary radio microphone. (Courtesy Lockheed Aircraft Company.)

Gatty had participated in a transoceanic flight three years before, when he and Harold Bromley attempted to fly the Pacific in 1930. After they had covered 1,200 miles, a broken exhaust ring forced them back to Japan. Almost overcome by carbon monoxide, Gatty spent several weeks in a hospital. Wiley was aware that a similar mishap would jeopardize his flight, so he paid careful attention to all of the mechanical details which would make his *Winnie Mae* safe.

The nine-cylinder, air-cooled Pratt & Whitney Wasp C engine, number 3088, received special care. It was a standard model, equipped with an internal engine-driven supercharger (blower), which had an impeller that turned ten times faster than the engine. The accessories were also standard except that Post decided to remove the starter, in order to save weight. The engine turned a fixed pitch propeller, and at 2,000 revolutions per minute, the combination produced 420 horsepower. In April 1931 Transcontinental and Western Air (TWA) in California overhauled the *Winnie Mae's* Wasp, which by this time had logged 245 hours of operation. Wiley's confidence in the Wasp was underscored when he told a reporter from the Associated Press that during his around-the-world dash the engine should require only minor servicing.[9]

Earlier, in preparation for 1930's National Air Races' air derby, Post had lowered the angle of incidence of the *Winnie Mae's* wings, which served to increase her speed by ten miles per hour.[10] He had learned this trick while working at Lockheed, that decreasing the angle of incidence would reduce the airplane's overall air resistance. However, this modification also resulted in a faster landing speed, increasing it to about 80 miles per hour. This may not sound like much in a day when ordinary jetliners land at more than 100 miles per hour, but in 1931 not even fighter planes had landing speeds of 80 miles per hour. Wing flaps were not designed into the Vegas in 1931, and to have attempted their installation by way of a modification would have been terribly expensive, so Post had to live with the higher landing speed. In any case, he was more than prepared to make the trade and master its hazards. He discovered, however, that by shortening his tail skid four inches, he could touch down with a higher angle of attack, which offset any tendency to nose-over while landing.

Another modification was the installation of a special hatch in the top of the fuselage, with a folding windshield, which allowed Gatty to make celestial sightings. Because of these structural changes, the government issued a restricted license to the *Winnie Mae*. The NC 105W license (the "C" stood for "Commercial") was changed to NR 105W ("R" meant "Restricted"). Later, when restored to her original condi-

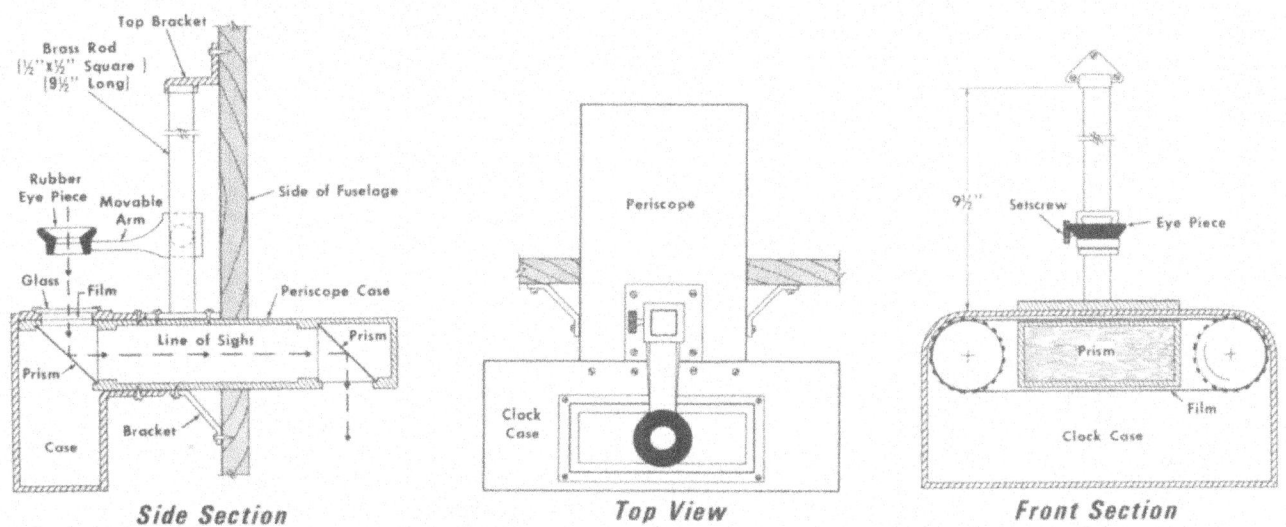

FIGURE 21.—*The Gatty Navigation Instrument.* Harold Gatty invented a special combination wind drift and ground-speed indicator to assist with his navigation duties during the 1931 world flight. The principle utilized for determining ground speed was based upon comparing the rate of passage of terrain, as viewed through an eyepiece and two prisms, with the rate of passage of a series of red marks placed on a film strip, moved by a clock mechanism at a fixed speed. The eyepiece was raised or lowered until the two rates were optically the same. Gatty then read off the distance above the film to which the eyepiece had been moved and consulted a table he had previously made in test flights with the *Winnie Mae* at known altitudes and ground speeds. All Gatty needed to know to use the instrument for ground speed was the altitude of the airplane above the ground (which could be determined by flying down and climbing to the cruise altitude or by using the altimeter that was set in accordance with the previous takeoff point). The instrument was useful over land or water. For wind drift, grids of the eyepiece were turned until objects on the earth's surface flowed parallel through the lines of the grids. The angle of "crab" across the surface could then be directly read by Gatty. The instrument was mounted near Gatty's seat in the *Winnie Mae* and the ground viewing portion extended through the right side of the fuselage where the external portion was encased in a teardrop fairing. (*Aero Digest,* January 1932, p. 57–58.)

tion, the NC 105W license would again be used.[11] While in the restricted category, an aircraft cannot be used for commercial passenger transport and can carry only the pilot and special-purpose crew members.

Innovations were necessary to provide Gatty with quarters among the cabin tanks. His seat was intentionally left unattached so he could move forward or backward and help balance the ship by altering the load with respect to the center of gravity. A special speaking tube, recommended by Gatty, was supposed to let them communicate; however it subsequently proved difficult to use except when the engine power was low, because the noise of the engine usually masked the voices. Also during flights, Post was temporarily partially deafened, because he sat immediately behind the engine; his feet actually straddled the rear end of the engine's crankcase. Post and Gatty had the option of exchanging written messages with a wire through the tube, and this proved to be their usual means of "conversation."

Several new instruments received special attention. On the advice of Jimmy Doolittle, the famous speed and aerobatic pilot who had pioneered in 1929 the first "blind flight take-off and landing" radio and instrument system, and Roger Q. Williams who had flown the Atlantic with Lewis Yancy in 1929, Post carefully grouped the bank-and-turn indicator, rate-of-climb instrument, and artificial horizon, for better scanning during times of "blind flight."[12] Duplicate flight instruments, including airspeed and compass, were available to Gatty, plus a "master" aperiodic compass located on the floor in front of Gatty.

In addition to the "blind flight" instruments, the *Winnie Mae* had the standard airspeed indicator, altimeter, tachometer, fuel gauges, oil-temperature gauge, cylinder-head temperature indicator, oil-pressure indicator, fuel-pressure indicator, and an outside air-temperature indicator.

A wind drift and ground-speed indicator was developed by Gatty especially for the flight. This instrument consisted of an adjustable optical tube through which the ground was viewed. A small motor-driven device produced a series of images that were superimposed upon the ground image; when no motion was apparent on the superimposed images, Gatty had a reading of the actual ground speed by virtue of previously made calibrations of the equipment. Simultaneously, a rotating grid was turned until the ground image flowed parallel to the grid lines, giving the degree of ground drift occurring. The external portion of this optical device protruded beneath the second and third windows on the *Winnie Mae's* starboard side and was surrounded by a teardrop streamlined fairing, and its small window was enclosed within the fairing.

Radio equipment was carried for use in emergencies, just in case they had to crash-land and needed to guide rescuers; however, it later proved impractical and was essentially "extra weight." The bulky two-way continuous wave radio was solely for communication purposes (by telegraph key) and had no navigational capabilities.

Post anticipated the physical strain that the flight would impose upon the body. It is reported that he spent long hours training himself to keep his mind blank, in hopes that such self-induced relaxation would combat the slowed-up reactions that can prove fatal to exhausted pilots. He developed a conditioning program for his mind and body. During the winter preceding the flight, he slept at different hours each day in an effort to break regular sleeping patterns and to alleviate fatigue.[13] He discounted the need for an exercise-training program, believing instead that he needed to practice what he would have to do most—*sit!*[14] Accordingly, Post had a more comfortable seat installed in the cockpit, which included a folding armrest.

In his book, *Around the World in Eight Days,* Post states: "I knew that the variance in time as we progressed would bring on acute fatigue if I were used to regular hours." This is the first documented literature reference to the important matter of "time zone fatigue," a syndrome encountered years later in commercial aviation.

A major problem that Post and Hall faced was in the political realm. In 1931 the United States had not yet recognized the Russian government, so special steps had to be taken to obtain permission to fly in Russia. For a time, the prospect of gaining permission was discouraging, but Hall began to get on the right path when he called Patrick J. Hurley, an Oklahoman who was the Secretary of War in President Hoover's cabinet. Hurley advised Hall that Senator William E. Borah of Idaho was one of the few men in the United States who could possibly get permission from the Russians. Hall then sought Senator Borah's assistance.

Post and Hall decided to retain the aviation public relations firm of Dick Blythe and Harry Bruno to assist with the news media. Blythe and Bruno were early pilots, who had helped with Lindbergh's 1927 flight as well as with some flights of other aviation pioneers. With adequate press coverage, the flight of the *Winnie Mae* could assume more significant proportions. The *New York Times* bought the rights in advance to the Post-Gatty saga and promised its readers a real scoop in aviation history. An agreement with Pathé News was made and Gatty took a Pathé News motion-picture camera and considerable film in order that he could document the flight; what is more, a "Pathé Rooster" emblem was placed on the *Winnie Mae.*

Hall was optimistic and predicted a fortune for Post

FIGURE 22.—On June 23, 1931, Post and Gatty landed at Harbour Grace, Newfoundland, after a 6-hour 47-minute flight from New York City. After refueling, they were given a hand start (one man pulled another, who held the lower propeller blade) and took off for England. The aircraft at this time did not have a starter motor. Gatty's drift and ground-speed indicator ports are seen just to the rear of the Pathé News emblem. Note the windsock, which indicates a strong wind down the dirt runway. The two small, square inspection windows are shown on the underside of the right wing. (Courtesy Lockheed Aircraft Company.)

if he succeeded in breaking the existing records. In an interview with the *Daily Oklahoman,* Hall estimated that Post would make $75,000 from the flight alone. In addition, he felt Post could expect more than $100,000 through barnstorming tours. Advertising contracts for the hundred or so "test" parts that the *Winnie Mae* carried were potentially worth about $125,000, Hall reported. Gatty, who had a guarantee of $5,000, was to receive 25 percent of the take.[15] As an added measure, Post and Gatty carried several hundred autographed envelopes which they hoped to have postmarked in each country they visited. Upon return, they planned to sell these to collectors.

Post and Gatty took off from California in early May 1931 and pointed the *Winnie Mae's* Wasp eastward for New York City. This was not meant to be a speed trial and they stopped in Oklahoma en route. Upon visiting the Chickasha Rotary Club with F. C. Hall, the oilman described Post as the "best pilot in the world"[16] and told friends that he had wanted the world flight to begin and end in Chickasha, but it turned out that east coast weather-reporting facilities made New York more feasible as the point of departure.

The two airmen hurried on from Oklahoma to Washington, D.C., where they visited the embassies of Great Britain, the Netherlands, Germany, Poland, China, and Japan, to obtain the final permissions necessary to fly over their countries. Although Japan and China were not on the planned route, Post wanted approval to land in them just in case the *Winnie Mae* was forced off course.

On May 23, Post and Gatty and the *Winnie Mae* finally arrived at Roosevelt Field, Long Island, their jumping-off point for around the world. Named in memory of Quentin Roosevelt (the son of Theodore Roosevelt), who was killed as an aviator in World War I, the soil of Roosevelt Field cradled a wealth of aeronautical history during the 1920s. Among other things, it was there where Rene Fonck had crashed in takeoff, in the first attempt at winning the lucrative Orteig Prize for a nonstop flight from New York to Paris; and it was from this same airfield that Charles Lindbergh took off a year later in 1927 for his phenomenally successful transatlantic flight that won the Orteig Prize. By 1931, however, expensive concrete runways were displacing grass fields and Roosevelt Field's golden age was almost at its end.

Ahead of Post and Gatty stretched a 15,000-mile track that would pierce the North Atlantic's terrible weather barrier and take them to Berlin and Moscow, across Siberia with its many unknown hazards of mountains and weather, to the usually fog-shrouded Bering Sea and Alaska, then across the width of Canada and the United States, and back to New York. Oscar Leiding, a writer for the Associated Press, remarked that the proposed flight resembled a fictional adventure from the world of Jules Verne. Emphasizing the similarities, he wrote: "Jules Verne sent mythical Phileas Fogg around the world in 80 days. Two hardy fliers hope to make the trip in one tenth, or maybe one-eighth of the time." [17] Indeed, although Post talked about flying around the world in ten days, he and Gatty really hoped to fly the circuit in eight days, and their most secret hopes were fixed on the round figure of one week.

F. C. Hall, his daughter Winnie Mae, and her husband Leslie Fain traveled to New York City by train and checked into the Biltmore Hotel where Post and Gatty were staying. Mae Post stayed in Oklahoma and made plans to go to New York only when the world flight neared the end of its mark. Mrs. Gatty also thought that her arrival in New York by the end of the flight would be time enough.

Word was finally received through the Amtorg Trading Corporation that the Soviet Union had granted permission for the fliers to land in Russia. Amtorg was a Soviet commercial organization that also functioned as the USSR's unofficial embassy in the United States, prior to diplomatic relations being established between the two countries in 1933. With the USSR's permission in hand, the only obstacle that remained was the North Atlantic's weather.

Post and Gatty spent all of a month in New York waiting for a favorable transatlantic weather forecast. At first they were anxious, but soon became resigned to the frustrations created by that malignant body of water. Several times they climbed into the *Winnie Mae* and were prepared to take off when a last-minute weather report of fog, storms, or icing conditions would come to hand, and they wearily taxied the *Winnie Mae* back to her hangar.

The two airmen met daily with Dr. James K. Kimball, the U.S. Weather Bureau's meteorologist in New York, who since 1927 had come to be referred to as the "guardian angel" of transatlantic fliers. It was Dr. Kimball, with his instruments, charts, and the meager data received from ships at sea, who gave transatlantic aviators the word "Go!" from his office in the top of Manhattan's 17 Battery Place. Without a favorable forecast from him, all the aviators could do was sit on the grass at Roosevelt Field and restlessly contemplate a sky that might be beautifully blue overhead, but was filled with fog, rain, or sleet somewhere out over the Atlantic. Flying the Atlantic was not simply a matter of having a reliable airplane. The key to transatlantic flight was adequate weather intelligence, but it did not become available until World War II.

In July the Hungarians Alexander Magyar and George Enders would dash from New York to Biscke, Hungary, via Harbour Grace, in their Lockheed 8A Sirius, named *Justice for Hungary*; Russell Boardman and John Polando would fly from New York to Istanbul nonstop in a Bellanca J–300 Special, named *Cape Cod*; and Hugh Herndon and Clyde Pangborn would fly from New York to Cardigan, Wales, in a Bellanca CH–400 Skyrocket, named *Miss Veedol,* on a projected around-the-world flight that was thwarted by the suspicious military authorities in Japan. They had hoped to beat the time of Post and Gatty; their consolation prize was in making the first transpacific flight, from Sabishiro Beach, Japan, to Wenatchee, Washington, 4,558 miles in 41 hours and 13 minutes, October 3–4, 1931.

Nor was that all. In August, Wolfgang von Gronau landed his twin-engine Dornier Wal flying boat *Gronland Wal* in New York harbor after a 13-day flight across the Atlantic via Iceland and Greenland; a few days later Parker D. Cramer and Oliver Paquette landed in the Shetland Islands after a successful flight across the Atlantic's subarctic wastes in a Diesel-powered, Bellanca J–300 Pacemaker seaplane. Unfortunately, after they took off from the Shetlands for Norway, they disappeared over the North Sea. All these flights, however, came in the wake of the *Winnie Mae*. On this morning of June 23rd Wiley Post, Harold Gatty, and their *Winnie Mae* had the North Atlantic's air corridors all to themselves.

On Tuesday, June 23, 1931—exactly a month after their arrival at Roosevelt Field—Dr. Kimball's forecast finally appeared satisfactory. When this message came to him shortly after midnight, Wiley considered an immediate takeoff; but a glance at the field, wet with rain, convinced him that the risk involved in a takeoff with his heavy fuel load would be too great.[18] After waiting a few hours for the field to dry, Post and Gatty climbed into the *Winnie Mae* and roared off into a still-dark sky. Post turned the hub of her Wasp toward the black Atlantic where the sun was still hidden beyond the eastern rim. In the darkness of his cubicle in the *Winnie Mae's* after cabin, Gatty noted in his log: "Took off 4:55 daylight-saving time, set course 63°, visibility poor." Then he checked over the motion-picture camera that Pathé News had given him for the flight; it is worth noting that this was the first time a movie camera had been carried on a transatlantic airplane flight.

The *Literary Digest* observed that Post and Gatty were the first of 1931's ocean hoppers, an activity which had become a summer perenniel since Lindbergh's flight of 1927. Immediately behind the *Winnie Mae* were Otto Hillig and Holger Hoiriis in a single-engine Bellance J–300 Pacemaker named *Liberty,* with Copenhagen as their destination. Hoiriis, the pilot, became lost at night, partly due to excessive fatigue, and finally landed at Krefeld, Germany; but they ultimately flew on to Copenhagen.[19] Ruth Nichols of Rye, New York, took off a few days later in her Lockheed Vega named *Aki a,* but crashed while landing to refuel at St. John, New Brunswick, luckily surviving the accident. She had hoped to become the first woman to solo an airplane transatlantic, but as it turned out this was a performance reserved for Amelia Earhart in 1932.[20]

With Gatty providing the heading, Post pointed the *Winnie Mae's* nose for Harbour Grace, Newfoundland. Ever since William Brock and Edward Schlee had used Harbour Grace as their jumping-off place for a flight to England in their Stinson Detroiter *Pride of Detroit* in August 1927, the landing strip provided by this little fishing village became a regularly used fuel stop for transatlantic fliers.

Six hours and 47 minutes after liftoff from Roosevelt Field, Post floated the *Winnie Mae* down onto Harbour Grace's rocky and pebbled runway. Ted Carlyle, the Pratt & Whitney field service representative present at Harbour Grace, wanted to remove the *Winnie Mae's* cowling so he could check over her engine. But Post would have none of that. "Not a thing wrong with the motor—I believe in letting well enough alone," he insisted.[21] Gatty made some movies during the refueling, and as soon as the tanks were topped off Post wasted no time in getting the *Winnie Mae* airborne again. Within a few minutes they were "streaking across the Atlantic," as the *New York Times* told its readers the next morning. Ahead of the two fliers was 1,900 miles of ocean, and with most of its airspace clogged with instrument weather. Post had to rely upon his gyroscopic instruments for long stretches of time. All alone in the *Winnie Mae's* after cabin, Gatty found himself unnerved by Post's practice of running each wing tank dry, which caused a chilling moment of engine sputtering and coughing while the fuel-selector valve was being switched and until the fuel pump got its drag on the fresh tank. Post always used the last drop of fuel in a tank so he could be sure of the *Winnie Mae's* exact fuel status.

After hours of blind flying, Post brought the *Winnie Mae* down through broken clouds to what he discovered after landing was the Royal Air Force's Sealand Aerodrome, about ten miles from Liverpool. The fliers had made the crossing in 16 hours, 17 minutes.[22] Post and Gatty had accomplished the 28th transatlantic flight (including airplane and airships) and the first crossing in an aircraft powered by a Wasp engine.

Following lunch with the English airmen, during which time the *Winnie Mae* was partially refueled, Post and Gatty took off for Germany.[23] Gatty filmed some excellent aerial motion pictures over Holland. The strange terrain presented navigational problems and Post later admitted that he was very tired and had trouble keeping a magnetic course.[24] They landed at Hanover, Germany, which was almost halfway to Berlin. The fliers got directions to Berlin and immediately took off. Post admits that he and Gatty were so tired they forgot to check their fuel, and had to return to Hanover to be on the safe side. After having some fuel pumped aboard, they flew on to Berlin as planned.

The arrival of the *Winnie Mae* in the German capital caused a great deal of excitement at Tempelhof Airport where a large crowd waited. Kendal Foss of the *New York Times* reported from the scene that in anticipation of the *Winnie Mae,* the crowd was excited by every airplane which came into view. At one point, a band prematurely played the "Stars and Stripes Forever," mistaking another airplane for the *Winnie Mae.* That evening in a special interview with the *Times,* Post stated he would have preferred better flying weather on the Atlantic leg. Post credited the successful flight to the blind-flying instruments and his comments appeared on the front page of the *Times* the next morning. Throughout the flight, Post and Gatty received prominent attention in the *Times* and other newspapers, usually on page one. This had the effect of further awakening the public to the potentialities of air travel.

After a much-needed full night's rest, Post and Gatty took off early the next morning on their 994-mile leg to Moscow. A low ceiling with heavy rains and some stiff headwinds complicated their navigation across Poland and eastern Russia. Gatty deliberately took them off course slightly to the north so that when they sighted the Volga River they would know that Moscow was off to the south. As they approached Moscow, Gatty shot some excellent aerial views of the ancient seat of government of Muscovy, now capital of the new Soviet state. When they landed, there were only a few dozen persons at the airfield to greet them, including American and Western European newsmen, but that evening they were feted at a gala nine-course banquet. The Russians made numerous speeches and many, many toasts were drunk to the success of the flight. Post and Gatty responded by drinking water. Post refused to hazard any impairment of his flying abilities by alcohol, however small, during the course of the flight.[25] He also made it a habit to eat lightly, which was not easily done in Russia.[26]

Publications for general distribution during the 1930s did not mention in-flight excretory considerations because of the social taboos of the day. However, Post and Gatty were well aware of the problem. Their practice was to partake only of light meals, which reduced uncomfortable periods between opportunities to visit toilets to a minimum. Otherwise, during flight it was their practice to use wax-coated ice-cream cartons and toss them overboard.

The next morning, after only two hours' sleep, a misunderstanding brought the first major delay. The Russians fueled the *Winnie Mae's* gasoline tanks with Imperial gallons (277 cubic inches, 7.2 pounds each) instead of U.S. gallons (231 cubic inches, 6 pounds each). With a Moscow-to-Novo-Sibirsk leg of 1,579 miles and a fuel consumption of 18 U.S. gallons per hour at 120-miles per hour ground speed, the *Winnie Mae* would hypothetically require about 13 hours air time to reach Novo-Sibirsk and would consume 234 U.S. gallons of fuel. Assuming five hours additional flight reserve (an additional 90 U.S. gallons), the *Winnie Mae* would require a total of 324 U.S. gallons of gasoline. At six pounds per gallon, this is 1,944 pounds of fuel. The *Winnie Mae* at this time could hold 540 U.S. gallons (3,240 pounds), but Wiley did not want too heavy a weight for the takeoff due to the nature of the field. The Imperial gallon is 20 percent larger than the U.S. gallon, which meant that instead of 1,944 pounds of fuel in the hypothetical case, the *Winnie Mae* would have received an additional 389 pounds, giving a total fuel weight of 2,333 pounds.

When Post learned of the mistake, he feared that the additional weight would make the plane too heavy for a safe takeoff from the Moscow field. Factors to consider included field roughness effects on landing-gear strength and field traction in relation to total airplane and fuel weight. It was necessary to siphon some fuel from the tanks, a time consuming process, which was accomplished largely by Post and Gatty themselves. The engine was then started by Gatty and several mechanics who pulled a rope attached to a boot that was fitted over the tip of one of the propeller blades.

The flight from Moscow to Novo-Sibirsk in Siberia was assisted by up-to-date maps given to Gatty in Moscow by representatives of Ossoaviakhim, a Soviet organization for the promotion of aviation and aeronautical careers among young Russians. During flight, Gatty filmed the Russian terrain. On reaching Novo-Sibirsk on June 26, the three clocks carried by Post and Gatty showed 1:32 p.m. Greenwich time, 6:32 p.m. local time in Novo-Sibirsk, and 9:32 a.m. New York daylight saving time. Gatty explained to Russian newsmen that it was lunchtime in London, midmorning in New York, and suppertime in Novo-Sibirsk. He also noted that all of these hours are on the same day, and that the next day, which began at the International Date Line (the 180th meridian), already was 1 hour and 32 minutes old.[27] A female professional interpreter assisted with the translations.

The weary fliers were taken to a hotel, had a sponge bath, and were given a banquet, of which they took sparingly. They got to bed about 10:00 p.m., local time. The beds were uncomfortable and Gatty didn't sleep well because of bedbugs. They were awakened on schedule at 1:00 a.m., with only three hours of sleep. The *Winnie Mae* roared off the sod at Novo-Sibirsk at 4:45 a.m. local time, which Post noted was dinner time in New York (5:45 p.m.).[28]

Wiley picked up the railroad track to Irkutsk, and Gatty got some snatches of much-needed sleep over the next two hours. Prior to landing at Irkutsk, Wiley asked Gatty to shift his chair back as an aid to holding the tail down on approach and landing.[29] The flight took six hours. Annie Polikof, a 16-year-old girl, who had lived her first six years in England, served as interpreter. Wiley sent his wife a two-word cable, "Feeling fine." After 2 hours, 19 minutes ground time, the fliers took off for Blagoveschchensk at 2:09 p.m. Irkutsk daylight time. Gatty was concerned that any delays in starting this next seven-hour flight would mean an attempted night landing at an airport lit by oil flames, and he wanted to avoid this, if at all possible. The primitive Siberian airfields were bad enough by daylight.

The *Winnie Mae* crossed the tip of Manchuria and flew under an overcast as it reentered Siberia. The distance to be covered to Blagoveshchensk on the Amur River was about 1,000 miles and the map showed indistinguishable features along the way. However, the town was on the Amur River, and Gatty and Post set a course which was intentionally too far to the left (Figure 23). This enabled the fliers, upon reaching the river, to know that the airport would be reached by a turn to the right. Otherwise a straight approach to the river would result in a 50/50 probability of turning in one direction over the over direc-

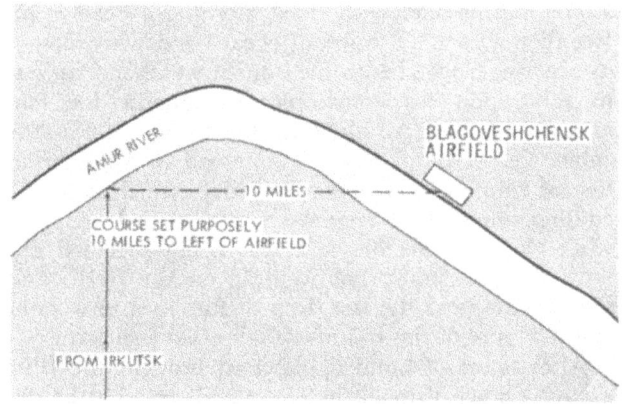

FIGURE 23.—*Gatty Navigation Strategy*. Post and Gatty departed Irkutsk at 2:09 p.m., Irkutsk daylight saving time, June 27, 1931, for Blagoveschchensk, which lay 1,100 miles away to the east. The flight course traversed long distances of featureless terrain and crossed the tip of Manchuria. Since Irkutsk was on the Amur River, Gatty plotted a course that purposely took them ten miles to the left of the Blagoveshchensk airfield, so that when the river was reached they would know that a right turn would bring them to the destination airfield. Since they would arrive at dusk, it was doubly important that they know exactly in which direction the field lay, upon reaching the river. (From Gatty's *Nature Is Your Guide*.)

tion with respect to finding the airport. This was one of Gatty's many "navigation tricks" which had important application in aviation.[30]

Darkness came fast and Gatty was the first to see the string of oil flames at the airport. An all-day rain had almost transformed the Blagoveshchensk landing field into a swamp; six inches of "ooze" was covered by two inches of water. Wiley made a slow "backside-of-the-power curve" soft-field approach, easing his way through the darkness to the rectangle of lights.[31] The plane rolled less than 400 feet as the wheels sank deeper and deeper into the mud.

An early-model Ford with Ossaviakhim men arrived, accompanied by two Danish telegraph operators who spoke English and assisted in making arrangements for a tractor to pull the *Winnie Mae* from the mud. Wiley was drowsy, fatigued, and became irritable, so much so that Gatty quit attempting to raise his spirits by humor.[32] This irritability is characteristic of sleep deprivation and is aggravated by time-zone dislocation. Wiley stayed with the plane and Gatty went into town to bring back food. Wiley wanted to be present when the tractor arrived, and stretched out in Gatty's fuselage seat, getting four hours' sleep.

Gatty was taken to the homes of the Danish telegraphers, where he had a hot meal and his first tub bath since leaving New York. He got two hours' sleep and then proceeded back to the field. The tractor failed to arrive. Finally, Post talked the Russians into using two horses, but the ground, although drying, was still too

FIGURE 24.—Winnie Mae Fain (formerly Winnie Mae Hall, now Mrs. Leslie Fain) is flanked by Clive Brook (English motion picture star, standing to her right) and her father, F. C. Hall, the backer of Post's 1931 world flight. (Courtesy Winnie Mae Fain.)

FIGURE 25.—A fatigued Wiley Post is supported by a tall New York City policeman just after stepping out of the *Winnie Mae* with Harold Gatty, following their 8:47 p.m. landing, July 1, 1931, at Roosevelt Field. Both men have lost weight and are considerably disheveled. Floyd Gibbons stands just to Gatty's left. (Courtesy Acme Newspictures, Inc.)

FIGURE 26.—Post and Gatty clutch hands with their backer, F. C. Hall, following their 8-day, 15-hour, 51-minute record, around-the-world flight, July 1, 1931. Post and Gatty took rooms with their wives at the Ritz-Carlton Hotel in New York City. Post and Gatty have not yet changed their clothes, which show the wear and tear of the trip. Although very fatigued, they were temporarily revived by the flush of success, and the satisfaction felt by Mr. Hall is evident in his facial expression. Post and Gatty have both lost several pounds of weight during the eight-day trip. (Courtesy Winnie Mae Fain.)

FIGURE 27.—Post and Gatty carried souvenir, stamped envelopes and had them canceled at various points along their around-the-world route. (Courtesy Lockheed Aircraft Company.)

muddy. After waiting five more hours (which allowed Post some extra sleep), the horses tried again and this time pulled the plane free.

After a careful soft-field takeoff, Post and Gatty were on their way to Khabarovsk, 363 miles away. The ground time at Blagoveshchensk had been 12 hours and 21 minutes; some precious sleep had been gained, but half a day was lost. The takeoff at Blagoveshchensk was at 1:21 p.m. (local time) and the landing at Khabarovsk was at 3:56 p.m.

When the *Winnie Mae* landed at Khabarovsk, she was five and one-half days out of New York, and ahead stretched the hazardous leg of 2,441 miles from Khabarovsk to Solomon, Alaska, filled with unknown mountains and wide stretches of water. Post commented on his fatigued feelings after landing, and the need, therefore, for the exercise of extra caution prior to jumping off on this long and hazardous leg of the flight.[33]

The *Winnie Mae* had functioned perfectly. As a preventive maintenance measure, Post had changed the four lower spark plugs at Khabarovsk. He also pulled the propeller through in a fashion that enabled him to feel the compression on each cylinder.

Gatty received a Japanese weather report by radio that stated that a low-pressure area with cloud banks was leaving the planned route across the Sea of Okhotsk, but another low was moving toward the route and could create headwinds several hours later.

Wiley felt that enough surface wind to enable a takeoff from Khabarovsk would exist and decision was made to fill all tanks and fly nonstop to Solomon, by-passing a fuel stop at Petropavolovsk. He and Gatty went into town and got two hours' sleep. When they got back to the field, the wind was an exact crosswind, so they took advantage of the situation and slept on cots in a hangar for another few hours. In their sleep-deprived state, this was a critically needed rest period.

They took off at 6:56 p.m. local time and met some rough flying conditions, sometimes skimming along rivers and trees to avoid higher headwinds (allowing ground speeds of 140 miles per hour), sometimes climbing on top of the clouds so Gatty could get a "moon and sun line" fix. At times, mountains were found which were higher than shown on the maps, necessitating rapid climbs and detours.

The *Winnie Mae* temporarily broke out over St. Lawrence Island, with two hours' remaining fuel. In 30 minutes they let down through a thin-cloud layer near Fort Davis. Wiley spotted Solomon, Alaska, and landed on the nearby soft beach sand at 2:45 p.m. The fuel tanks were nearly empty. They brought the fuel up to 100 gallons and planned to fly to Fairbanks to spend the night. The takeoff attempt was unsuccessful, however; the soft sand caught the *Winnie Mae's* wheels, nosed her over, and bent the tips of her propeller.

Wiley managed to straighten the tips, for a short flight, with a hammer, wrench, and stone. Then, while attempting to start the engine by swinging the

FIGURE 28.—Shortly after their 1931 flight, following a period of rest and cleaning up, Gatty and Post pose with their wives. The emotional strain of the post-flight demands is evident. Gatty and Mrs. Gatty were divorced not long after, and he joined the U.S. Navy as a navigation instructor. Mae Post was a little amazed at Wiley's rocket-like climb in three years from an unknown Oklahoma barnstormer to one of the world's most famous pilots. (Courtesy Winnie Mae Fain.)

propeller, Gatty was hit by a blade when the engine backfired. When he recovered from the shock in a few moments (with a bad bruise and a wrenched back), he got in and Post made a successful takeoff.

Upon reaching Fairbanks, the two fatigued fliers told newspapermen that they would be back in New York within two days.[34] Alaskan Airways personnel installed a new propeller, while the fliers logged slightly more than three hours of sleep. Six hours later they took off for Canada.

The *Winnie Mae's* takeoff from Fairbanks was made at 3:25 a.m. local time, in the eerie dawn created by the "midnight sun." Gatty gave Post the course, and they were on their way to Edmonton, Alberta. Considerable rain and fog were met, and some care had to be taken with mountains shrouded in fog; but there were patches of clear weather along the track and Gatty got some aerial movie coverage of this leg of the flight. The Canadian National Railway's tracks finally came into sight and they provided an "iron beam" that guided them into Edmonton. The Fairbanks-Edmonton leg was a difficult one, and Gatty remarked that both he and Post were exhausted.[35]

Post had barely braked the *Winnie Mae* to a stop when he was already concerned about his takeoff from Edmonton. Rains had soaked the field and it was dangerously soft. A Canadian airmail pilot suggested that Post might use the paved surface of Portage Avenue, Edmonton's main street, and the City Fathers proved eager to cooperate. While Post and Gatty slept that night, work crews were busy removing telephone wires and power lines along Portage Avenue's "runway," while at the airport a gang was busy washing the *Winnie Mae* to have her all prettied up for her return to New York. The next morning Post raced the gleaming white and purple airplane down Portage Avenue and climbed out over Edmonton's rooftops for

FIGURE 29.—Wiley Post and Harold Gatty receive the largest ticker-tape deluge in New York City's history, July 2, 1931, in recognition of their record around-the-world flight. The fliers' achievement exerted a tremendous stimulus to aeronautics the world over. (Courtesy Wide World Photos.)

Cleveland—and New York.

A few hours later the glittering surface of Lake Superior came in sight and 26 minutes later the *Winnie Mae's* shadow was speeding among the pine forests of the United States. Lake Michigan came in sight, fell behind, and then the length of Lake Erie appeared ahead. Post brought the *Winnie Mae* down onto Cleveland's Municipal Airport at 5:15 p.m. eastern daylight time. There was a huge crowd at the airport and the airmen received a rousing welcome; but it was only a sample of what was awaiting them in New York. Among the persons to greet them at the airport was the then-famous boxer Bill Stribling who was challenging Max Schmeling for the world's heavyweight title. Stribling himself was a licensed pilot and an active aviator, and he reportedly gave Post and Gatty tickets for ringside seats at the forthcoming championship flight. It is not known if the two fliers attended the fight, but it is well known that Stribling lost it!

Meanwhile, fuel was flowing into the *Winnie Mae's* tanks and as fast as they were filled, Post and Gatty were gone. Post lifted the *Winnie Mae* clear of Cleveland's runway only 30 minutes after her touchdown. Now there was only one more stop—New York City, the beginning and the end.

Post and Gatty took off for New York, aided by the revolving beacons of the Department of Commerce's lighted airway en route. These beacons were routinely turned on as they crossed Bellefonte, Pennsylvania, and the Alleghenies. The New York skyline came into view, and Hal MacMahon, flying a Breese monoplane fitted for photography, was the first pilot to spot the *Winnie Mae*. This airplane had belonged to Martin Jensen who had flown it from Oakland, California, to Hawaii in the 1927 Dole race. As Post neared Roosevelt Field, numerous other photographic planes were in the air. Post made an extra turn for the photographers and stated that he deliberately came in high over the hangars since he and his eye were tired.

Although they had anticipated some fanfare, Post and Gatty were amazed at being met by the more than 10,000 persons who broke into a complete state of pandemonium. Floyd Gibbons handled the broadcast microphones, but in the confusion, about all Post said was, "We had a great time." [36] Walter Mullins of Pathe News was filmed trying to induce Post to be more talkative. Post and Gatty were very tired and in

FIGURE 30.—New York City Mayor Jimmy Walker, Post and Mrs. Gatty to the right, Gatty and Mrs. Post to his left, greet the news media on the steps of City Hall. Behind Mrs. Gatty is Dick Blythe, noted pilot and aviation public-relations specialist in association with Harry Bruno (with spectacles—just behind man holding WOR microphone), who handled publicity for Charles Lindbergh's 1927 Atlantic Ocean solo flight. They were retained by F. C. Hall, and Post, for the public-relations aspects of the 1931 world flight. (Courtesy Winnie Mae Fain.)

FIGURE 31.—Wiley Post and Harold Gatty are welcomed by President Herbert Hoover at the White House following their 1931 around-the-world flight. (Courtesy Associated Press and the Herbert Hoover Presidential Library.)

an attempt to enliven the activities, Floyd Gibbons donned Post's eye patch. In answer to questions, Post said he had no real difficulties going through customs during the trip, but that Cleveland and Roosevelt Field customs took longer than all the other stops put together. He also commented that persons at all stops were helpful and gave specific commendation to the Russians who were "especially nice to us."

The *Winnie Mae* had touched down at Roosevelt Field at 8:47 p.m. on July 1, and an official timer of the National Aeronautics Association was on hand. Post and Gatty now held many new records. Their time was 8 days, 15 hours, and 51 minutes, which was more than 12 days faster than that of the *Graf Zeppelin*.[37] The "two young men in a hurry," as one periodical called them, had covered a total of 15,474 miles in a total elapsed time of 207 hours and 51 minutes. Averaging 146 miles per hour, they had spent 107 hours and 2 minutes in the air.[38] It was reported in *The Pilot* of October 1931,[39] that the *Winnie Mae* consumed 3,455 gallons of fuel during her flight. A total of 14 stops were made (not counting the double departure at Hanover as two). The longest leg of the circuit was from Khabarovsk to Solomon, a distance of about 2,500 miles; the shortest was from Hanover to Berlin, approximatey 154 miles.

The events of the next few days kept Post and Gatty from catching up fully on sleep. These included a radio interview over the National Broadcasting Company network in which Post and Gatty told of their flight experiences and thanked the public for its support; there was a ticker-tape parade along Broadway; a scheduled visit with President Herbert Hoover in Washington; and a luncheon given by the Aeronautical Chamber of Commerce, among many other activities. During the New York welcome,

FIGURE 32.—Post, President Hoover, and Gatty pose at the White House with Government officials, following the President's invitation after the record around-the-world flight. (Courtesy the Herbert Hoover Presidential Library.)

FIGURE 33.—Harold Gatty and Wiley Post hold their bronze plaque awards which read:

"Wings Around the World, June 23-July 1, 1931"
"Presented to Wiley Post and Harold Gatty by the Aeronautical Chamber of Commerce of America." (Courtesy Washington Studio Newark, New Jersey.)

Mayor Jimmy Walker punned that Post's plane was "the 'Winnie May' before the flight started, the 'Winnie Must' while in progress and the 'Winnie Did' now." Another popular suggestion had been that the name stood for "Win He May." Post and Gatty were filmed by Pathe in the Ritz-Carlton Hotel in New York City, being interviewed by Claude Collins.

Mrs. Post had arrived at the Ritz-Carlton Hotel where newsmen reported her comment that "wives should be seen and little heard from." [40] Reservations had been made for Mrs. Post and Mr. Gatty at the Biltmore, but the Mayor's Committee wanted the aviators at the Ritz, and their rooms were duly changed to the Ritz. Mrs. Gatty didn't arrive until the day after the two fliers landed (her plane had been forced down at Pittsburgh). Mrs. Post remarked how impressed she was by her visit to the White House and the gracious hospitality extended by Mrs. Hoover.

Wherever Post went, his admirers wanted to know how he had stayed awake. For a man who had slept only 15 hours in the last eight and a half days, his answer was simple: he didn't get sleepy. Although he admitted being tired, the one-eyed pilot said that he had little trouble staying awake. As the flight progressed, he found it easier to stay awake—and without the aid of any stimulants.[41] Part of his secret was his ability to relax completely and take catnaps when away from the airplane. It is reported that he went to sleep at Edmonton as soon as he entered the automobile that carried him away from the airfield.[42] He also found that the practice of eating lightly during the flight definitely helped him to avoid drowsiness.

The physical stamina demonstrated by Post and Gatty drew an editorial in the *New York Times*. Entitled "A Feat of Endurance," the *Times* said that the flier's skill and daring were overshadowed by their ability to undergo prolonged physical strain; the flight was proof of what men could endure when necessary.[43] To many, Post's flying was especially significant because of his lost eye. Clarence M. Young, Assistant Secretary of Commerce for Aviation, noted at a banquet in honor of the one-eyed pilot that in 1931 Post was one of three one-eyed men in the United States who held an air-transport pilot license.

The performance of the *Winnie Mae* and her Pratt & Whitney Wasp engine had been outstanding. The aircraft made the flight with a minimum of mechanical attention; from New York to Khabarovsk, a track of 9,010 miles, the only servicing required was fuel, oil, minor lubrication, and attention to the rocker arms. As noted earlier, Post had changed a few spark plugs at Khabarovsk. He also paid special attention to the fuel since the engine required high-quality gasoline (87 octane for takeoff and 80 octane for cruise, constituted the usual procedure). Throughout the trip the fuel he acquired was good, although in Russia it contained no ethyl compound. However, the Ethyl "anti-knock" compound was an American development, and although available in Western Europe it was still not widely used, even there, as early as 1931. The Pratt & Whitney Wasp's qualities became clear when it was found to need no special attention even after the Winnie Mae's return to New York.[44]

The flight by Post and Gatty was praised by newspapers and magazines throughout the nation and offered editors an opportunity to comment on aeronautical progress. Oklahomans were especially excited and local pride was high. Editor Showen of the *Maysville News* was quick to realize the advantages of having a home-town boy become an international hero; the town promptly claimed Wiley because his parents farmed there and he was a frequent visitor. Two days after the flight began, Showen wrote that some of Wiley's early flying was over Maysville when Wiley was still a barnstorming parachute jumper. After the flight ended, the editor made the following observation: "Maysville has been placed on the map of the world along with such places as New York, Berlin, Blagoveshchensk, Khabarovsk and Irkutsk." [45]

One of the biggest thrills for Maysville residents was

Figure 34.—Wiley Post taxis in, after landing the *Winnie Mae* at Chickasha, Oklahoma, July 9, 1931, for a triumphal homecoming following the around-the-world record flight. The return flight to Oklahoma was made nonstop from Columbus, Ohio, with Harold Gatty and F. C. Hall aboard. The "dust-bowl" environment of the southwest of the period is obvious in the *Winnie Mae's* prop-wash. A police motorcycle escort guides the fliers to the ramp. (Courtesy Winnie Mae Fain.)

the arrival of newsreel crews five days before the flight ended on Wednesday, July 1. Showen reported the novel experience for Post's parents, to be filmed for movies and talk into the "mike." In his editorial, "A Notable Achievement," Showen paid high compliments to Post and Gatty. Citing the revolutionary exploits of Columbus, Magellan, and Lindbergh, he reflected:

None of these received greater acclaim than the two men who flew around the world in less than nine days. Aviation has been given a tremendous impetus by this epoch-making flight and there will be others to break this new world record as bigger and better ships are made.[46]

A few weeks later, the following toast by William T. Lee appeared in the *Maysville News:*

Here's to the birdmen of the air,
Who were not afraid to take a 'dare'.
They laughed at danger, and challenged death,
While they circled the globe in almost a breath.
So to these Colonels I give this toast,
The heroes of the day—Gatty and Post.[47]

In the same issue, the editor observed that Post had proved himself the world's greatest aviator and the world's briefest orator: "He would rather fly around the world than make a five minute speech." Then the *News* gradually dropped into its regular country routine, filled with accounts of local people, religious revivals, and economic hard times. Carl Jenkins wrote in the *Daily Oklahoman* of July 11, 1931, that Wiley wanted to "return to the days back when," and Post slipped away to Maysville in his 1929 Ford coupé with Mae.

The *Daily Oklahoman* of Oklahoma City had covered each day of the flight, but its editorial page did not comment until four days after the flight. An editorial entitled "The Commonplace Approaches" then

FIGURE 35.—Post, Gatty, and Hall pose with Oklahoma figures just after stepping out of the *Winnie Mae* on July 9, 1931, Chickasha, Oklahoma. Chickasha was the first Oklahoma landing point, following Post's return to his home state. The four-cylinder motorcycle parked just forward and to the left of the *Winnie Mae* was popular with police departments. (Courtesy Winnie Mae Fain.)

appeared in the *Daily Oklahoman*. It highlighted the technical advances made in aviation and cited the flight as a graphic illustration of the vast improvement made in flying following the Army around-the-world-trip in 1924. The prophetic editorialist declared:

Such feats as that of Post and Gatty are destined to become commonplace before the world is very much older. Ere long, the world will pay no more attention to the feat cheered so insanely at Roosevelt Field Wednesday than it will to a morning flight from New York to Philadelphia. The future of the human race is in the air.[48]

Edith Johnson, an editorial page columnist for the *Oklahoman*, praised Mrs. Post and Mrs. Gatty for encouraging their husbands to "enter upon one of the greatest adventures in the world's history."[49] In Chickasha, F. C. Hall's former headquarters, the *Daily Express* proclaimed under a heading of "Brave, Bold Boys!" that Post and Gatty were now world heroes: "They won a unique place in the history of aviation by making a new record for circling the globe by air. It was an achievement worthy of all the popular acclaim that has been accorded to it."[50] A few days later, the *Daily Express* predicted that Post and Gatty's pioneering accomplishment would "stand out as one of the milestones in the progress of aviation."[51]

The *New York Times*, having a deep involvement in the flight, devoted several editorials to its progressive accomplishments. On June 27, while the flight was still in progress, the *Times* praised it as a profitable experiment that would speed intercontinental travel by air. The day after Post and Gatty returned, the *Times* described the feat as a "test of men, fabric, and engine," and two days later, on the Fourth of July, the New York newspaper commented that Post came from Oklahoma, "an interior State of America"

FIGURE 36.—William H. "Alfalfa Bill" Murray, homespun popular Governor of Oklahoma, poses on July 9, 1931, in Chickasha, with F. C. Hall, Wiley Post, and, far right, Harold Gatty. The admiring youths of the period, for whom Post felt a special affection, are interested onlookers (the Governor autographed the original). (Courtesy Winnie Mae Fain.)

FIGURE 37.—Wiley and Mae Post pose with their 1929 Model A Ford, shortly after Post's 1931 flight. Wiley had a desire to get away for awhile with Mrs. Post. He had expressed a specific wish to drive to his hometown of Marysville, Oklahoma. (Gordon Post snapshot and scrapbook). (Courtesy Gordon Post.)

that had been a part of the Union for only about 25 years (Oklahoma became a state on April 22, 1907). The *Times* considered the flight to have significance for all mankind: "It was as if messengers had come out of the skies to the earthdwellers with promise of greater victories, for man has not yet come to the limit of his striving with the forces of sea and air and land." [52]

Other newspapers had praise for the aerial journey. The New Haven *Journal-Courier* considered the flight significant because it would lead thousands of people to feel safer while flying. To the Philadelphia *Evening Public Ledger,* the flight was proof of aeronautical progress through better equipment. A day of relative safety in the air was the vision of the Springfield *Republican*.[53]

In aviation circles, the endorsement of *Aviation Magazine* revealed the feelings of aeronautical experts. *Aviation* considered the flight to be the great achievement of the last three years, comparable to the achievements of Lindbergh and Australia's Kingsford-Smith. It felt that the nation should be grateful to Post and Gatty for offering forceful and dramatic evidence that air transportation was encroaching upon the last frontier.[54] *Outlook Magazine* congratulated the two "brave and skillful men" but noted that the Post-Gatty flight around the world was about 15,000 miles in length, whereas the earth's circumference is 25,000 miles.

An interesting comment was made by the Russian

Figure 38.—Gatty and Post are seen after their 1931 around-the-world record flight. Note the oil-streaked cowling of the *Winnie Mae*. The small hole in the cowling above the trim is for the crank that spins the hand-inertial starter. The venturi tube just aft of the cowling above Gatty's head is for Gatty's duplicate set of gyroscopic flight instruments. The airscoop for cooling Post's feet is seen just above Gatty's right ear. The Pathé rooster emblem on the fuselage has been painted over but still shows slightly through. Gatty's drift and ground-speed instrument ports are shown under the rear windows. The propeller is a fixed-pitch Hamilton Standard. The right-wheel pant has a metal cover on top for a fuel-handler step. The attachment point to the wheel axel is shown with eight screws, while below this, the cover for the tire inflation valve is shown. The aircraft is roped off for protection. On this flight, Post confirmed his theory that the "variance in time" would disrupt his body biological rhythms and derogate flight performance. He was the first to publish on this phenomenon, which later became known as "circadian rhythm disruption." (Courtesy Lockheed Aircraft Company.)

newspaper, *Isvestia*, which stated that Russia could produce a corps of airmen just as skilled in blind-flying techniques as Post. In Joseph Stalin's view, there was "no fort which the Bolsheviki could not storm." [55] It is interesting that about a week after Post and Gatty landed in New York City, the Russians announced the establishment of a new air route from Moscow to Irkutsk, along the course worked out by Post and Gatty, with airmail flights beginning in August.[56]

Oklahomans prepared for Post and Gatty's return with high spirits, reminiscent to some of the excitement that accompanied the land openings of 1889. Shortly after the flight had started, the *Chickasha Daily Express* made a contract with F. C. Hall which provided that when the *Winnie Mae* returned to Oklahoma, Chickasha would be the site of the first landing.[57] Immediately after Post and Gatty landed at New York City, the Mayor of Chickasha wired Hall that Chickasha was "preparing for the biggest event in Oklahoma since the opening of the Cherokee Strip." [58] The gala day came on July 9 when Post, Gatty, and Hall arrived in Chickasha after a nonstop flight from Columbus, Ohio. Several State officials, including Governor William H. "Alfalfa Bill" Murray, were on hand to greet the fliers.[59] Mrs. Post and Mrs. Gatty came from New York in a Lockheed Vega flown by Marshall Headle, chief Lockheed test pilot; however on July 8, their Vega ground-looped at Columbus, Ohio, causing a day's delay.

On the next day, a celebration was held in Oklahoma City, and a portion of the banquet in honor of the fliers was transmitted over the Columbia Broadcasting System network. However, a prior contract that Post and Gatty had signed with the National Broadcasting Company prevented the two from saying anything for CBS.[60] A few days later Post and Gatty were feted at a banquet in Claremore, the hometown of Will Rogers, where they listened to comments by the humorist-philosopher, who had a deep interest in aviation.

The NBC contract was arranged by NBC's Artists' Service, the same group that brought Ignace Paderewski, Rudy Vallee, and Paul Whiteman to the nation.[61] It provided for a nationwide speaking tour

FIGURE 39.—For a short period in the fall of 1931, Post held title to the Lockheed Vega he had flown around the World, having come to terms regarding its purchase from F. C. Hall. Post sought sources of economic sponsorship, but discovered that the depression era was a tough time for independent operators. Note that the fuselage is still loaded with the long-distance fuel tanks. (Courtesy Winnie Mae Fain.)

utilizing the *Winnie Mae,* and cities desiring an appearance were required to put up as much as $1,500 in advance.

On July 21, 1931, Post and Gatty met in Boston at the State House with Massachusetts Governor Joseph Ely and the always-colorful James Michael Curley, mayor of Boston. A parade started at Beacon Street and Mayor Curley rode with Post and Gatty in a large touring car. Pathé News recorded the group passing along Tremont Street. Mayor Curley made a welcome speech at the following reception and banquet and presented Post and Gatty with flowers.

The good-will tour continued, with a stop in a different city each day. The Oklahoma City *Times* described Post and Gatty as follows: "Almost broke, their plans for the future a little indefinite, a couple of young men who were in a hurry around the world a few months ago, slowed down considerably Monday and took an accounting of their adventures." [62] Post reportedly said that he would clear about $500 for his part of the flight.

Soon after the round-the-world flight, Post and Hall had some strong differences of opinion concerning the use of the *Winnie Mae* in conjunction with Post's personal appearances. When Post and Gatty were in Columbus, Ohio, prior to departing for the homecoming celebrations in Oklahoma, Hall finally agreed to sell the airplane to Wiley. A sales contract dated July 8, 1931, written on stationery of the Deshler-Wallich Hotel, provided that Post would pay $3,000 cash within thirty days and accept a note for $18,200 at eight percent interest per annum.

One paragraph in the contract provided for the removal of Winnie Mae Fain's name from the airplane, if she so desired. Happily, she did not. The purple-trimmed white Vega had carried her name around the world in record time and across the front pages of the world's press; she was content to permit Wiley Post and his Vega to carry her name on into history. After Post and Hall signed the contract, it was Harold Gatty who witnessed the document.[63]

After selling the *Winnie Mae* to Post, Hall bought another Lockheed Vega, second hand from Ben Wofford in Tulsa, and named it *Winnie Mae of Oklahoma City, Okla.* On August 31, the Associated Press reported that he had hired Frank Hoover, a former Braniff pilot, who he would sponsor for an around-the-world flight to break the record set by Post and

FIGURE 40.—Wiley Post, left, at the Lockheed factory in Burbank, studies the fuselage-construction method used for Vega fuselages. The two half shells of the wooden fuselage were glued together as shown. Second from left is Bill Parker, third is Carl B. Squier, general manager, and on the far left is Richard Von Hake, works manager. (Courtesy Lockheed Aircraft Company.)

Gatty. While attending the National Air Races at Cleveland, Hall boasted to newsmen that his new airplane had a top speed of 218 miles per hour as compared to the *Winnie Mae's* 210.[64] Perhaps Hall's new Vega could beat the *Winnie Mae'* time, but he never tried to find out. Within a year he had sold the airplane, and thereafter his name fades from the scene of aviation.

On August 29, 1931, Wiley remarked that he might undertake a nonstop from Tokyo to Seattle in the spring of 1932.[65] No one had as yet flown transpacific. He proposed several possible modifications to the *Winnie Mae,* including a jettisonable landing gear.[66] Meanwhile, in October, Herndon and Pangborn made their successful transpacific flight from Japan to Wenatchee, Washington, which made Post's transpacific plans superfluous. Wiley Post always tried to do new things, and in new ways, that would leave a historic milestone along the path of progress of manned flight. He was not a man who poured old wine into new bottles; it was not his way to fly in the tracks of other men, simply for the sake of setting a new record.

In a November 21 Chicago dateline report, the North American Newspaper Alliance described Post during an interview in his hotel room as being "a little hard of hearing, plump, genial and disillusioned." The temporary deafness was due to the high noise level of the Vega cockpit. He had flown to Chicago from Oklahoma City the night before, and had spent a few weeks hunting in Texas and Mexico with Mae, where they shot some ducks and quail. Post described his world flight as a "stunt" which "didn't advance the mechanics of aviation an inch," because only equipment already proved sound was acceptable to a long-distance flier. However, Post reported that he had some offers in aviation.[67] In the same article, Post was quoted as saying that the economics of the time made it difficult to make money in aviation. He observed that Lindbergh had been the big money-maker. He also said he might write a book, "Behind the Scenes in Aviation," and he thought it might be a real eye-opener. It is a pity he did not, but perhaps the prospect of libel suits (even truth may be judged "libelous") discouraged him.

Post and Gatty's account of the 1931 flight, published as a book in August of that year by Rand McNally and Company, and entitled *Around the World in Eight Days,* was rather hastily written, but is very readable. Leo Kieran, a New York writer assisted Post and Gatty in writing the book, which took about three weeks to complete.[68] In his close labors with Post and Gatty, Leo Kieran evidently did not learn much about how to speed around the world by air. Five years later in October 1936, Kieran himself raced around the world for the *New York Times,* using commercial airlines in competition with two other journalists. The object of the race was to demonstrate how quickly any person could fly around the world by regularly scheduled airlines. Kieran came in third.

The Smithsonian Institution showed an interest in acquiring the *Winnie Mae* and Post helped initiate a drive for funds; however, the idea of another flight around the world was beginning to seize Post's mind. Such a flight, employing newly developed equipment, would provide a dramatic demonstration of the new capabilities of modern aircraft. The *Winnie Mae* could not become a museum piece just yet; she had another great labor to perform before her retirement.

Post and Gatty continued on their lecture circuit of various American cities, and sometimes local pilots would treat them to a hop. In Cincinnati, Blanche Noyes took them up for their first flight in an autogyro. After five months, Gatty went back to business in San Diego. The economic depression, which had become worse than ever, made things extremely difficult; the *Literary Digest* noted in August 1932 that many ocean fliers were unable to "raise the price of gasoline to fill the tanks, let alone make any profit on the trip."[69] In 1932 there were only five transatlantic flights made. One of them was simply to get the monster 12-engine Dornier Do.X flying boat back to Germany after its dismally unsuccessful "sales" flight to South America and the United States that began

FIGURE 41.—Wiley Post stands before the beautifully reconditioned *Winnie Mae,* August 1932, Burbank, California. The propeller is of the fixed-pitch variety, and the lower right wing sports a retractable landing light (the light and the other, in the left wing, was extended manually or by an electric motor). The airplane is now in the "commercial" category (NC 105W). Note that the listing of the 1931 landings is lined up on the left margin, and that the exhaust is emitted at the lower side of the cowling. The *Winnie Mae* is on a "compass rose" at the airport. (Courtesy Lockheed Aircraft Company.)

FIGURE 42.—Billy Parker's Lockheed Vega is started by hand-craking the inertial starter at the National Air Races, 1932. The mechanic on the right is Fidel "Pancho" Vela, who maintained Parker's plane. (Courtesy Phillips Petroleum.)

the year before. One of the other transatlantic flights was subsidized by the German airline Deutsche Lufthansa. Only three were made by individuals.

In such straitened circumstances Post had little hope of promoting the funds for another expensive around-the-world flight. Indeed, it would seem that even he may have been having difficulty in keeping the *Winnie Mae's* tanks full. Post's Department of Commerce pilot records show that he had 3,100 flight hours on September 15, 1931, and that this reached 3,500 hours by March 15, 1932. However, between March 15 and September 15, 1932, his records show only 14 flight hours. During the six-month period after September his flying time increased by 235 hours, but 1932 ended for Wiley as definitely an "in-between" year from the standpoint of flying.

The challenges of another around-the-world flight, nevertheless, continued to fill Post's mind. He wanted to fly the circuit again, faster than before—and alone.

NOTES

1. WILEY POST AND HAROLD GATTY, *Around the World in Eight Days* (London: John Hamilton, Ltd., circa 1931), hereafter abbreviated as Post and Gatty, *RW*.
2. POST AND GATTY, *RW*.
3. POST AND GATTY, *RW*.
4.
5. F. C. Hall to Snetcher and Pitman, April 15, 1931. Mrs. Hall died in the fall of 1930; *Daily Oklahoman*, July 2, 1931.
6. F. C. Hall to J. Edwin Pool, *Chickasha Daily Express*, May 22, 1931; Fain scrapbook.
7. *New York Times*, June 24, 1931.
8. HARRY BRUNO, *Wings Over America* (Garden City: Halcyon House, 1944), pp. 196–206.
9. *Aviation* (August 1931), p. 469.
10. *New York Times*, July 2, 1931, p. 4.
11. *Aviation* (August 1931), p. 468.
12. POST AND GATTY, *RW*, p. 27.
13. POST AND GATTY, *RW*, pp. 18–19.
14. Billy Parker interview.
15. *Daily Oklahoman*, June 28, 1931.
16. *Chickasha Daily Express*, May 15, 1931.
17. *Chickasha Daily Express*, May 29, 1931, p. 1.
18. *New York Times*, June 24, 1931, p. 3.
19. For a summary of this and related flights, see C. R. Roseberry, *The Challenging Skies* (New York: Doubleday, 1966). A good summary account of transatlantic flights, 1919–1939, may be found in F. H. Ellis and E. Ellis, *Atlantic Air Conquest* (Toronto: The Ryerson Press, 1963), 223 pp; and a similar account, but beautifully illustrated, is Kenneth McDonough, *Atlantic Wings, 1919–1939* (Hertfordshire, England: Model Aeronautical Press, 1966), 132 pp.
20. *Literary Digest* (July 4, 1931), p. 11.
21. *Bee Hive*, vol. V, no. 8 (August 1931).
22. *Literary Digest* (July 4, 1931), p. 11.
23. Post highlights this point in his book, *Around the World in Eight Days*, by indicating that it was only breakfast time in New York, his recent point of departure, and the thought of lunch was strange. This time-zone displacement contributed to the developing fatigue.
24. POST AND GATTY, *RW*, p. 88.
25. Gatty drank a glass of wine immediately after the later landing at Novo-Sibirsk, but he did not have the psychomotor pilot duties of Post; related in *RW*, p. 119
26. *New York Times*, June 27, 1931, p. 2.
27. POST AND GATTY, *RW*, p. 118.
28. POST AND GATTY, *RW*, p. 125.
29. POST AND GATTY, *RW*, p. 129.
30. HAROLD GATTY, *Nature is Your Guide* (New York: E. P. Dutton and Co., 1958).
31. POST AND GATTY, *RW*, pp. 133–134.
32. POST AND GATTY, *RW*, pp. 137–138.
33. POST AND GATTY, *RW*, p. 143.
34. *New York Times*, July 1, 1931, p. 1.
35. POST AND GATTY, *RW*, p. 165.
36. *Daily Oklahoman*, July 2, 1931.
37. Emme, *Aeronautics*, p. 28.
38. *Aviation* (August 1931), p. 455.
39. *The Pilot*, vol. 4, no. 10 (October 1931), p. 50.
40. Jane Eads, AP, Gordon Post scrapbook.
41. *New York Times*, July 3, 1931, p. 6.
42. *New York Times*, July 1, 1931, p. 1.
43. *New York Times*, July 1, 1931, p. 26.
44. *Aviation* (August 1931), p. 469.
45. *Maysville News*, July 3, 1931, p. 4.
46. *Maysville News*, July 2, 1931, p. 4.
47. *Maysville News*, July 16, 1931, p. 1.
48. *Daily Oklahoman*, July 5, 1931, p. 8c.
49. *Daily Oklahoman*, July 4, 1931, p. 8.
50. *Chickasha Daily Express*, July 3, 1931, p. 8.
51. *Chickasha Daily Express*, July 7, 1931, p. 8.
52. *New York Times*, July 4, 1931, p. 12.
53. *Literary Digest* (July 11, 1931), p. 5–6.
54. *Aviation* (August 1931), p. 450.
55. *New York Times*, July 14, 1931, p. 3.
56. *New York Times*, July 11, 1931, p. 13.
57. *Daily Express*, June 26, 1931.
58. Fain scrapbook.
59. *Daily Express*, July 9, 1931.
60. *Daily Oklahoman*, July 11, 1931.
61. *Daily Oklahoman*, July 1, 1931.
62. *Oklahoma City Times*, September 14, 1931.
63. Fain scrapbook.
64. *Daily Express*, August 31, 1931.
65. *Oklahoma City Times*, August 29, 1931.
66. Gordon Post scrapbook.
67. *New York Times*, November 22, 1931, II, 2.
68. Harry Bruno, Post's agent, recalls that Kieran "had to work fast and get the information bit by bit whenever the two fliers could be held long enough for them to talk"; Harry Bruno, personal communication, August 19, 1963. Kieran later joined the *New York Times* and was on its staff until his death.
69. *Literary Digest* (August 13, 1932), p. 30.

3 / Epic Solo Flight (1933)

ON JANUARY 14, 1933, Gilbert Budwig wrote to Winnie Mae Fain in Oklahoma City and stated that the semiannual inspection of her aircraft, Lockheed Vega, serial number 122, license NC 105W, was due February 15, 1933. She was told to see Robert I. Hazen of Love Field, Dallas, Texas, for this inspection. And yet another development in ownership of the *Winnie Mae* occurred at this point.

On February 5, 1933, Lockheed Vega number NC 105W, was listed in the record, transfer, and reassignment form as having been purchased from Winnie Mae Fain by the Fain and Post Drilling Company of 706 Northwest 29th Street, Oklahoma City, Oklahoma. A request was made for a restricted license for the aircraft by the Fain and Post Drilling Company. Leslie Fain was listed as president of the company and Wiley Post and L. B. Thompson were listed as directors. In addition, Wiley Post was listed as secretary-treasurer of the company. The purpose for requesting a restricted license was in order to make a solo around-the-world flight. The aircraft was stated as being at Curtiss-Wright Airport, Oklahoma City.

A few weeks later the *New York Times* reported that Wiley Post was planning to make another trip around the world, and this time he would fly alone. Post refused to discuss the matter with the *Times*. The *Times*, however, provided alleged details of the flight, and observed that the aviator would use a new "robot" pilot. The same issue of the *Times* reported that another pilot, James J. "Jimmy" Mattern, would also attempt to fly solo in a Vega around the world that year.[1]

In July 1932, Bennett Griffin and Jimmy Mattern had attempted to beat the time of the 1931 Post-and-Gatty flight. The Vega used by Griffin and Mattern had a blue fuselage with white trim, a white tail, and white wings; it was named *Century of Progress* in honor of the forthcoming World's Fair in Chicago. Arrangements for this representation were made through Rufus Dawes, a Chicago businessman.[2]

Griffin and Mattern bought the cabin fuel tanks used in the *Winnie Mae,* in the 1931 flight, from Post and installed them in the fuselage of their Vega. They put a set of dual controls and flight instruments behind the fuselage tanks so the "aft pilot" could spell the front pilot during long flight legs. The aft pilot could only see out of the side of the fuselage, and in effect was a human autopilot. This arrangement was almost exactly the same as that used by Kelly and MacReady in their immortal coast-to-coast, nonstop flight of 1920 in the Fokker *T-2*. Mattern also installed a voice tube for interpilot communications, and it proved to work well.

Griffin and Mattern took off from Floyd Bennett Field on July 5, 1932, but, after successfully reaching Harbour Grace and Berlin, they were forced down inside Russia when their cabin hatch flew off and seriously damaged the vertical stabilizer. The crash landing resulted in the fuselage breaking in half and the wings being ruined. The engine, fuel tanks, and the instruments were brought back by the two pilots when they returned to the United States.[3]

Griffin and Mattern planned early in 1933 to make another attempt at an around-the-world flight. When they learned that Post was going to fly solo, they matched coins to see which of them would make the attempt. Mattern won,[4] and he purchased one of the three Lockheed Vegas which the Standard Oil Company of New Jersey owned. These Vegas had the unusual decoration of a giant, red eagle painted on a blue fuselage with eagle wings painted on the white wings of the airplane, and giant claws were painted over the wheel pants. The result was a truly bizarre-looking airplane. The Mattern airplane contained a sign on the right and left of the fuselage, at the forward side of the eagle's neck, stating, "Mattern and Griffin World Records." It also referenced that they had made the first American (i.e., Newfoundland) to Berlin nonstop flight in 1932.

Department of Commerce records document the following:

On March 14, 1933, S. L. "Sandy" Willits, Supervising Inspector, Aeronautics Branch, Department of Commerce, with offices at Roosevelt Field, Long Island, New York, wrote to the Chief of the Inspection Service of the Aeronautics Branch, Washington, D.C., and stated that Wiley Post was in on March 14 and had installed a Sperry automatic pilot in the Lockheed Vega, NC 105W.

Willits wrote that:

"He [Post] would like to leave the C license on this air-

FIGURE 43.—Rare photo of Wiley Post, second from right, with L. E. Gray (arms on Post), and Braniff mechanics, who repaired the *Winnie Mae* after its April 21, 1933, accident at Chickasha. The *Winnie Mae* is being prepared for the solo around-the-world flight. To the far left is George Brauer, who accomplished much of the repair work on the aircraft. Photo taken at Curtis-Wright Field, Oklahoma City. Note the hand crank for the inertial starter (man standing on tire has left hand on the crank). (Courtesy L. E. Gray.)

plane for about two months, at the end of which time the airplane will be overhauled and will be equipped for long distance flights. At that time he will apply for a restricted license. In the memorandum, he has assured me that he will not haul any passengers for hire. I have given him permission to fly this airplane to Oklahoma City without removing the C. Will you please communicate with him directly at 706 29th Street, Oklahoma City, Oklahoma, and advise him whether or not he can continue the operation of this airplane with the C license."

Willets also said that he had inspected the airplane on March 14. On March 16, 1933, Budwig wrote to Post giving him authority to install and operate a Sperry automatic pilot in NC 105W during a 60-day period, extending from March 14, 1933. Budwig stated that this authority was valid only with the provision that no passengers would be carried for hire in the aircraft.

In latter March of 1933, when Post tested the Sperry automatic pilot in the *Winnie Mae*, on a flight from Oklahoma to Mexico City, it became apparent that he was preparing for an unusual flight. The *Daily Oklahoman* on April 5, 1933, reported that Post still refused to verify the rumors of another world flight. The paper noted that Post had previously told New York newsmen that if he flew around the world again he would "go it alone." But Post offered no comment.

On April 21, 1933, an accident almost ended Wiley's plans. Wiley persuaded his close friend, "Red" Gray, to fly the *Winnie Mae* and to try the new Sperry automatic pilot. Gray was reluctant for fear that he would crash the special airplane, but Post persisted. When Gray climbed into the pilot's seat at the airport south of Chickasha, he noticed that the gasoline gauges showed the plane's tanks to be almost empty. However, Wiley felt that there was sufficient fuel for a short hop since he had recently partially fueled the plane; unknown to him, however, some youths had slipped in and siphoned off some fuel for their car. Post, Frederickson, and another passenger climbed into the cabin. Gray gunned the engine and headed down the turf runway. When the plane reached an altitude of about 50 feet, the engine suddenly quit. Gray hoped to bring the *Winnie Mae* back to earth, and ground-looped before running into a peach orchard at the end of the field. Gray's experience in flying Vegas for Braniff Airways apparently saved the *Winnie Mae* from complete destruction when she finally did strike the trees. The *Winnie*

Mae's occupants were fortunate: Post had a cut finger, Frederickson two cracked ribs, while Gray and the third passenger were uninjured.

Post had the *Winnie Mae* hauled to Oklahoma City, where a crew of Braniff Airways craftsmen immediately set about rebuilding her. George Brauer, a German woodworker who had come to the United States from Russia just before World War I, supervised the bodywork. A master woodworker, Brauer had developed some unique techniques while repairing Braniff's six-ply, plywood Vegas, and he put his best into the *Winnie Mae*.

In his *Oklahoma City Times* column, "The Tiny Times," Harrison revealed that four Braniff Airways persons had put up their back salaries so that Post could get his plane out of the shop, following the accident at Chickasha. The necessary modifications and repairs had amounted to $1,763.92, but Post had only $1,200 cash when the plane was completed. The four men who came to his aid were Tom Braniff, operating manager; Luther E. "Red" Gray, and Claude Seaton, pilots; and Sterling E. Perry, head mechanic.[5] In addition, several other Braniff employees, led by chief overhauler, George Brauer, donated their off-hours to the *Winnie Mae,* and Post later saw that they were paid double for their efforts.[6]

Brauer installed larger gasoline tanks in the *Winnie Mae's* wings. Because Post would fly solo, the airplane was able to lift more fuel than in 1931, and the entire cabin was filled with fuel tanks, raising the plane's capacity to 645 gallons. To duplicate the type of balance changes that Getty had provided in 1931 when he moved backward or forward, a means of pumping fuel between fore and aft fuselage tanks was installed. A radio mast made of one-inch diameter streamlined tubing, six feet long, was installed in the

FIGURE 44.—George Brauer, left, master woodworker, and Post stand before the rebuilt *Winnie Mae*, Oklahoma City, May 1933. Note that the 1931 flight stops are painted so that the right margin is lined up from top to bottom (contrast with the earlier photos.) (Courtesy George Brauer.)

fin and a new Breeze radio-shielded ignition harness was put on the engine.[7]

The *Winnie Mae's* Wasp now had approximately 780 operational hours, so Braniff mechanics began getting her engine ready for the flight, under the supervision of Raymond Peck of Pratt & Whitney. The Wasp was built under Airworthiness Type Certificate number 14; it was originally approved for 420 maximum continuous horsepower at 2,000 revolutions per minute, sea level, and it could use fuel with octane as low as 58. Its original bore and stroke were each 5.75 inches, and its original displacement was 1,344 cubic inches. The engine's dry weight (without accessories or oil) was 745 pounds. It had a direct-drive crankshaft and now a supercharger with an impeller gear

FIGURE 46.—Portrait made of Wiley Post on June 9, 1933, shortly before his solo around-the-world flight. For this photo he substituted his glass eye on the left, for his traditional eye patch. (Courtesy Phillips Petroleum Company.)

FIGURE 45.—The Winnie Mae's instrument panel as prepared for the solo world flight. The Sperry autopilot is shown in the center of the instrument panel. The magnetic compass is shown on the right of the autopilot, and below the compass is shown the sensitivity knob for the radio compass. The airplane's control stick is in the center, and behind it is the pneumatic servomechanism that is part of the autopilot mechanism. The openings to the left and right rudder pedals are shown in the lower portion of the picture. The cockpit door opened into the fuselage and was pushed to the open position by hand through a hole in the left side of the bulkhead lateral to the door. (Courtesy George Brauer.)

ratio of 7:1 (a 10:1 impeller was used in 1930 for the air derby race, but it raised the fuel consumption too much for long-distance flying). The carburetor was a two-barrel, updraft Bendix Stromberg NAY–7B, with a 1¾-inch verturi diameter. The ignition had dual scintilla VAG–9D magnetoes.

All cylinders had been replaced in June of 1932 with Series C1 cylinders and 6:1 compression-ratio pistons were utilized. The previous compression ratio had been 5.25:1; the new 6:1 ratio provided for a more smoothly running engine and a better-fuel economy. The new cylinder heads provided a cooler operation and new type, sodium-cooled exhaust valves were used. The rocker boxes were provided with special fittings and lines that enabled Wiley to use a grease gun in the cockpit during flight, to grease the rocker arms.[8] This innovation—unique in its day—reduced the likelihood of an inflight emergency and decreased the need of ground maintenance en route.

The *Winnie Mae's* Wasp engine, series C, serial number 3088, had originally been built during April–May 1930 at the Pratt & Whitney factory in Bridgeport, Connecticut, and shipped to Lockheed in Burbank for installation. The 1930 *Winnie Mae* was a

Figure 47.—Wiley Post stands before the newly rebuilt *Winnie Mae*, ready to fly, on June 14, 1933, to Floyd Bennett Field, Long Island, New York. This photograph was made in Oklahoma City. Above the wing is a fuel container that was used for topping off the wing tanks just prior to departure. (Courtesy Winnie Mae Fain.)

Vega Model 5B, factory serial number 122, before her later modification to a 5C model in mid-1932. Her airworthiness was based on the Department of Commerce Airworthiness Type Certificate number 227. The takeoff and normal power rating of her engine, as originally delivered, was 420 horsepower at 2,000 revolutions per minute at sea level. A gear-driven internal 7:1 supercharger served to provide a sea level, horsepower rating up to an altitude of 9,000 feet. But if Post used 87 octane fuel from a special tank for takeoff (as he usually did), the engine produced 500 horsepower at 2,200 revolutions per minute. After takeoff, as previously noted, he would then switch tanks to cruise on ordinary 80-octane gasoline.[9]

The *Winnie Mae* rolled out of the Braniff shops a much-improved airplane. With the modified engine and certain other new equipment, she was one of the finest outfitted airplanes in the world. It should be noted, however, that the *Winnie Mae* was rapidly becoming obsolescent. New, all-metal, twin-engine aircraft were in the process of development and would take to the air in 1933; the sleek Boeing 247, the sensational Douglas DC-1, and shortly thereafter the incredibly successful Douglas DC-2. The Lockheed Company itself was moving away from the plywood on which it had built its reputation and was designing a twin-engine, all-metal airplane with a retractable landing gear that would take to the air as the Lockheed 10 Electra. Post was well aware, even in 1931, that the *Winnie Mae* would soon be obsolete, but a new airplane was far beyond his slim finances.

On May 19, 1933, Clarence M. Young, Assistant Secretary of Commerce, wrote to the Secretary of State announcing that Wiley Post proposed to make an around-the-world flight, to depart on some date after June 15, 1933. Young pointed out that Post held transport pilot license number 3259, and would pilot a Lockheed airplane with license NR 105W, and that this airplane was registered in the name of Winnie Mae Fain, 624 Culbertson Drive, Oklahoma City, Oklahoma. He asked the Department of State to request the necessary permissions from Newfoundland, Free State of Ireland, Great Britain, Belgium, and Poland for Post's flight, and a check in the amount of $100 payable to the Secretary of State was enclosed to cover the cable charges. No firearms or cameras were to be carried in the aircraft during the flight. The Department of Commerce saw no objection to the flight and approved the airplane as airworthy and the pilot as competent. This formal paperwork was standard operating procedure for making a flight beyond the Western Hemisphere after 1929.

In May, another story in the *New York Times* discussed Post's plans in more detail. Lauren "Deac" Lyman, aviation editor, stated that Post hoped to fly nonstop from New York to Berlin, about 3,900 miles away. This range was normally considered a thousand miles more than the Lockheed Vega could handle. Post hoped to achieve the longer range through certain mechanical alterations of his craft, which included a Smith controllable-pitch prop and extra fuel tanks. The Smith hollow-steel propeller was similar to

FIGURE 48.—The Wasp engine of the *Winnie Mae* is readied for the 1933 solo world flight by Pratt and Whitney mechanics, as Post watches. (Courtesy Pratt and Whitney Aircraft.)

the one used by Jimmy Doolittle in the Granville brothers' Gee Bee R-1 racer, in which he set a new land-plane speed record in 1932.

The Smith propeller was entirely mechanical in operation; it required no hydraulic or electrical systems, and was quickly recognized by the three-sixteenths-inch hole drilled in the front of each blade, near the tips, which served to drain water out of the hollow blades. There were two shafts at the boss ends of the blades and a sliding sleeve with a worm gear that turned the shafts and changed the propeller pitch by disengaging the blades. The propeller rotation provided the energy to change the pitch of the blades and the pilot could set them at any pitch he wished.[10]

In the 1930s the variable pitch propeller was often described as the "gearshift of the air," and the simile is accurate; a low-pitch setting took a relatively small "bite" on the air (corresponds to low gear in an automobile) and was used for takeoffs and landings; a high-pitch setting took a larger "bite" on the air and was used for cruising. The controllable pitch propeller not only allowed Post to choose optimal pitch settings to gain many extra miles from his fuel, but also gave the *Winnie Mae* a much better climb performance out of any short fields that Post might have to use en route.

Wiley had been quietly making his plans for several months. Although he planned to follow almost the same route he and Gatty used in 1931, he now scheduled only five refueling stops: Berlin, Nova-Sibirsk, Kharbarovsk, Fairbanks, and Edmonton. This was possible as a result of the *Winnie Mae's* new fuel tankage and the economy provided by the controllable pitch propeller.[11]

After the 1931 flight, some persons had suggested that Gatty was the "brains" of the operation. Implied here was that all Post did was sit up front and "steer." This was utter nonsense, and no one would have labeled it as such faster than Harold Gatty; but it was typical of the nonsense in which newspaper reporters are wont to peddle for the sale of an "angle" on their story. Wiley gave Gatty credit for the success of their flight in their book, but later developed the desire to circle the world alone.[12] He encountered many problems in finding money to support his second around-the-world flight. For one thing, F. C. Hall's purse was no longer at hand to be tapped, and by 1933 the Great Depression was at rock bottom and the resources of the wealthy oilmen who assisted in financing the 1931 flight were no longer available.

Earlier in 1933, Post made an arrangement with Harry G. Frederickson, a young Oklahoma City businessman, who would help him raise the funds from Oklahomans and from various companies concerned with aviation. Post stipulated that the money should not come from any one source, but rather those Oklahomans interested in the progress of aviation. Frederickson would receive ten percent of the funds he raised. They went to the Oklahoma City Chamber of Commerce and Stanley Draper, its managing director, agreed to cooperate by appointing a committee, and he made the first donation by check toward the proposed flight. The project was presented to the community at a luncheon, and although it was received with enthusiasm, the subscriptions came in slowly. New impetus came when Walter Harrison, managing editor of the *Oklahoma City Times,* enthusiastically

FIGURE 49.—A trim, bushy-headed Wiley Post is shown at Floyd Bennett Field, New York, at the time of his solo around-the-world-flight, summer, 1933. (Courtesy Sperry Gyroscope Company.)

endorsed the flight, and 41 persons and business concerns eventually contributed.

A major source of support came from John Kroutill, a miller from Yukon, a town located a few miles west of Oklahoma City. When funds became low, Post and Frederickson would drive out to Yukon and come back with enough money to continue their preparations. In all, Kroutil donated about $5,000. Among other contributors was a newspaper reporter named "Mike" Monroney, who ultimately became a Congressman and then a distinguished United States Senator from Oklahoma. Monroney subsequently authored the Federal Aviation Act of 1958, and served in the 1960s as chairman of the Senate Committee on Aviation Affairs and the Civil Service and Post Office committees.[18]

The list of donors to the 1933 flight, which appeared in the *Daily Oklahoman,* included: John Kroutil, Frank Phillips, Lew Wentz, T. E. Braniff, J. F. Owens, Harrison Smith, Oklahoma Publishing Co., Steve Anderson, Westgate Oil Co., Homer Smith, Frank Buttram, Streeter B. Flynn, G. G. Sohlberg, W. E. Hightower, Stanley Draper, Moss Patterson, John R. Baker, Home State Life Insurance Co., R. T. Stuart, Virgin Browne, T. C. Thatcher, Oklahoma Natural Gas Co., Reinauer Brothers Motor Co., Chauncey Nichols, M. J. Stooker, O. A. Cargill, E. E. Westervelt, W. E. Grisso, Kerr Dry Goods Co., W. R. McWilliams, H. G. Frederickson, Ancel Earp, James Brazzell, J. R. Keaton, John A. Brown, Mike Monroney, S. F. Veazey, L. C. Pollock, B. C. Housel, L. A. Macklanburg, F. E. Northway, and three "Friends of Aviation."

As the cash contributions came in from the Oklahomans, Post and Frederickson approached the large aeronautical companies for donations of equipment and supplies; these donations were essential to the flight. Pratt & Whitney not only furnished the parts needed to improve the *Winnie Mae's* Wasp engine; they also provided a technical specialist, Lionel B. Clark, to help Post with mechanical problems after reaching New York. The Sperry Gyroscope Company donated the automatic pilot and provided technical assistance. One of the largest hurdles was overcome when Socony-Vacuum (Mobil Oil) agreed to furnish fuel and oil (Mobilgas and Mobiloil); the company also provided Socony-Vacuum Mobilgrease for the engine rocker arms, Socony-Vacuum Compass Liquid, and aircraft instrument oil for lubrication of the automatic pilot. The Roosevelt Hotel in New York City donated to Post and his party a $35 per day hotel suite for use prior to and after the flight and gave a 50-percent discount on food.

Post and Frederickson thus succeeded in obtaining basic financial and other support for the flight. Post was almost prevented from making the flight, however, when the Amtorg Company demanded a $1,000 cash advance to handle any emergencies that might occur while he was in Russia. It will be recalled that in 1932, Mattern and Griffin were forced down in Russia; their rescue and the salvage of their aircraft created certain costs for the Russians. Through friends in Oklahoma, Post came into contact with C. B. Ames, head of the Texas Company (Texaco Oil); Ames, whose company traded with the Amtorg Company, persuaded the Russians to agree to a $1,500 letter of credit.[14]

A key item of equipment was the new Sperry automatic pilot that Wiley referred to as "Mechanical Mike" and which he had tested for about 85 flight hours.[15] Developed by Elmer and Lawrence Sperry in the early 1920s, the "robot pilot" used two gyroscopes and was only 9 by 10 by 15 inches in size. One of these was an azimuth (directional) gyroscope, which provided a datum for the heading control of the airplane. The other was a horizontal gyro, providing a datum for longitudinal and lateral control of the airplane. The two gyros were air driven and ran at a speed of

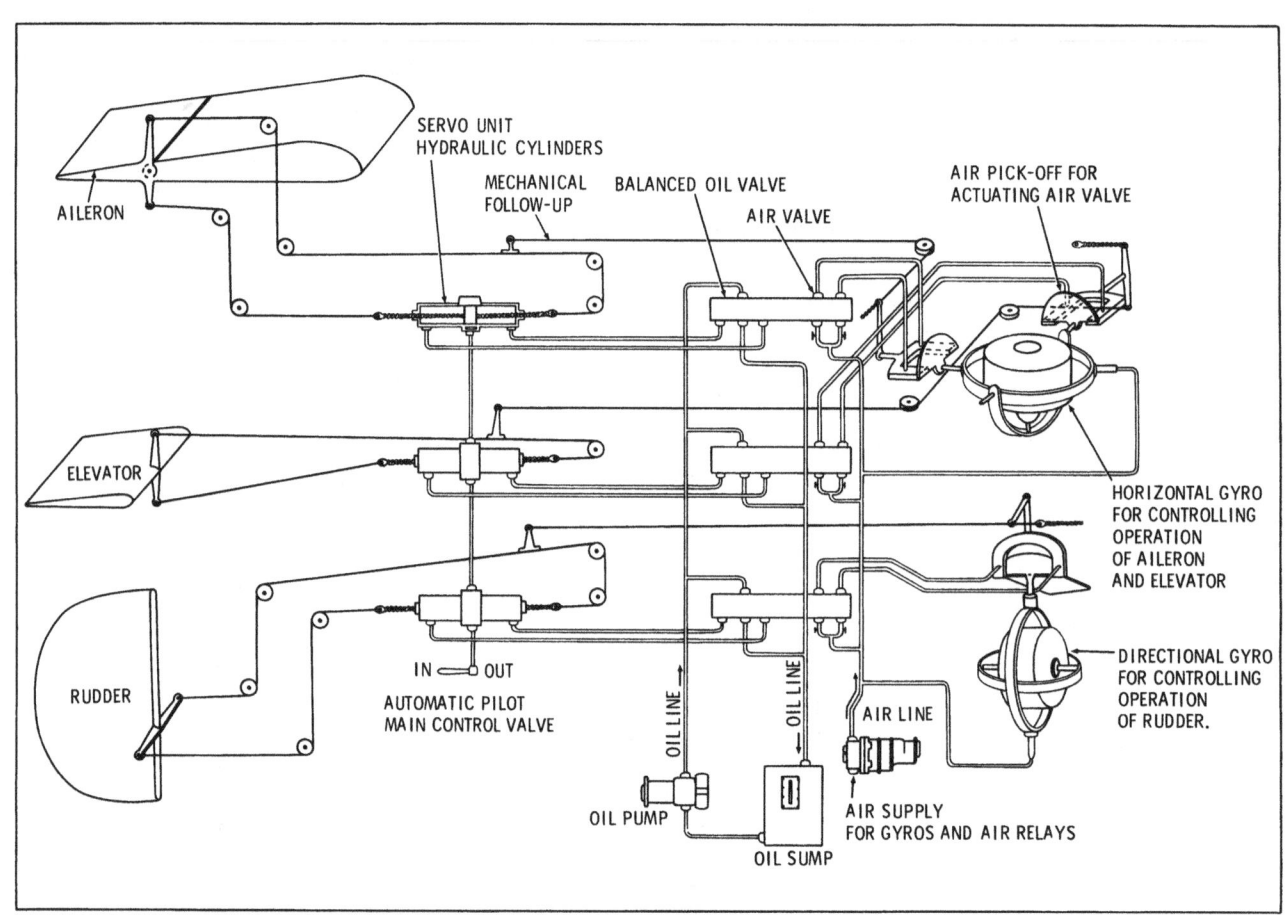

FIGURE 50.—*"Mechanical Mike," the Sperry Autopilot.* The Sperry autopilot, used by Post during the 1933 solo world flight, incorporated two gyroscopes and operated upon compressed air and hydraulic pressure. It was a "three-axis" autopilot, that is, one gyroscope sensed pitch changes and roll (bank) changes by the aircraft, and the other gyroscope sensed heading changes (yaw). The air compressor and the hydraulic pump were engine powered. The gyroscopes were driven by compressed air. Compressed air was also used to correct changes of aircraft attitudes in relation to pitch, bank, or yaw, through a system of small air ducts and semilunar plates. Attitude changes of the aircraft, produced pressure differentials in airflow in the ducts ending near the discs. The result was a proportional change in air valves that was transmitted to the appropriate hydraulic system which, in turn, moved the proper-control surface (elevator for pitch, aileron for bank, and rudder for yaw). The autopilot, which Post called "Mechanical Mike," required no electrical power and functioned very well. (Courtesy Sperry Gyroscope Company.)

15,000 revolutions per minute. The human pilot could shift from automatic pilot to manual control at will, but he could also change course, climb, or dive by turning remote controls to the autopilot, thus effecting flight changes without disengaging the autopilot. The apparatus was provided with a hand-operated clutch for disengaging the autopilot for takeoffs and landings.

A mechanism was incorporated so that when the airplane banked about its longitudinal axis, the stabilized gyroscope resisted the bank, and an airjet, activated valve opened, which, through an oil-operated servo mechanism, moved the control cables to remove the resistance by adjusting the ailerons to roll the airplane wings level. A similar mechanism on the same gyroscope controlled airplane pitch about the lateral axis (nose up, nose level, or nose down) by moving the control cables forward and backward as necessary to adjust the elevators. The other gyroscope controlled the directional gyro (which was set periodically in accordance with the magnetic compass) and through its oil-operated servomechanism made small adjustments on the rudder to yaw the aircraft back to maintain a predetermined heading. The entire apparatus weighed 70 pounds and it deserves appreciation that such devices had not received extensive trials at the time Post was planning his world flight.[16]

The Sperry automatic pilot used by Post for the 1933 flight differed from previous autopilots in an important manner. Other automatic pilots of the time used electrical "pick-offs" to determine the relative motions of the aircraft and the "fixed" axes of the spinning gyroscopes, and utilized a slip-stream, "wind-powered" spinning gear device as the motive power to enable the autopilot to move the control surfaces. An externally placed small propeller blade was necessary to achieve this motive power. This type of device created drag and was relatively inefficient as a source of power.

Post's automatic pilot used airjet pick-offs closely associated with the gyroscopic platforms, a system less liable to mechanical troubles that were common in other autopilots which used varying electrical contacts. The airjet pick-off mechanism used in the *Winnie Mae* was the first autopilot with this new mechanism. The autopilot was completely mechanical and did not use electrical power. The diagram of the autopilot (Figure 50) illustrates the relationships of the various mechanisms constituting the autopilot.

The horizontal gyroscopic air pick-offs consisted of two hemispherical discs that were fixed to the gyroscopic platform, and, with the airplane flying straight and level, the edges of the discs received equal pressure from the air jets. If the airplane nose up, and/or banked, as by a gust, one or more of the jets of air would not encounter a portion of the disc, allowing more air to flow out of the respective jet. The difference in airflow activated the associated air valve which then opened a hydraulic valve and caused pistons to be moved which were attached to the respective aileron or elevator surfaces. The proper surfaces moved to return the aircraft to the position where the airflow pickoffs were equal.

The heading gyroscope, which controlled the rudder, was arranged in such a way that the mounting of the hemispherical disc caused the airjets to move with the airplane rather than with the gyroscope. This enabled the pilot to fix the airplane on various headings in the 360° azimuth from North. Otherwise, the mechanism operated identically to that of the horizontal gyroscope.

An "elevator" knob at the right of the gyro horizon on the control panel enabled Post to establish a given "pitch attitude" of the airplane to be held by the autopilot. An aileron knob, just above the gyro horizon, permitted a similar setting for bank and a rudder knob, immediately above the direction indicator, was used fo azimuth. A "directional gyro compass" display was mounted immediately to the left of the "artificial horizon," both being centered on the panel in front of the pilot's seat. The lever that shifted the autopilot from manual to automatic was located immediately under the servo-unit hydraulic cylinders, which were mounted just beneath the autopilot gyroscopes in the instrument panel. The hydraulic cylinders were in plain view.

A "caging" knob for the artificial horizon was placed just to its left, and a similar caging knob was just below the directional gyro indicator. The gyros were "caged" during periods of manual, visual flight to save wear and tear on their bearings.

Another new device was reviewed and selected by Post for the upcoming flight. In 1931, Gerhard R. Fisher, research engineer for Western Air Express, reported that he and G. G. Kruesi (also Western Air research engineer) were testing a new "automatic radio compass" for navigational use, with standard commercial broadcast stations.[17] Fisher reported that Dr. J. H. Dellinger of the U.S. Bureau of Standards had devoted the previous five years to developing an improved directional radio system which consisted of special ground stations that transmitted specifically directed radio beams. The original system had been developed in 1926 by Eugene Donovan of the Ford Motor Company. The radio beams enabled pilots to stay on a predetermined course, regardless of visibility and wind conditions.

This system was adopted by the Department of Commerce and was of immense value, but Fisher pointed out that the fixed beams did not permit pilots to leave their courses sufficiently to travel around large storms. Also, its necessary ground system was not yet available outside of the United States.

So that a pilot could be entirely independent of a special ground system and could find the way by homing anywhere that radiobroadcast stations existed, Fisher supported the "automatic radio compass" as an answer to the problem—an instrument which is also referred to as the automatic direction finder (ADF). The mariner's radio compass of the day used a rotating loop, while Fisher and Kruesi adapted a fixed directional loop antenna for use with aircraft, and these loops could be as small as 10 to 12 inches in diameter.

Their system consisted to a special vacuum tube dual circuit, which when balanced gave a zero reading on an indicator on the instrument panel, which had a needle that could move from left to zero to right (resembling the automobile ammeter display of the day). When a station ahead and on the left of the long axis of the airplane was tuned, its signal added to the left circuit and the needle moved to the left, indicating that the station ahead was to the left. By turning the aircraft to point to the left until the needle was centered, the pilot would then have the aircraft pointed at the station. The system allowed pilots to home on stations 200 miles or more away, while the Department of Commerce system was limited to 125 miles. The radio compass electronic equipment that plugged into a standard radio receiver could consist of four tubes, or, if the two oscillator tubes were combined in one, three tubes.

An ADF radio was installed in the *Winnie Mae* by the Army at Wright Field, near Dayton, Ohio. Involved was a fixed "loop" antennae, installed within the wooden fuselage of the *Winnie Mae* and a "sense" antenna which ran downward from an extended mast on the fin to the midpoint of the fuselage, just aft of the wing trailing edge. The radio signal detected by the "loop" would "build" or "decline," depending upon the relation of the long axis of the *Winnie Mae* to the station. The loop-signal reception strength was thus compared with the relatively nonchanging "sense" antenna-signal reception and displayed on the left-right indicator. The indicator needle was placed immediately above the automatic pilot.

Because the science of radio electronics was relatively new and somewhat mystifying to much of the public, and because ADF was still in the experimental stage (and certain details classified by the military), little technical information was given by the news media on this aspect of the equipment.[18] The public received this simple explanation: by tuning to a standard broadcast station, Post could determine the bearing from his position to the station and turn so as to fly toward (or away from) the station. Post believed that this device would be a valuable aid to navigation. The *Scientific American* reported that once under way, he would fly on a signal from St. John's, Newfoundland, and then on signals from Machester, England, other European and Russian stations, Army stations in Alaska, and commercial stations in Canada and Chicago. The direction finder and robot proved to be an unusual combination in 1933, leading the *New York Times* to remark: "He will ride around the world on radio waves while the robot flies the plane." [19]

The specific ADF utilized by Post was based on circuitry patented by G. G. Kruesi [20] for a "Radio Direction Finder," which became known as a "right-left" radio compass.[21] The indicator for the device consisted of the needle that was centered in the nose or tail of the airplane, pointed directly to the turned radiobroadcast station. As the nose or tail was turned away from the station, the needle swung to the side on which the station was located. The bearing to the sta-

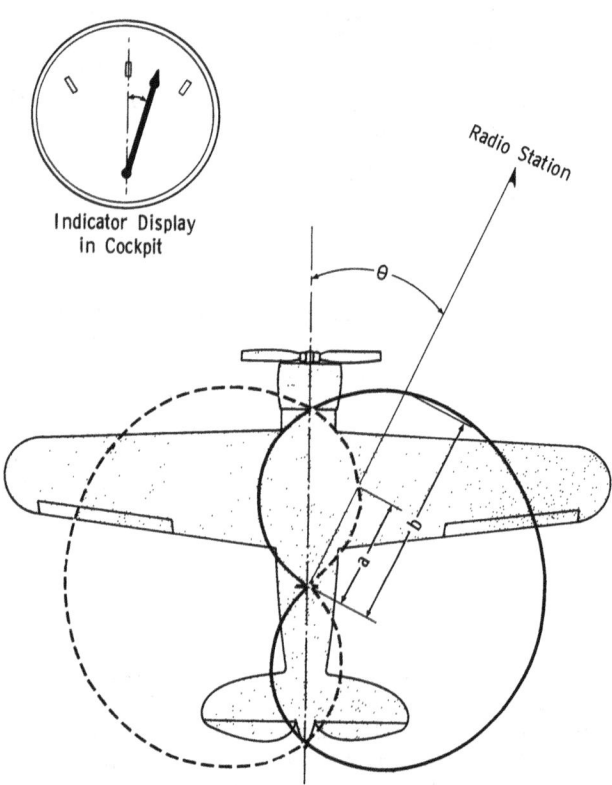

FIGURE 51.—*Principle of Post's Radio Compass.* The U.S. Army Signal Corps installed a new radio direction finder in the *Winnie Mae* shortly before the 1933 solo world flight. The Kruesi circuitry was utilized and involved a fixed loop mounted within the aft fuselage of the wooden *Winnie Mae*. A "cardioid" antenna-radiation pattern was utilized that alternated from side to side at a fixed frequency between 40 to 90 cycles per second. The incoming signal energy derived from the tuned radiobroadcast station added to the energy of the oxcillating antenna circuit. A cockpit indicator display needle integrated with the circuitry moved to the side of the scale toward which the radio station lay. The amount of needle movement in degrees was proportional to the amount of offset in degrees from the nose of the aircraft of the station. (After P. C. Sandretto.)

tion was obtained through the characteristics of the antenna system field pattern, as illustrated in Figure 51.

The principle of operation of this radio compass is shown in Figure 52. Within the *Winnie Mae*, the fixed loop was mounted with its plane at right angles to the major axis of the airplane. This loop antenna was "directionally sensitive" and connected to the radio receiver as was the "nondirectional sense" antenna which stretched from the fin antenna post to the top midline of the fuselage near the wing trailing edge. The sense antenna was of the "end-fed" type and was nondirectional to low frequency, long radio waves. The loop antenna was connected with the receiver through an electronic "reversing switch." The loop antenna and the sense antenna, together, yielded a field pattern of a "cardioid" a heart-shaped pattern illustrated in Figure 51. The loop antenna alone would yield a symmetrical "figure of 8" pattern that was used on earlier radio compasses by indicating the "null" point or point of lowest signal strength when the loop plane was at right angles to the line to the station. The Kruesi radio compass took a more sophisticated approach. When the reversing switch is thrown from side to side, the cardioid pattern of the antenna system "flips" alternately from right to left and back.

A meter having two opposing windings was connected to the rectified output of the radio receiver, and the connections to the meter were reversed in coordination with the loop-reversing switch as is shown in Figure 52. The loop-reversing switch in one position caused the meter needle to move to the right, and the amount of receiver output to the meter was related to this connection through the loop antenna. For the other position of the reversing switch, the needle moved to the left, indicating the amount of receiver output to the meter for the alternate connection of the switch. If the switch were reversed very rapdily, the mechanically mounted needle could not follow the individual oscillations, but would deflect to a position proportional to the differences in the receiver outputs to the meter, with respect to the two alternative connections on the loop.

In Figure 51, a radiobroadcasting station located at an angular distance from the long axis of the *Winnie Mae* would result in an influence of the loop-antenna system upon the receiver output to the meter as follows. The receiver output for one loop-antenna connection is *a*, while for the second connection, it is *b*. Because the amount *b* is greater than *a*, the meter-needle deflection will be proportional to the difference between the magnitude of *b* and the magnitude of *a*; and because the station is on the right the needle will deflect to the right. The instrument was ad-

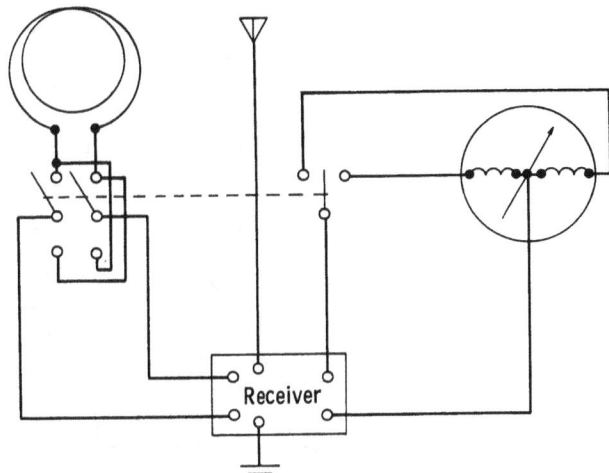

FIGURE 52.—*Schematic General Plan of Post's Radio Compass*. The loop-directional antenna is shown connected with the alternating reversing switch (which in actuality was a "push-pull" oscillating electronic circuit). The circuit then connects with the receiver that is tuned through the "sense" antenna to a broadcast station (the sense antenna stretched from a post on top of the vertical fin to a point on the top of the fuselage just aft of the trailing edge of the wing). The cockpit indicator was attached as shown by the needle pointer on the right. (After P. C. Sandretto.)

justed so that a deviation of 5° from directly ahead gave a full-scale deflection of the instrument.

The reversing accomplished by the system was done electronically. The reversing circuit was an "oscillator" connected to the grids of two tubes, each grid connected to one side of the loop antenna. The loop antenna had a "center tap" and the schematic diagram of the associated circuitry is portrayed in Figure 53. When the oscillator voltage reached a fixed negative valve, one of the tubes V_1 or V_2 was cut off and would not conduct until the oscillator cycle reversed. The center tap of the loop connected to radio-frequency amplifier tubes V_1 and V_2. The grids of these tubes received connections from the "push-pull" audio oscillator made of tubes V_3 and V_4 and coil L_0. The oscillator coil was also part of the indicator Meter I.

The oscillator coil was tuned by a condenser, C_0, producing an audio frequency of a relatively low value, fixed somewhere between 40 and 90 cycles per second. The voltage from the audio oscillators V_3 and V_4 alternately cut off the grids of V_1 and V_2 at a fixed pace between 40 and 90 cycles per second. The energy from the radio-frequency oscillator tubes V_1 and V_2, fed alternately into the radio receiver, and was mixed with the energy from the sense "fixed" antenna A. Since the output of the reciever was rectified, the resultant was an audio voltage with a frequency similar to the frequency of the oscillator. The output voltage was connected to the other coil by the indicator. Thus, the indicator served as a "phase meter" and

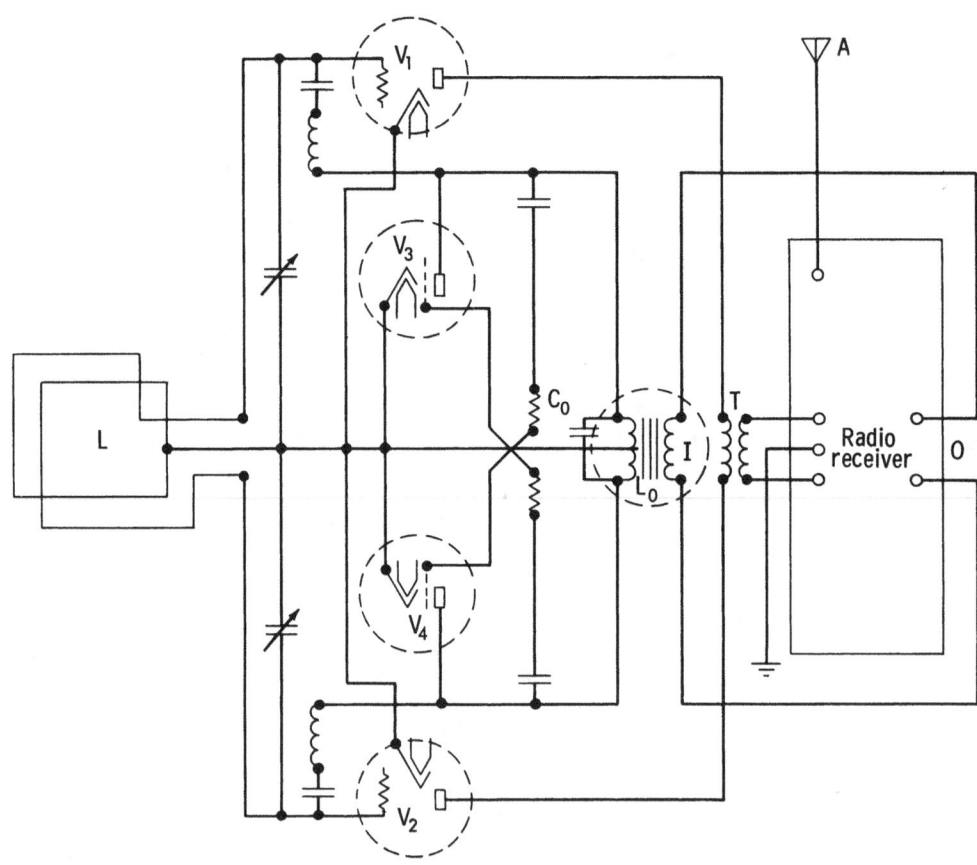

Figure 53.—*The Circuit Diagram of the Kruesi Radio Compass.* The vacuum tube circuitry utilized in the radio compass used by Post is illustrated and involved an electronic vacuum tube "push-pull" circuit. The center-tapped loop antenna (L) was integrated into the oscillating circuit. The radio receiver and its sense antenna (A) were linked with the oscillating circuit through the indicator (I). (After P. C. Sandretto.)

moved the indicator pointer in a matter that was proportional to the relative intensity of the energy picked up by the two "cardioids."

Because the rectifier output was tuned to the audio frequency at which the receiver was reversed, the effect of static was minimized and the radio compass indicated accurately, even with very poor "signal-to-noise" ratios.

Post followed the same training method he devised and used in 1931. He attempted to break regular sleeping and eating patterns by changing them from day to day. Often he would eat only one meal a day and spend all night at the airport, sitting in the cockpit of the *Winnie Mae* with his eye open.[22] Post carefully sought to determine his own physical tolerances to fatigue prior to the solo flight. On at least one occasion, he had several persons take turns walking with him throughout the night in self-evaluation of his condition after varying periods of physical exertion and sleeplessness. He also devised a "Rube Goldberg" means of waking himself, should he begin to doze. This consisted of a lead ball held in his hand and tied to his finger by a length of string; if he dozed off, he hoped that his hand would open, the ball would fall, jerk the finger, and awaken him.

On June 1, 1933, Post made a series of flight tests in which he determined the *Winnie Mae's* new flight characteristics and fuel consumption.[23] Time was now becoming painfully short because Jimmy Mattern of San Angelo, Texas, was also planning an around-the-world solo flight. It will be recalled that Mattern and Griffin had tried unsuccessfully to beat Post and Gatty's record in 1932, only to crash in eastern Russia. Now Post and Mattern were direct competitors in the around-the-world solo dash, and a friendly rivalry had developed between them. Wiley Post was not about to be rushed by a lot of hot air in the newspapers about rivalry, however; he let it be known that he had no plans for a takeoff before July 1st, and he did not in-

FIGURE 54.—As perfect a match of man and machine as ever found in aviation is embodied in this picture of Wiley Post and his beloved Vega. The photograph was made at Floyd Bennett Field, just prior to Post's 1933 solo around-the-world flight. (Courtesy Lockheed Aircraft Company.)

tend to advance his date of departure, regardless of what Mattern might do.

Jimmy Mattern flew out of New York's Floyd Bennett Field on June 3 in his bizarre-looking Vega named *Century of Progress,* and 23 hours and 55 minutes later landed at Jomfruland, Norway. Until he climbed out of his airplane, Mattern was certain that he had landed in Scotland! He refueled, and hurried on eastward to Oslo, Moscow, Omsk, and Chita. The nation's press gave Matttern's flight a great deal of publicity,[24] but even while Mattern was on his way across the Atlantic, Post stated again that his plans were unchanged. Even if Jimmy Mattern made it around the world in four days, he was not going to be rushed.

Meanwhile, on June 10, 1933, S. E. Perry, superintendent of maintenance for Braniff Airways in Oklahoma City, signed a Certificate of Repairs with the Department of Commerce for the *Winnie Mae*. The certificate cited the following items:

The fuselage received one-half of a new shell and diaphragms Nos. 4678 and 4679 were replaced by new ones.
  Diaphragms 1, 12 and 13 were rebuilt and strengthened.
  The entire fuselage was covered with Balloon Cloth.
  The cockpit was completely rebuilt.

All new control cables were installed.
  Fuselage fuel tanks were installed, totalling 410 gallons.
  With respect to the wing, the right wingtip was completely rebuilt. Seven stringers were installed between spars and the entire top side was covered with 1/8-inch plywood between spars. The rest of the wing was covered with 3/32-inch plywood.
  No windows were installed in the cabin except for one standard emergency exit between Nos. 7 and 8 diaphragms.
  All ribs and spars were taped on their upper sides.
  Five standard fuel tanks were installed in the wings, 48 gallons each, for a total of 240 gallons.
  With regard to the empennage (tail surfaces), the stabilizer was recovered on its underside and one-half of its topside. The stabilizer actuating gear was completely rebuilt. A radio mast consisting of one-inch streamline tubing, 6-feet long, was installed inside the vertical fin. The elevators and rudder were completely rebuilt and a new stabilizer was installed.
  The entire landing gear was rebuilt by the Lockheed Aircraft Company in Burbank, and two new belly fittings were installed. All bolts and nuts were replaced with new ones, and the landing gear contained shock cord-wrapped shock struts.
  The Pratt & Whitney SC-1 Wasp 450-horsepower engine was completely overhauled, and nine new cylinders with 6:1 compression pistons were installed.
  New supercharger bearings were installed.
  New magnetos were installed.
  The carburetor was overhauled by the Bendix-Stromberg Company.
  A new Breeze radio-shielding ignition harness was installed, as well as magneto coupling gears.[25]

The next day, June 11, Robert Hazen paid a visit to Oklahoma City's Curtiss-Wright Airport and filed an operation-inspection report for the Department of Commerce's Aeronautics Branch on his inspection of the *Winnie Mae*. He noted that the airplane now had 11 fuel tanks installed, with a total capacity of 645 gallons, while the oil capacity was 26 gallons. No baggage compartments were installed in the aircraft, and he noted that the *Winnie Mae's* log showed a total of 825 hours of flight time. Since her previous overhaul, however, the airplane had experienced only two hours' flight time. Among the accessory equipment on board, Hazen noted:

No. 6 Eclipse inertia starter.
Bosch starter magneto (15 pounds)
No. 19 Exide battery.
One radio (visual type)
Two 2-quart water containers.
One 1-quart fire extinguisher.
One U.S. Army Air Corps type radio compass.
One Sperry automatic pilot.
One Kollsman altimeter.
One auxiliary directional gyro.
One magnetic compass.
One aperiodic compass.

Hazen remarked on the three extra fuel tanks in the wings (48 gallons each including a center wing tank and two lateral tanks), the six new cabin tanks, and that shock-cord landing gear had been installed. In conclusion, he noted that a final inspection of the

FIGURE 55.—The *Winnie Mae* is shown ready for the around-the-world solo record flight attempt. The "sense" antenna post on the fin is clearly evident. (Courtesy Jimmy Gerschler and Smithsonian Institution.)

Winnie Mae's instruments would be made in Washington, D.C., before Post flew on to his takeoff point in New York.

After Hazen had gathered his information, the following day Post applied for a restricted license for the *Winnie Mae*, noting that the airplane had been completely remodeled for a special around-the-world flight.

With the *Winnie Mae's* new license approved, Post took off from Oklahoma City on June 14, with Harry Frederickson on board, stopped off at Washington, and flew on to New York's Floyd Bennett Field the next day.[26] Floyd Bennett Field is located on Long Island's Jamaica Bay; it was named in honor of the great aviator who was Richard E. Byrd's pilot on their flight to the North Pole—the first flight to the Pole —in 1926, and who died while attempting a rescue flight to assist the downed aviators of the transatlantic airplane *Breman* in 1928. It was New York City's first municipal airport, and when it opened in 1931 it had the longest runways in the world.

While Post had been preparing the *Winnie Mae*, Jimmy Mattern had sped across Russia to disappear in the wilds of the Siberian Arctic. On June 14th Mattern took off from Kharbarovsk for Nome, Alaska, and after that—nothing.

Upon arriving in New York, Post had no full-time engine and airframe mechanic, and was pleasantly surprised when Lionel B. Clark of Pratt & Whitney appeared and offered to give important assistance. Clark was actually in charge of all of these aspects, freeing Post for important planning activities. The Wasp engine of the *Winnie Mae* at this point had operated for 846 hours. Later, Post flew the *Winnie Mae* to Wright Field, Dayton, Ohio, where the Army Air Corps worked on the ADF installation, after which he returned to Floyd Bennett Field.[27]

In a June 27, 1933, *Daily Oklahoman* article, Bennie Turner stated that guards were thrown around the flight equipment of Wiley Post and an attendant was placed on duty in the hotel suite, following receipt by Post of threatening letters and attempts to tamper with the *Winnie Mae*. At Floyd Bennett, mechanics prevented one attempt to tamper with the engine of

FIGURE 56.—Fay Gillis leaves Moscow for Novosibirsk in a Russian Junkers airplane, June 25, 1933, in anticipation of assisting Wiley Post with expeditious refueling service. Post requested by cable that Miss Gillis, who lived in Moscow, meet the *Winnie Mae* in Novosibirsk and assist with aircraft servicing. (Courtesy Fay Gillis Wells.)

the *Winnie Mae*; another attempt by an unidentified person was made to damage the carburetor. In addition to the civil guard, soldiers were added because of the experimental ADF installed with the assistance of the United States Army. Post's skyrocketing popularity was enjoyed by almost all who knew him, and his fellow aviators held him in very high regard. Human nature, however apparently generated in some a feeling of jealousy, for as Wiley attempted new achievements, lesser persons, hiding in the shadows, were anxious to attempt sabotage.

The same article by Turner reported an attempt by an individual to get some of Post's blood. The requestor claimed that he had made a "radio machine" that would keep contact between Post's blood in a bottle and Post himself anywhere in the world; this charlatan (or mental case) claimed that he would keep the world informed of Post's health. Lee Trenholm, Post's business representative, reported on June 28 that a larger guard was being established.

Meanwhile, on July 5, word came from Russia that Jimmy Mattern was alive. He was speeding across the Siberian wastes with the Bering Sea almost in sight, Nome only four hours away, when his engine packed up and quit. He made a crash landing near the Anadyr River, built a raft and floated down the river with hopes of finding some civilization. It was two weeks before some Eskimos found him. Wiley announced his pleasure at hearing this news.[28]

On July 6, 1933, E. Y. Mitchell, Assistant Secretary of Commerce, wrote to Post, c/o Roosevelt Hotel, and stated that under the Air Commerce regulations, authorization was granted for an around-the-world flight, subject to the following conditions: The air-

FIGURE 57.—Russians flank Fay Gillis in Novosibirsk. She holds a special map prepared by the Russians for Post's continuing flight across Siberia. Post landed in Novosibirsk at 6:27 a.m. on July 18, 1933. He told Izvestia that "due to poor meteorological conditions I will continue to Khabarovsk only by daylight. I will spend the next night in Irkutsk." Fay Gillis was in Novosibirsk at Post's request to ascertain that no mixup in the servicing of the aircraft occurred, as happened in Russia in 1931 when the language barrier lead to overfueling of the *Winnie Mae*. May Gillis' fluency in the Russian language was very helpful in assisting translation during the Novosibirsk stop. (Courtesy Fay Gillis Wells.)

craft license number is NR 105W, the owner is Winnie Mae Fain of Oklahoma City, Oklahoma (by this time, however, the aircraft had been changed to the Fain and Post Drilling Company), the pilot is Wiley Post. The authorization would remain in force until the 31st day of December, 1933, provided that the pilot and aircraft license remained in force, and that the Entry and Clearance of Aircraft Regulations of the Department (Aeronautics Bulletin number 7C) were followed. Mitchell enclosed the written authorizations from Great Britain and Northern Ireland which were necessary because there was as yet no agreement between the United States and the United Kingdom that allowed reciprocity with regard to airworthiness certificates.

On July 6, 1933, the Secretary of Commerce wrote to the Secretary of State and acknowledged receipt of the communication from the Secretary of State concerning Wiley Post's proposed solo around-the-world flight. Acknowledgment was made of copies of decisions referenced by the Secretary of State that were received from the American Embassy at Paris, which stated that permission for the flight had been granted by the governments of Belgium, Iceland, Great Britain, and Northern Ireland. The Secretary of Commerce stated: "Our files disclose that Post has obtained all the necessary permissions for his flight, and therefore, authorization for such flight from this Department is approved to him today. Your cooperation in this matter has been greatly appreciated."

Reports of bad weather over the North Atlantic track kept Post grounded for four weeks in New York before a favorable forecast came to hand. This was not because the North Atlantic's weather was any worse in 1933 than it would be a quarter of a century later, nor that the meteorologists of 1933 were mediocre men; the difficulty was that there was no weather-reporting system operating on the North Atlantic, nor around its northern rimland. The weather information with which the Weather Bureau's meteorologists in New York had to work in 1933 was pitifully inadequate, and in retrospect it is remarkable that they even dared make a forecast, favorable or unfavorable.

Once again, as in 1931, it was Dr. Kimball who kept Post informed on meteorological conditions. On

FIGURE 58.—A crew of Russians energetically and efficiently refuel the *Winnie Mae* at Novosibirsk on July 18, 1933. Note that the left- and right-wing tanks are being filled through chamois cloths to remove any contaminating water. A photographer in the left foreground records the event. Post stated that he got excellent service in Russia and received a very warm welcome at each stop, including Moscow, the preceding stop, where he made an unscheduled landing. The Chief of Transaviation, Mr. A. Petrov, requested the chief of the West Siberian Administration and the chief of the Far Eastern Administration to give full assistance to Fay Gillis and Wiley Post regarding the flight. (Courtesy Fay Gillis Wells.)

July 9 the weather appeared to be breaking up, but a last-minute conference with Kimball, in his eyrie atop 17 Battery Place, led Post to hold off. Two days later, he again postponed an imminent takeoff because of instability over the North Atlantic. Finally, after midnight on Saturday, July 15, Kimball's reports became encouraging and Wiley decided to go.

Wiley had nothing but the greatest respect for weather, and repeatedly demonstrated it in his cautious but sound judgment in his takeoff decisions. When in doubt, he stayed on the ground.

After so many false starts during the past few weeks, it is remarkable that almost 500 persons had maintained a vigil at Floyd Bennett throughout this night, in the hope of witnessing Post's takeoff.

When Wiley appeared on the field he was dressed in a snappy new dark gray double-breasted suit, which was worn over a white shirt with a blue necktie.[29] Post's refusal to wear the customary flying clothes and to "look like an aviator" was frequently remarked upon by the press. Many aviators of the late 1920s and early 1930s wore cavalry boots and carefully tailored riding breeches with fancy leather jackets, and helmet and goggles always; they looked like someone out of the "Smilin' Jack" or "Tailspin Tommy" comic strips. But not Wiley Post. The only thing that prevented Post from looking like a New York businessman en route to the office this morning was his lack of a hat, but Post almost never wore a hat and it was said that he never had even owned one.

Over his left eye Wiley wore a white patch, which was a precaution against the discomfort this his glass eye caused him during the flight of 1931. In cold air the glass eye had become so cold that it gave him a headache.

Among the small knot of close firends who stood with him under the nose of the *Winnie Mae* were Mae Post, Harry Federickson, Lee Trenholm, and the Oklahoma newspaperman, Bennie Turner. In a last-minute gesture to his Oklahoma supporters, Wiley called for a pad and pencil and dashed off a telegram to Editor Walter Harrison, expressing his appreciation to those persons who were making the flight possible.

Then in a rare public display of emotion, Wiley kissed Mae goodby, said, "See you in six days or else," climbed up on the *Winnie Mae*, and dropped through the hatch into her cockpit.

As a hint of daybreak began to spread itself across the low marshes and swampland that have long since

FIGURE 59.—The *Winnie Mae* is shown at Novosibirsk receiving the final servicing touches in 1933. One Russian is standing on the extendable steps on the left side of the cockpit, cleaning the windshield. Just below the fuselage window is an empty can of oil and the sense-antenna post may be seen on top of the fin, with the antenna running to the center of the fuselage at the trailing edge of the wing. Post landed in Novosibirsk at 6:27 a.m., and slept in the terminal building for two hours while the airplane was serviced. He took off at 8:55 a.m., the stop taking only 2 hours, 28 minutes. The efficiency of the stop service was responsible for assisting Post in beating the 1931 around-the-world flight. (Courtesy Fay Gillis Wells.)

FIGURE 60.—The *Winnie Mae* has nosed over on July 20, 1933, Flat, Alaska, after a long nonstop leg from Khabarovsk, Siberia. A block and tackle was erected to lower the tail. (Courtesy Stephen E. Mills.)

been transformed into John F. Kennedy International Airport, the *Winnie Mae* stood poised at the Flatbush Avenue end of the Floyd Bennett runway that pointed toward Jamaica Bay. She was fueled to her caps with 645 gallons (3,870 pounds) of gasoline, and during these final minutes, two gallons of heated oil were added to her engine's sump, to encourage the Wasp in its warmup.

At 5:10 a.m., July 15, 1933, Wiley Post checked the 14-degree pitch setting of his propeller, ran his eye over the instrument panel, and opened his throttle to bring the Wasp up to 2,200 turns. He released the brakes and the *Winnie Mae* went charging down the runway. Her tail came up, and after a 1,900-foot run of only 29 seconds, the hard-working rubber of her tires left the runway. She was airborne—and on her way around the world, again.[80]

Friends, supporters, well-wishers, and just plain curiosity-seekers stood quietly on the tarmac, watching the small, white airplane climb out over the bay, grow smaller in the sky, and gradually fade into the light of the new day that was coming up out of the east.

Wiley Post and his *Winnie Mae* were not alone in the North Atlantic's air corridors on this July morning. Shortly after he roared off of Floyd Bennett's runway, two Lithuanian pilots, Stephen Darius and Stanley Girenas, made an unauthorized takeoff in a single-engine Bellanca CH–300, named *Lithuanica*. Their destination was Kaunas, Lithuania.

Five minutes after liftoff from Floyd Bennett, Wiley flew into a great wad of fog and immediately turned on his Sperry autopilot. He was out of the fog within 20 minutes, but then ran into a thick cloud at higher altitudes. For the next hour and a half, he plowed through them on instruments. He flew out of the cloud tops 90 minutes later over Cape Cod, and the next land he saw was the rockbound coast of Nova Scotia. Past Nova Scotia, he was able to tune in a broadcasting station at St. John's, Newfoundland, and then put his radio compass to work as a navigation

FIGURE 61.—The *Winnie Mae* nosed over at the end of the short, primitive strip, Flat, Alaska, on July 20, 1933, during Post's record solo around-the-world flight. The controllable pitch propeller and landing gear were damaged, nearly ending the record attempt. Post caught up on some much-needed sleep, while members of the Flat Mining Company raised the airplane with a block-and-tackle rig. Joe Crosson, chief pilot of Alaskan Airways flew in a new fixed-pitch propeller and on the next day Post was on his way to New York. Note that the stabilizer is trimmed for a slow-speed, nose-high, short-field approach, and that the wheel pants have been removed. (Courtesy Stephen E. Mills.)

aid. St. John's also supplied further weather reports, which he was pleased to have for his flight planning.

The sky remained clear until halfway across the Atlantic, during which time he flew at an altitude of only 2,000 feet. But halfway across, he caught up with the weather front that had kept him grounded for the past few days. There was fog, the clouds mounted in steps, and the clouds were full of rain. Wiley climbed to 11,000 feet, but found only more clouds and rain.

Somewhere past the halfway mark, Wiley's radio picked up a British radio station, G2LO of Manchester, and heard the welcome words through his receiver, "This is a special broadcast for Wiley Post—" [31] Charles A. Lindbergh never had anything like that in 1927." Trans-atlantic flight had come a long way in only six years. But then Post himself had nothing like this, either, when he flew the Atlantic with Gatty—only two years before! The British voice sounded good to Wiley and immediately brought his radio compass to bear on its pleasant signal.

As Wiley neared the British Isles and his radio was able to pick up more stations, his ADF set (radiocompass) became an invaluable assistant to his navigation. Ireland was overflown in cloud, but the clouds began to break up and he was able to catch a glimpse of the Emerald Isle's eastern shore. He dropped through the broken clouds and flew under their base across the Irish Sea.

As Wiley flew across England, he was in a race with a lowering cloud base that almost put him on the deck, but he held his low altitude across the North Sea. Some of this time he used the autopilot, but now problems began to appear in its operation. The low coastline of norther Europe appeared below and then he was speeding across a flat terrain quilted with neat farms. The Elbe River passed below, and a few minutes later the low skyline of Berlin took shape on the horizon beyond his propeller arc.

Twenty-five hours and 45 minutes after his takeoff from Floyd Bennett, Post and his *Winnie Mae* touched down on Berlin's Tempelhof Aerodrome. It was Sunday, July 16, and the local time was 11:55 a.m. But when Wiley looked at his wristwatch, it still showed eastern daylight saving time, and told him that it was 6:55 a.m. in New York.

This was the first nonstop airplane flight from New York to Berlin; the *Winnie Mae's* average speed was 153.5 miles per hour.

Post had just completed the longest solo flight from the United States to a point in Europe. The distance from New York to Berlin is 3,942 miles. No one would fly this track again, much less exceed Post's time over the route, until August 11, 1938, when the 4-engine Focke-Wulf FW.200 Condor airliner D–ACON, under the command of Alfred Henke with a crew of three, flew from Berlin to New York in 24 hours and 57 minutes. Two days later they sped back over the route—the "Wiley Post Route"—New York to Berlin, in 19 hours and 54 minutes. What is to be appreciated here is that when Post touched down at Berlin in 1933, the design of the formidable FW.200 was hardly a vague idea in the mind of its designer, Kurt Tank, much less an airplane that was taking shape on the drawing boards. Yet there are only five years between the two flights.

Upon checking his fuel at Tempelhof, Post was pleased to note that there were still 160 gallons remaining in the tanks. Transatlantic the *Winnie Mae* had consumed only 485 gallons. His fuel consumption had been an economical 19 gallons per hour, but Wiley knew that this was with a prevailing west wind, and that he could not always count on the same between Berlin and Kharbarovsk.

Among those who were present at Tempelhof to personally congratulate Post was Herman Goering, a famous German ace of World War I, who had succeeded to the command of Baron Manfred von Richthofen after the "Red Baron" had been shot down in 1918. When Goering greeted Post, he was the Chief of the German Air Ministry, appointed to the position by Adolph Hitler only a few months before.

Besides setting a new transatlantic record over the first leg of his world flight, Post confirmed a remark —and a prediction—by his wife Mae, that sending messages to him en route would be unnecessary, because he would be back in New York so soon.[32]

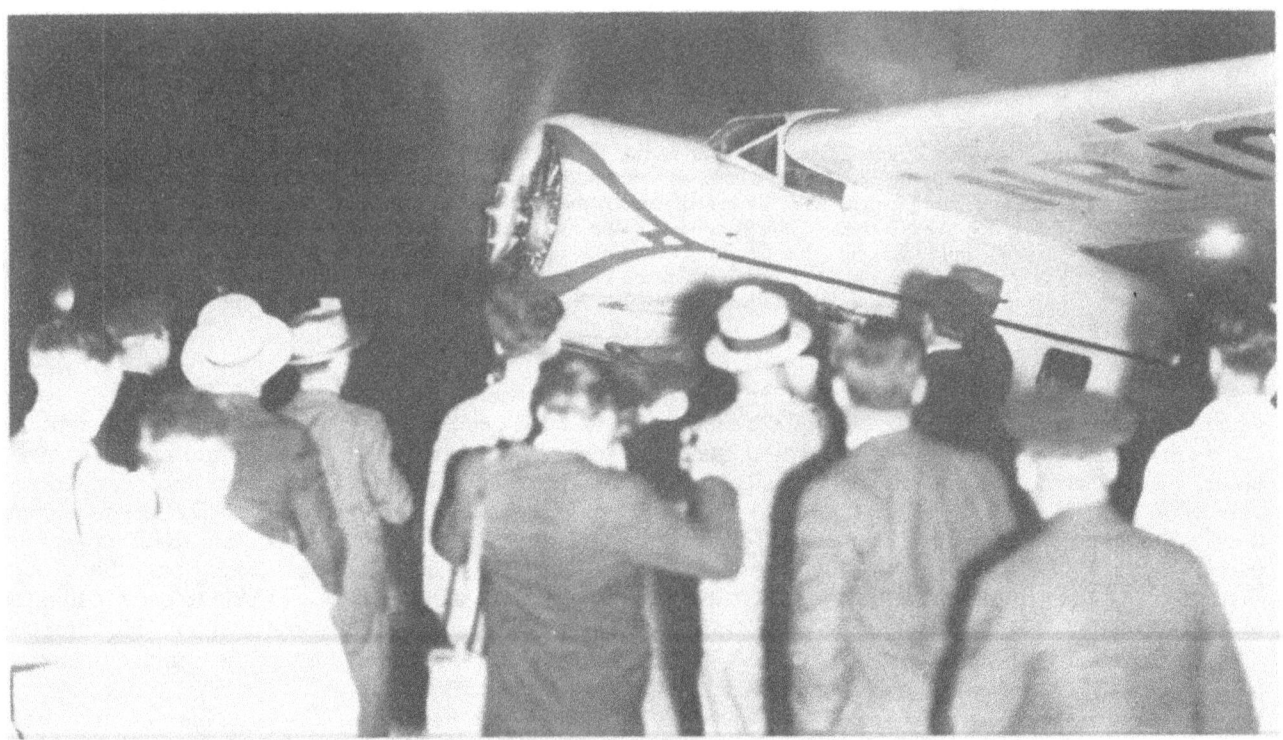

FIGURE 62.—The *Winnie Mae* has just landed at Floyd Bennett Field, New York City, 11:59½ p.m., July 22, 1933. Post is just switching off the Wasp engine as the crowd of 50,000 persons begins to swarm around the airplane that has just completed another record around-the-world flight. The extendable step is out (seen just aft of the cowling, above the fuselage trim). (Courtesy Lockheed Aircraft Company.)

Posts' New York-to-Berlin leg of 1933 was the 66th transatlantic flight made by any type of aircraft, and it was the 27th transatlantic flight made from west to east. However, the distinction of being the first transatlantic flier of 1933 does not belong to Wiley Post.

The first to fly the Atlantic in 1933 was Jimmy Mattern, on the initial leg of his abortive around-the-world flight. Second were two Spaniards, Captain Mariano Barbaran and Lieutenant Joaquin Collar, who flew from Seville to Camaguey, Cuba, in a Breguet XIX Special, named *Quatro Vientos* (Four Winds), figuratively retracing the route of Christopher Columbus. The third transatlantic flight of the year was in fact a package of 24 flights, when General Italo Balbo led a massed formation of two dozen Savoia-Marchetti flying boats from Orbetello, Italy, to Chicago, to participate in Chicago's "Century of Progress" World's Fair. The Italian seaplanes flew via Amsterdam, Northern Ireland, Iceland, Labrador, and Canada, and with their arrival they ran up the number of transatlantic flights from 41 to 65; The Italians arrived in Chicago on the day Wiley Post took off for Berlin, so Post's transatlantic flight proved to be the 27th of 1933. And, of course, right on Post's tail came Darius and Girenas. They succeeded in making the nonstop ocean crossing, only to crash to their deaths in the dark of a rainstorm after they exhausted their fuel over a forest in East Prussia.

The year 1933 remained a big one for transatlantic flights. After Post returned from around the world, Balbo led his formation back across the ocean (losing one aircraft in the Azores) to Italy, running up the total transatlantic score to 91 flights. In August, Charles and Anne Morrow Lindbergh flew to Europe via Labrador, Greenland, and Iceland in their Lockheed Sirius seaplane named *Tingmissartoq*; Jim and Amy Mollison flew from Pendine, Wales, to a crash landing at Bridgeport, Connecticut, in a twin-engine DeHavilland DH. 84, named *Seafarer*; and the French aviators Maurice Rossi and Paul Codos flew from New York to Rayak, Syria, nonstop, in their Bleriot 110 Special, named *Joseph LeBrix*. The year's "transatlantic season" ended by the German *Graf Zeppelin*, under the command of Dr. Hugo Eckener, cruising from Brizil to Akron, Ohio, via Miami, and on October 28th taking off from Akron to fly nonstop to Seville, Spain, in 80 hours, 31 minutes. When

FIGURE 63.—Just after shutting down at Floyd Bennett Field, July 22, 1933, Post climbs out of the *Winnie Mae* and views the huge crowd that greet him following his record solo around-the-world flight of 7 days, 18 hours, and 49½-minutes. Police try to hold back the crowd. Six hundred New York City policemen were required to handle the influx of 50,000 congratulators. Five thousand automobiles jammed the airport and surrounding roads, producing New York City's largest traffic jam of the time. Post's eye patch was dirty, so he requested and donned a clean handkerchief to cover his left eye socket. (Courtesy Pratt and Whitney Aircraft Company.)

FIGURE 64.—Post examines the *Winnie Mae* at Floyd Bennett Airfield, New York, after completion of the 1933 solo world flight. The lower cowling reveals the dents placed there in the Flat, Alaska, nose over. The propeller is the fixed-pitch Hamilton Standard substituted at Flat for the controllable pitch propeller damaged in the nose over. (Courtesy Pratt and Whitney Aircraft.)

1933 came to its end, 96 flights had been made across the North Atlantic since that overcast day in May 1919 when the U.S. Navy's NC flying boats took off from Rockaway, New York, to demonstrate that it could be done in the first place.[33]

To Wiley Post it seemed as if there were nothing but delays at Tempelhof. The refueling of the *Winnie Mae* went quickly enough; the troubles were created by difficulties in servicing her Sperry Autopilot. Post did not get away from Berlin until 2 hours and 15 minutes after his arrival. His plans called for a direct flight to Novo-Sibirsk, but when he was almost to the Russian frontier he discovered that certain maps were missing and turned back to land at Koenigsberg in East Prussia. He also discovered further difficulties with the Sperry Autopilot: the oil supply line to the autopilot's servo unit had begun to leak badly, which disabled the instrument. However, he could still fly "blind," manually, by using the autopilot's horizon and directional gyro. His time over this 340-mile leg was 4 hours and 30 minutes, with a ground speed of only 77.77 miles per hour. Upon landing at Koenigsberg, there were further problems with the autopilot; then the weather moved in and grounded him for the night.[34] It was perhaps just as well; he needed the sleep.

No one at Koenigsberg could repair the autopilot. The delay, however, had the benefit in that it allowed Post to sleep for six hours, which was one of the longest rest periods he would take on the entire flight. His bad eye bothered him some; a physician put boric acid in it, which helped a little.[35]

Now behind schedule, Post faced a difficult decision: Should he stop at Moscow and have the autopilot repaired or go directly to Novo-Sibirsk as planned? Although he desperately wanted to break his previous record, Post also wanted to complete the flight, so he decided to make an unscheduled landing at Moscow and to seek mechanical air. He took off from Koenigsberg in great haste, forgetting his suitcase of clothing, and flew five hours through rain and low clouds, to land at Octobrisky Field, Moscow. An oil line near the sump (the sump had a gauge to indicate the oil level), located by Post's knees, had loosened, resulting in a loss of oil flow to all three of the servo units.

While Russian mechanics worked on the loose joint in the oil line, three Russian doctors examined Post for fatigue. One doctor was surprised that the flier

FIGURE 65.—This view shows the *Winnie Mae* at Floyd Bennett Field with a battered wing leading edge and dented wheel pants and cowling, illustrating the scars of the 1933 solo world flight. The two steps for mounting or climbing down from the cockpit are extended. The steps could be moved in or out from either inside the cockpit or outside the aircraft. An unusual feature is the tail wheel, which Post did not prefer. His traditional tail skid gave much more stability with respect to ground handling during landing roll-outs, especially in crosswinds at short fields. However, some "grass-strip" airport operators objected to tail skids, due to the "furrowing" that was produced. The top of each wheel pant is metal clad to withstand foot-pressure without damage to the finish. (Courtesy Mobil Oil Corporation.)

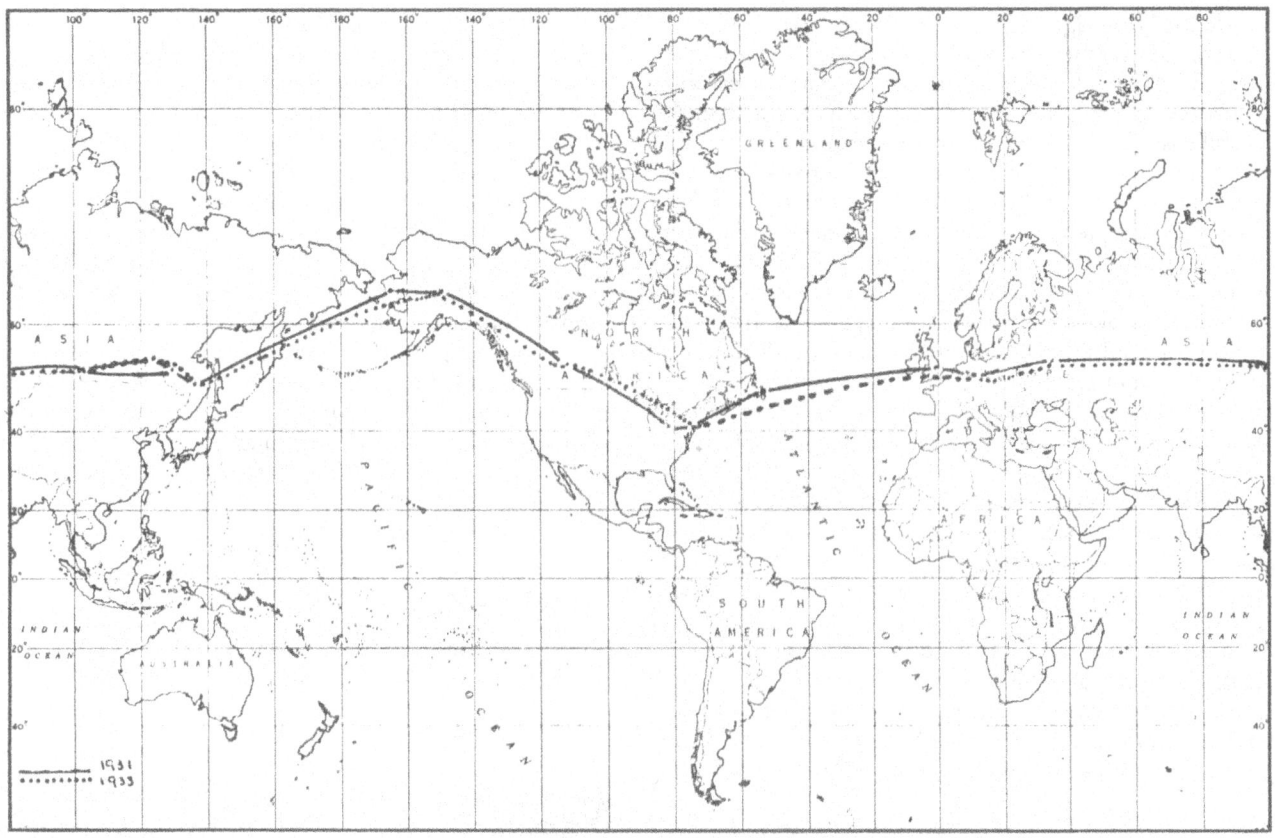

FIGURE 66.—Itineraries of Wiley Post's around-the-world flights in 1931 and 1933.

1931		1933
New York, U.S.A.	40° 39′ N, 73° 47′ W	New York, U.S.A.
Harbour Grace, Newfoundland	47° 42′ N, 53° 17′ W	
Chester, England	53° 12′ N, 2° 54′ W	
Hanover, Germany	52° 23′ N, 9° 44′ E	
Berlin, Germany	52° 23′ N, 13° 25′ E	Berlin, Germany
		Koenigsberg, Germany (now Kalingrad, USSR) 54° 41′ N, 20° 31′ E
Moscow, Russia	55° 45′ N, 37° 42′ E	Moscow, Russia
Novosibirsk, Siberia	55° 04′ N, 83° 05′ E	Novosibirsk, Siberia
Irkutsk, Siberia	52° 18′ N, 104° 15′ E	Irkutsk, Siberia
		Rukhlovo, Siberia (now Skovorodino) 54° 00′ N, 123° 15′ E
Blagoveshchensk, Siberia	50° 19′ N, 129° 30′ E	
Khabarovsk, Siberia	40° 3′ N, 135° 08′ E	Khabarovsk, Siberia
Nome, Alaska (Solomon Beach)	64° 30′ N, 165° 30′ W	
		Flat, Alaska 62° 28′ N, 158° 01′ W
Fairbanks, Alaska	64° 50′ N, 147° 50′ W	Fairbanks, Alaska
Edmonton, Canada	53° 34′ N, 113° 25′ W	Edmonton, Canada
Cleveland, U.S.A.	41° 30′ N, 81° 41′ W	
New York, U.S.A.		New York, U.S.A.

showed so little sign of being tired and asked Post how he avoided fatigue. Post told the representative of the *New York Times* to tell the Russians that Americans of pioneer stock could do without sleep for a week.[36] Despite his boast, Post knew that exhaustion would catch up with him if he met many more serious delays. He had already lost a day, and the trip was less than half completed. He took time to have a Russian barber shave his two days' growth of beard. Post praised the Russian mechanics who labored to fix the automatic pilot, but it was still not in perfect order.

Post took off from Moscow 2 hours and 15 minutes after the landing and encountered a stressful flight to Novo-Sibirsk in Siberia. Once, while flying blind, he almost scraped a hillside that loomed up through the fog. By climbing to 21,000 feet for a brief time, Post hoped to get above the bad weather but he failed to climb out on top. This climb to such a high altitude, without any oxygen equipment, may seem reckless, but Post had carefully predetermined his tolerance to hypoxia for brief periods.

It took 13 hours and 15 minutes to get to Novo-Sibirsk, 7 hours of which were spent in blind flight. Some periods of apprehension occurred, because he had to work his way through a pass in the Ural Mountains at a point where the mountains were 6,000 feet higher than he was flying.

Upon landing at Novo-Sibirsk, Post was met through prearrangement by Miss Fay Gillis of New York. Fay Gillis' father, Julius H. Gillis, was an American engineer who had gone to Russia in 1930 to build two electrolytic zinc plants for the USSR's first five-year plan. Fay had begun flying at the age of 19 and in September 1929, while piloting a training plane with her instructor over Curtiss Airfield at Valley Stream, Long Island, the tail surfaces had parted from the plane, forcing her and her instructor to bail out. Miss Gillis thus became the first female member of the famed Caterpillar Club.[37] At the cabled request of Wiley, she had left Moscow on June 25 for Novo-Sibirsk to supervise the refueling of the *Winnie Mae* and to help with any other needed aircraft attention. The cable was sent from New York by Wiley to Fay Gillis in Moscow and stated:

> LIKE YOU ARRIVE NOVOSIBIRSK BY JULY FIRST [to] ARRANGE [to] GAS PLANE IN TWO HOURS WHILE I SLEEP [and] THEN FLY WITH ME TO KHABAROVSK TO DIRECT SERVICE THERE [stop] GET ME BEST

FIGURE 67.—Wiley Post is congratulated by President Franklin Delano Roosevelt at the White House on July 26, 1933 following the solo around-the-world flight. To the right is Navy Captain Walter Vernon, aide to the President. This was Post's second invitation by a President to the White House. (Courtesy INS and the Franklin D. Rossevelt Library.)

FIGURE 68.—The autopilot used by Wiley Post in 1933 was placed on display by the Smithsonian Institution (bottom panel of exhibit). In the upper panel, the viewers were able to practice with a working model of the autopilot to learn how it functioned. This was a very popular exhibit for many years. (Courtesy Sperry Gyroscope Company.)

FIGURE 69.—Post was an avid hunter. Here he straddles a Kodiak Bear, bagged during an Alaskan hunting trip. (Courtesy L. E. Gray.)

MAPS NOVOSIBIRSK [to] KHABAROVSK [stop] WILL PAY YOUR EXPENSE [stop] REGARDS [stop] WILEY POST.

Fay Gillis' mastery of the Russian language was absolutely priceless to Post.[38] She tells that each night during the week prior to Post's landing, the Russians brought a hot meal to the airport in anticipation of his arrival.[39] Fay Gillis also told of Post having to land twice because of poor visibility while enroute from Moscow to Novo-Sibirsk.[40] Post's New York agent, Lee Trenholm, announced that Fay Gillis would fly in the passenger cabin of the *Winnie Mae* from Novo-Sibirsk to the next landing point in Rusia to assist with refueling there,[41] but these plans were dropped shortly after Post's New York departure.[42] It was explained later that this would have spoiled the solo nature of the flight.

Post stopped in Novo-Sibirsk only two hours, just long enough to refuel, and left in such a rush that he did not have time to eat a meal. However, this was consistent with Wiley's practice of eating lightly on these long flights.

A hand-lettered page of instructions was prepared by the Russians to accompany maps they collected for "pilot-Post" for his remaining flight through Russia. On the instructions were such items as "the safe height in feet when flying in fog for a given region and heights of artificial obstructions and radiomasts in large populated points." The heights were given with the "height of the aerodrome of departure" for the reference point, not mean sea level; however, Moscow airport was cited as being 512 feet and Novo-Sibirsk as 492 feet above sea level. The aerodromes where landing was permitted were listed as Moscow, Sverdlovsk, Omsk, Novo-Sibirsk, Krasnojorsk, Irkutsk, Chita, Rukhlovo, and Khabarovsk.

Some problems continued to plague Post after he left Novo-Sibirsk. More trouble with the automatic pilot forced him to make another unscheduled landing at Irkutsk. However, the 1,055-mile distance was flown in 6 hours and 33 minutes at a ground speed of 161.7 miles per hour, which was his fastest leg. The Russians had reports of storms to the east over the Baikal Mountains, so Post stayed several hours in Irkutsk. During this delay, Russian mechanics repaired the automatic pilot and refused to take any pay for their services.[43] Post finally took off, with a nonstop flight to Khabarovsk as his goal. But rain began to fall; the evening darkness deepened; the railroad tracks below could not be seen. He finally decided that if his fuel gave out during the night he would bail out. After 7 hours and 32 minutes he spotted Rukhlovo, 370 miles northwest of Blagoveshchensk, and he was dismayed to discover that his ground speed had been only 99.55 miles per hour. At this point, however, Post found that he was only an hour behind his 1931 flight.

Upon landing at Rukhlovo, Wiley was thirsty, but the Russians were unable to understand him when he asked for a drink of water. They thought he wanted liquor. Finally, after an animated discussion, the Russians brought forth a samovar of tea.[44] This incident led Will Rogers to remark that Post had to fly 1,800 miles for a drink of water. After a few hours, Post took off for Khabarovsk; the headwinds over this leg were negligible; he was able to make a ground speed of 150 miles per hour, and touched down in Khabarovsk after a flight of four and one-half hours.

Two hours were spent refueling the *Winnie Mae* at Khabarovsk, and Post studied the Russians' weather reports carefully. Jimmy Mattern, who was still at Anadyr, assisted the Russians in preparing the weather reports of the Bering Sea area for Post. When Post took off from Khabarovsk, he faced a 3,100-mile flight to Fairbanks, a track almost as long as his flight from New York to Berlin, but by this stage of the flight he was by no means as fresh. And between Khabarovsk and his Alaskan landfall at Nome stretched the Sea of Okhotsk, the Kamchatka Peninsula, which had mountains that reached up to 15,000 feet, and then the long stretch of the Bering Sea. It was an arduous flight, even for a pilot who was well rested and who enjoyed good weather over the route, but Wiley Post teetered on the edge of fatigue, and the weather he met was bad.

Thick clouds stood like a barrier across the Sea of Okhotsk, but Post plunged into them and for the next seven hours he flew by instruments and autopilot. Post was unequivocal in his praise of the autopilot during these hours and credited it for his success between Khabarovsk and Fairbanks. When the *Winnie Mae* finally flew out of the murk, Post found himself flying at 14,000 feet above a great cloud layer above the Gulf of Anadyr; he was able to recognize the gulf by the smoothness of the clouds, where they covered the sea. Somewhere below that cloud layer, in the village of Anadyr, Jimmy Mattern sat by a radio, sweating out Post's passage, and pondering his own bad luck. An hour rolled around the clock and then another; then a purple fringe took shape across the monotonous horizon ahead, that was framed in the blur of the *Winnie Mae's* propeller arc—the mountains of the Seward Peninsula. With the coast of Alaska in sight, Post began a gradual letdown to about 3,000 feet and a few minutes later, the *Winnie Mae's* shadow crossed the Alaskan shoreline at Cape Prince of Wales. From the Cape, Wiley swung off to the southeast and followed the desolate coastline to Nome; he circled the Nome radio station to announce his arrival, and then sped off into the east for the Yukon and Fairbanks.

Now Wiley began to have troubles with his radio and ADF set; he could not pick up the Fairbanks radio station. About halfway between Nome and Fairbanks, Noel and Ada Wien, pioneer Alaskan bush pilots and the founders of Wien-Alaska Airways, were in the air in one of their Bellancas and spotted the *Winnie Mae*. She was circling over the Yukon River, as if lost. They flew toward the *Winnie Mae*, hoping to get Post's attention. But he never saw them, and flew off toward the southeast. The Wiens attempted to follow, but the Vega was much faster than their Bellanca, and the *Winnie Mae* was soon lost to sight.[45]

Post was flying southeast, toward McGrath, which was considerably off course from the correct heading for Fairbanks. As the *Winnie Mae* flew over McGrath, Oscar Winchell, a radio operator for McGee Airways of Anchorage, tried to get radio contact with Post, but with no results. The *Winnie Mae* flew off into the southwest, on a heading which was exactly the opposite from a course for Fairbanks.

Having troubles with his radio, being unfamiliar with the terrain, afflicted by poor visibility, and being crowded by fatigue, Post was wandering around Alaska's skies, looking for a landmark that would correspond to something on his charts and that would provide a bearing for a course to Fairbanks. Meanwhile, he also had to take care to dodge the 20,000-foot summit of Mount McKinley and its satellite peaks, which for all he knew could be hidden in the haze anywhere around him.

Post finally looked out his windshield and saw the small mining settlement of Flat below him. Flat is about 75 miles southwest of McGrath and 300 miles southwest of Fairbanks. The radio operator at Flat called Winchell at McGrath and notified him that the *Winnie Mae* was circling overhead. At this point in his flight, Post was 31 hours and 29 minutes ahead of the 1931 flight.[46] With luck, he might yet beat his 1931 record by all of one day. But Post was tired; he knew that he was lost, and in no condition to continue; he throttled back his Wasp and trimmed out the *Winnie Mae* for a landing at Flat.

The airfield at Flat was no more than a crude landing strip; it was 700 feet long and had a ditch across its end. Post brought the *Winnie Mae* lightly, touched down easily, and rolled out nicely—but was unable to brake in time to avoid running into the ditch. As the *Winnie Mae's* wheels skidded into the ditch, she lurched over on her right wing, and the right leg of her landing gear crumpled; her tail came up, driving her nose into the earth, bending the complex Smith propeller; and she finally came to a stop with her engine cowl stuck in the dirt. As Post studied the damage, he ruefully recalled that the accident was similar to the one he and Gatty had experienced at Solomon Beach in 1931. However, the two accidents probably had less to do with Solomon, Flat, or Alaska's primitive airfields, than it did with Post's state of fatigue in this final stage of his flights.

The weary Post was not injured and a careful inspection showed that the *Winnie Mae* had not received any irreparable damage. Joe Crosson of Pacific Alaska Airways, a PanAm subsidiary, was reached by radio in Fairbanks, and he promptly took off for Flat with Hutch Hutchison, one of his mechanics, and a serviceable fixed-pitch propeller for the *Winnie Mae*.[47] Post got some much-needed sleep, while Crosson was flying to Flat. Meanwhile, workers of the Flat Mining Company promptly volunteered their labors. They erected a tripod derrick of timbers, and hoisted the *Winnie Mae* out of the ditch with block and tackle; then they chocked the airplane up so Crosson and Hutchison could work on the damaged landing gear. After Crosson and Hutchison arrived, Post went over the damaged airplane with them, and then he went back to sleep, while the Pacific Alaska men put the *Winnie Mae* in repair.

Post was up with the dawn, Crosson had the *Winnie Mae* ready to go, and they took off together, with Post following Crosson to Fairbanks. The *Winnie Mae* was quickly refueled at Fairbanks, but bad weather over the route to Edmonton kept Post grounded at Fairbanks for eight hours. Post was anxious to go, but he had no desire to tempt fate with the wretched weather that can boil up over the mountains between Fairbanks and Edmonton. He was also too familiar with the shortcomings of the airfield at Edmonton and had no intention of attempting a landing there at night.

When Post finally got away from Fairbanks he, nevertheless, met a hostile sky over much of the 1,450-mile track to Edmonton. He flew this leg in 9 hours and 22 minutes, with an average ground speed of 154.8 miles per hour, and four of those nine hours were spent in heavy cloud, flying on instruments. Mountain peaks along the Fairbanks-Edmonton track often reach up to 15,000 feet, and to avoid them and some cloud formations, Post was often driven up 20,000 feet for periods of several minutes.

Post was in a hurry to be away from Edmonton, but it took an hour and a half to get the *Winnie Mae* refueled and serviced, the most important item being replenishing the oil in her Sperry Autopilot. This time the Edmonton Field was dry, so Post was able to make an ordinary takeoff, and the citizens of Edmonton were deprived of seeing the *Winnie Mae* roar down Portage Avenue again.

The Edmonton-New York leg was 2,044 miles, but the air was smooth, the sky was clear, and Post made most of the flight by his Sperry Autopilot. With his "Mechanical Mike" doing the flying, Post allowed himself to doze from time to time. To make sure that he would do no more than doze, he rigged his "Rube Goldberg" by tying a wrench to a finger with a length of string, holding the wrench in his hand; whenever he slipped off into a sleep deep enough to relax the hand, the wrench fell, jerked his finger, and woke him up.[48]

Speeding across Canada, over the Great Lakes, and into the United States, the *Winnie Mae's* passage proved to be an easy downhill run. Between dozing, Post checked his navigation with the ADF set, zeroing in on the scores of commercial broadcasting stations along his route. One of the news broadcasts he picked up said that the famous Russian Arctic aviator Sigmund Levanevsky had flown Jimmy Mattern from Anadyr to Nome in a Soviet seaplane; this was good news, and Post was very grateful to Mattern for his assistance from Anadyr. As the afternoon passed and the Ontario Peninsula slid by below, Post could detect a rising excitement in the New York City radio stations, which were keeping track of his passage, and speculating over the time of his arrival at Floyd Bennett.

As the *Winnie Mae* neared New York, a great popular clamor began to fill the radio airwaves and the "Extras" that flooded the city's newstands in anticipation of Post's return. Some newspapers portrayed Post as a one-eyed superman, who could fly an airplane as if he had mystical powers; one reporter stated that Post was part American Indian (not true); while another described Post as tough a Southwesterner who could use a tomahawk as well as any Indian (not true either!).[49] Aside from the nonsense, however, there was general appreciation that Wiley Post and his *Winnie Mae* had achieved something that was truly great, and that someday men would be able to fly around the world in as little time, or less time, and without having to be a Wiley Post.

A crowd estimated at 50,000 persons was jammed in and around Floyd Bennett Field when the sound of the *Winnie Mae's* Wasp sounded out of the darkness overhead. Then her landing lights could be seen floating through the night sky, across the field boundary and onto the runway.

When the Winnie Mae touched down, she was 13 hours and 18½ minutes out of Edmonton; Post had flown the 2,004-mile track with an average ground speed of 150.5 miles per hour.

More significant, in that same instant of touchdown at 11:50½ p.m. on July 22, 1933, Wiley Post and his *Winnie Mae* had circled the world in seven days, 18 hours, and 49½ minutes. Their total flying time was 115 hours, 36½ minutes. Post had broken his and Gatty's record of 1931 by more than 21 hours.

This was not to Post's satisfaction. It was his intention to fly the circuit in a minimum of seven days, something less than one week. But he could console himself that seven days, 18 hours and 49½ minutes sounded much better than eight days and one minute.

With his touchdown at Floyd Bennett on this evening of July 22, Wiley Post became the first person to circumnavigate the earth twice by aircraft. He was the first man to fly around the world alone, and he had done it with all possible speed. Post's record remains unique. Fourteen years later in 1947 his record was ostensibly broken; but it was done under such radically different circumstances that the new record was really meaningless.

When Post taxied the *Winnie Mae* up to the flood-lit terminal buildings, the airplane was engulfed by a swarm of humanity. About 600 policemen had been sent to Floyd Bennett to handle the throngs that swarmed over the airport, but it is doubtful if 1,600 would have been enough. An estimated 5,000 automobiles jammed the airport's parking facilities, spilling over into vacant lots nearby; and the roads leading out of Brooklyn and Queens to Floyd Bennett were a hopeless tangle of snarled traffic.

Upon lifting himself through the overhead hatch in the *Winnie Mae's* cockpit, Wiley was greeted by his wife Mae. And there was Harold Gatty, and a delegation of his Oklahoma supporters, including John Kroutil, Walter Harrison, Leslie Fain, and "Red" Gray. Wiley's first request was for a clean eye patch, but that was something that no one thought to bring; he had to settle for a clean handkerchief, which he tied around his head.

After several wild minutes, while the crowd jammed in around the *Winnie Mae*, Wiley was finally able to get out of the airplane only by crawling back over the wing to its trailing edge, where he slid over the curve of the after fuselage to the ground. Eventually, he made his way to a waiting automobile. Meanwhile, the Navy sent a detail of men in to surround the *Winnie Mae* to protect her from souvenir hunters; she was eventually rolled off to the protection of a Navy hangar. It was the ugly custom of souvenir hunters to almost literally tear an airplane to pieces in their frantic desire for a piece of fabric from it; fortunately for the *Winnie Mae* she was 90 percent plywood.

Despite the fact that he had very little sleep during the past week, Post remarked that he could hold his hand as steady as ever, and a doctor who examined him found him to be in good condition.[50] A few days later, Post told newsmen that he weighed his usual 171 pounds when he landed back at Floyd Bennett (it will be recalled that his 1930 pilot's license had given his weight as 155). He also told Walter Harrison that with good weather, the flight could have been made in five days.[51] In appreciation for Lionel Clark's assistance at Floyd Bennett during the weeks before takeoff, Post had a gold watch prepared with a special engraving, and gave it to Clark.

Post found little time to catch up on his sleep during the next few days. Some hours earlier on the day of his return to Floyd Bennett, General Italo Balbo had led his armada of two dozen Savoia flying boats from Chicago to New York, landing in Jamaica Bay. On the evening of Post's arrival, Balbo and some of his pilots tried to drive to Floyd Bennett to be on hand to extend him their congratulations when he landed, but the highways were so jammed that they finally gave up the effort as futile. On the following day, Balbo and Post finally got together, an event well covered by the newspapers.[52] Balbo's massed flight to the United States and back to Italy has been virtually forgotten with the passing of time, but it was no small accomplishment to fly two-dozen airplanes across the North Atlantic. The Balbo operation ranks as one of the great accomplishments of interwar aeronautics. Balbo relates that in his conversation with Post, Wiley expressed disappointment that his around-the-world solo had not been accomplished in four days or less.[53]

Wiley also visited the famous British husband-and-wife flying team of long-distance fliers, James and Amy Mollison, who were in the hospital at Bridgeport, Connecticut.[54] Jim Mollison had flown the North Atlantic solo in August 1932, from Port Marnock, Ireland, to Pennfield Ridge, New Brunswick, in a tiny, 2,754-pound DeHavilland DH. 80A Puss Moth named *The Heart's Content*. In 1933 he and his wife Amy became the first husband-wife team to fly the Atlantic. They had taken off from Pendine, Wales, on July 22, in a twin-engine DeHavilland DH. 84 Dragon Moth named *Seafarer*, with New York their destination. Short on fuel, they landed at Bridgeport. They had been in the air for 39 hours; it was dark and the airport was unfamiliar; they inadvertantly landed downwind and the result was a crash landing. But they climbed out of the wreckage of their *Seafarer* with none-too-serious injuries and a measure of immortality. The airport at Bridgeport was later named Mollison Field.

Port received the formal compliments of New York City, awarded by Mayor O'Brien, and was honored by another ticker-tape parade up Broadway, which brought rousing cheers from his fellow Americans— and several hours of overtime for Lower Manhattan's street cleaners. He was invited to the White House, and on July 26 flew to Washington for a visit with President Franklin D. Roosevelt.[52] Once again, Wiley Post was the Nation's reigning hero.

The *New York Times* considered the flight as more than simply a stunt executed by a man with "steady nerves and great courage." The *Times* called the flight a "revelation of the new art of flying," and added that it made a real contribution to technical aviation:

> By winning a victory with the use of gyrostats, a variable pitch propeller and a radiocompass, Post definitely ushers in a new stage of long-distance aviation. The days when human skill alone and an almost bird-like sense of direction enabled a flier to hold his course for long hours through a starless night or over a fog are over. Commercial flying in the future will be automatic.[56]

Post's solo achievements also reminded the paper of how much remained to be done before world flight would be safe. Without sufficient radio guidance from the ground, the paper warned, similar flights would remain hazardous in the extreme. Similarly, supply depots would have to be established in out-of-the-way places to alleviate emergency situations.

The *Daily Oklahoman* was impressed by the impact that Post's flight could have on future wars. "There will be no non-combatants in the war of the early future," the *Oklahoman* predicted. The writer observed that militarists saw the Post and Balbo flights as sufficient reason for building strong defensive protection. On the other hand, pacifists considered the flights as evidence of the need to scrap weapons and abandon war. In essence, Post's accomplishment revealed certain "deadly potentialities" of the airplane in warfare, including its reliability and long-distance capability.

In Maysville, Editor Showen of the *News* wrote about Post, the man, and the fame that had been brought to Maysville: Reminding his readers of the city's position in the eyes of others, he wrote:

> If they had forgotten that the town was one of the most important towns in the world by reason of its being the home town of Wiley Post, their memory was refreshed by Wiley's later super-human stunt. Nor is Wiley likely to allow the name of Maysville to be forgotten in the years to come.

Post predicted that other fliers using similar equipment would beat his record.[57] The record stood until 1938 when Howard Hughes and a crew of four circled the world in 3 days, 19 hours, and 8 minutes.

Hughes also recommended that radio homing beacons be placed at every major airport.

For his 1933 flight, Post received one of aviation's highest awards, the Gold Medal of the Federation Aeronautique Internationale. Annually awarded to the person who had made the greatest contribution to aeronautics, the medal had been won by only one other American at that time, Charles A. Lindbergh in 1927.[58] The medal was formally awarded on October 9, 1934, in ceremonies in Washington, D.C. Post also won the coveted Harmon International Trophy for 1933, which was awarded by the League of International Aviators; previous winners were: Shirley Short, 1926; Charles A. Lindbergh, 1927; Carl Ben Eielson, 1928; James Doolittle, 1929; Frank M. Hawks, 1930; Clyde E. Pangborn, 1931; and Roscoe Turner, 1932.

Post hoped to realize some financial gain from the 1933 flight, and Walter Harrison predicted that he would make $50,000.[59] For example, although he did not smoke, Post agreed to be shown holding a Camel cigarette in his hand. The Camel ad said, "It takes healthy nerves to fly around the world alone." Wiley was quoted as saying, "Smoking Camels as I have for so long, I never worry about healthy nerves." His agents also arranged for the Buick Company to give Post a new automobile. Magazine testimonials brought in some money; two such advertisements, boosting Mobilgas and Sperry gyroscopes, appeared in the August 1933 issue of *Aviation*. Post was also to receive $7,500 from Socony Vacuum for a two-month tour around the nation, promoting the company's products.

When the management of Radio City Music Hall approached him concerning personal stage appearances, Post accepted, although several persons advised against it. His appearances consisted of showing newsreels of the 1933 flight, making comments on various aspects of the flight and aviation in general, and displaying the *Winnie Mae* outside in Rockefeller Center, which in those days was still under construction. The *Winnie Mae's* Sperry Autopilot was concurrently on exhibit in the lobby of the Roxy Theatre.[60] During these theater appearances, Post predicted 500-mile hour flights at altitudes of 35,000 feet.[61]

Harry Frederickson and several other Oklahomans advised Post that his theater appearances might ruin his opportunities for serious endorsement-type advertisements, but Post persisted. He believed that he could make $40,000 from the theater; actually, he cleared less than $7,000, although capacity crowds turned up to see him. At heart, Wiley Post was something of a populist; he believed in "the people." But at the Music Hall the people finally let him down. This was not true of the people of Oklahoma, however; they never let him down, nor did they forget him after he was gone.

While helping Post to raise the money for the 1933 solo flight, Walter Harrison discovered to his dismay how expensive it was to conduct research in aviation. Accordingly, he suggested that Oklahomans raise $20,000 and buy *Winnie Mae* from Post. The airplane would then be presented to the Smithsonian Institution in the State's name and Post would have the funds to purchase a more modern airplane and to continue his experimental flying.[62] Meanwhile, Post had further plans for his *Winnie Mae*.

During both world flights, Wiley Post's greatest enemy had been weather. Indeed, if the weather had not been against him across Russia and Siberia, he surely would have girdled the globe in less than a week. Twice around the world the weather had driven Post and the *Winnie Mae* to altitudes of 15,000 and even 20,000 feet, altitudes where they trespassed on a new and hostile environment, and where they dared not trespass for long. Yet only by achieving greater altitudes, Post knew, could men hurdle the hazards created by clouds and the storm conditions that they harbored. Three days after he returned to the United States, Post told the Aeronautical Chamber of Commerce of his plans to begin high-altitude studies. This was his first public mention of his intention to penetrate the stratosphere.[63]

Post later visited several cities, including Hartford, Connecticut, the home of the Pratt & Whitney Wasp. A parade was planned, but weather delayed Post's arrival. Meanwhile, the mayor became impatient, and angry, and decided to leave. When Post finally arrived, he found among those waiting for him, Lionel Clarke, the Pratt & Whitney man who had been such a great help to the 1933 flight. Post waved Clarke into the seat in the waiting limousine that otherwise would have been occupied by the mayor, and they were driven off to join the parade and later meeting with the govenor of Connecticut. Post and Clarke got along just fine without the company of "his honor."

The Quincy, Illinois, Herald-Whig of September 21, 1933, related that Post was in town the night of September 19 under the auspices of Socony Vacuum, a trip arranged by Walter Chatten. Post told a dinner meeting of 200 held in his honor by the Kiwanis Club, that "it will be possible to fly and land blind with instruments", and that "there is no limit to the speed that will be developed by the plane of the future—the more than 300 mph now possible will be greatly expanded". "Regular transoceanic service is not far off", Post told the group.

During the introduction of Post by Quincy Mayor Leo Lelane at the banquet, the Mayor forgot Post's name. When the Mayor reached the point in his introduction where he stated, "I give you . . .," the Mayor leaned over to Post and whispered, "What's your name?" Post, somewhat irritated by this, refused to answer. The Mayor then continued his introduction, "That intrepid flyer, Mr. . . .," and once again leaned over, this time asking Post loud enough for the front rows to hear, "What's your name?" Wiley gave his name and, following the Mayor's introduction, stood up after the applause, and said: "It is a great honor to be asked to speak to the representatives of this great city of . . .," and at this point Post appeared to falter, leaned over, and asked in a loud voice, "Mr. Mayor, what city is this?" The audience loved it, an incident which illustrates once again the special style of the taciturn, yet spunky, Post, who engendered widespread affection.

Wiley experienced engine failure in the *Winnie Mae* while taking off from Quincy the next day. He narrowly escaped death when the plane came down in a wooded area.[64]

George Brauer, the Braniff Airways mechanic who had prepared the *Winnie Mae* for her world flight, went to Quincy to arrange for the plane's shipment back to Oklahoma City. Meanwhile, Post was recuperating in a Quincy hospital. The newspapers explained the crash in terms of simple "engine failure." But Brauer was suspicious. He knew that engines that received the care which Post lavished on the *Winnie Mae's* Wasp simply do not pack up and quit without reason. He suspected that someone had tampered with the airplane. The first thing Brauer did upon his arrival in Quincy was to check the *Winnie Mae's* fuel tanks. He was stunned to discover five and one-half gallons of water in the tanks.[66] Since his two around-the-world flights, Post had been the target of several crackpot threats of the type that invariably come to afflict famous persons, but the Quincy affair was something else. It was truly frightening to Post's friends and associates to realize that there was someone at large who was jealous and resentful enough of Post's successes to attempt to kill him. Nor would this be the last attempt to wipe out Post and his *Winnie Mae* by the cowardly instrument of sabotage.

Under the careful hands of George Brauer, the *Winnie Mae* was gradually restored to a condition as good as new in her Oklahoma City hangar. Department of Commerce records show that the *Winnie Mae* was subsequently licensed through to March 27, 1934, in a restricted category, with modifications for exhibition and special test purposes. Meanwhile, Post was discharged from the hospital, and once back in Oklahoma City, he turned his attentions to the new kinds of equipment that he and the *Winnie Mae* would require for cruising great distances across a realm that few men had probed, and where none had stayed for very long—that which existed above 30,000 feet—the stratosphere.

The initial years of Post's aviation career had been directed toward the achievement of flying farther and faster. No one can fly an airplane farther than around-the-world, and he had indeed succeeded in flying it the fastest. In 1931 and again in 1933 he startled the world by showing how really small the globe could be. Post was an air racer, but his most determined rival was himself. As an air racer he was unique; he not only competed against himself, but, where other air racers snarled their way around tight courses marked by pylons or were content to race across a continent, his race course was the world—his pylons were Berlin, Moscow, Khabarovsk, and Fairbanks.

Post's flights suggested to the man in the street that someday he too would be able to fly around the world, and without having to endure the rigors experienced by Post. Within three years of Post's solo flight, it finally became possible to walk into a travel agency and purchase an around-the-world air passage aboard commercial airlines. In October 1936, Herbert R. Ekins of the *New York World-Telegram* dramatized the fact by speeding around the world in 18 days, 14 hours, and 56 minutes, wholly by commercial airlines. Unfortunately, Wiley Post did not live to see that.

Post was by no means satisfied with his solo flight. He knew that his around-the-world circuit should have been flown much faster than it had been, but he had the wisdom to realize that any further attempts would be hit-or-miss affairs until flight could be achieved at high altitudes, where he would be "above the weather."

Having accomplished all that he felt practicable on the horizontal, Post now reached out over the vertical, toward a hostile environment where man could not live. But Wiley Post was not an ordinary man, and it was the extraordinary fire that burned within him that inspired him to challenge the stratosphere and to create the world's first successful high-altitude pressure suit.

NOTES

1. *New York Times*, February 19, 1933, p. 24.
2. Griffin communication.
3. Griffin communication.
4. Griffin communication.
5. *Oklahoma City Times*, July 31, 1933.
6. *Aviation* (September 1933), p. 294.
7. Report of S. E. Perry, Approved Repair Station #89, June 10, 1933, to the Department of Commerce.
8. Letter to Smithsonian from Harvey H. Lippincott of Pratt & Whitney, April 11, 1960, and *Bee Hive*.
9. Letter to Smithsonian from Harvey H. Lippincott of Pratt & Whitney, April 11, 1960, and *Bee Hive*.
10. *New York Times*, May 28, 1933, VIII, 8.
11. *New York Times*, July 4, 1933, p. 8.
12. Frederickson interview; *Oklahoma City Times*, June 7, 1933.
13. *Daily Oklahoman*, June 15, 1933, p. 11.
14. *Oklahoma City Times*, June 1, 1933.
15. *New York Times*, July 16, 1933.
16. A discussion of Sperry autopilots appears in William

C. Ocker and Carl J. Crane, *Blind Flight in Theory and Practice* (San Antonio, Texas: Naylor Printing Company, 1932).

17. Gerhard R. Fisher, "The Way Home," *Western Flying,* vol. 9, no. 3 (March 1931), pp. 26–68.

18. This type of radio compass subsequently was adopted by the Army Air Service as standard equipment, and was in general use at the beginning of World War II.

19. *New York Times,* July 16, 1933, p. 3.

20. U.S. Patent No. 1,868,945 (July 26, 1932).

21. A detailed description is given in P. C. Sandretto, *Principles of Aeronautical Radio Engineering* (New York: McGraw-Hill, 1942).

22. *Daily Oklahoman,* June 30, 1933.

23. *Daily Oklahoman,* June 1, 1933.

24. *Daily Oklahoman,* June 4, 1933.

25. *Oklahoma City Times,* June 3, 1933, p. 2.

26. *Oklahoma City Times,* June 14, 1933, p. 2.

27. *New York Times,* June 28, 1933.

28. Roseberry, *The Challenging Skies,* p. 268; and the *New York Times,* July 8, 1933.

29. *Oklahoma City Times,* July 15, 1933.

30. *New York Times,* July 16, 1933.

31. Lionel B. Clark interview.

32. *New York Times,* July 17, 1933, p. 1.

33. An excellent tabulation of transatlantic flights is to be found in a set of charts by Arthur Flury, *Transocean Flight Attempts 1910–1940* (Bern, Switzerland: published by the author, 1947).

34. *New York Times,* July 18, 1933, p. 3.

35. *New York Herald Tribune,* July 18, 1933.

36. *New York Times,* July 17, 1933, p. 3.

37. Membership in the Caterpillar Club is limited to those aviators who have saved their lives by parachute.

38. *Daily Oklahoman,* July 4, 1933.

39. Fay Gillis Wells interview.

40. *New York Times,* July 19, 1933, p. 2.

41. *New York Times,* July 5, 1933, p. 10.

42. *New York Times,* July 17, 1933, p. 3.

43. *New York Times,* July 19, 1933, p. 1.

44. *New York Times,* July 22, 1933, p. 2.

45. Stephen E. Mills and James W. Phillips, *Sourbough Sky* (Seattle: Superior Publishing Company, 1969).

46. *New York Times,* July 21, 1933, p. 3.

47. *New York Times,* July 21, 1933, p. 1.

48. *New York Times,* July 21, 1933, p. 1.

49. *New York World Telegram,* July 22, 1933.

50. *Daily Oklahoman,* July 23, 1933, p. 2.

51. *Daily Oklahoman,* July 23, 1933, p. 2.

52. *New York Times,* July 24, 1933, p. 2.

53. Italo Balbo, translated by Gerald Griffin, *My Air Armada* (London: Hurst & Blacket, Ltd., 1934).

54. *New York Times,* July 25, 1933.

55. *New York Times,* July 27, 1933, p. 8.

56. *New York Times,* July 24, 1933, p. 2.

57. *New York Times,* July 24, 1933, p. 2.

58. Emme, *Aeronautics,* 172.

59. *Oklahoma City Times,* July 31, 1933.

60. *New York Times,* July 27, 1933, p. 20.

61. *New York Times,* July 30, 1933.

62. *Daily Oklahoman,* July 24, 1933.

63. *New York Times,* July 26, 1933.

64. *Washington Star,* September 21, 1933.

65. George Brauer interview.

4 / The First Practical Pressure Suit

While Wiley Post and the *Winnie Mae* were speeding around the world, the Australian city of Melbourne was preparing to observe its centennial in 1934, and to properly mark the centennial, Sir MacPherson Robertson [1] offered a cash prize of £ 10,000 (about $50,000 at that day's rate of exchange), and a gold cup, worth more than £ 600, to the winner of an air race between England and Australia. The race would start at Mildenhall, Suffolk, on October 20, 1934, and would proceed over a course marked by Baghdad, Allahabad, Singapore, Darwin, and Charleville, Australia, to the center of the Flemington Race Course in Melbourne. The purpose of the race was to encourage aviation, which was regarded as Australia's most promising link with the rest of the world; and it would do much to liven Melbourne's centennial.[2]

This race had everything dear to Post's heart: it was an international route of 12,500 miles that transversed continents; there would be some first-class competition from the United States, the British Empire, and Europe; it would be a widely publicized event which would provide a further stimulus to aviation progress; and the generosity of the prizes made participation extremely attractive.

Post was well aware, however, that recent innovations in aircraft design and new developments in engines and fuels had done much to make his *Winnie Mae* obsolescent. If she were to be entered in the MacRobertson Race, she would be flying under a handicap, unless modifications could be made. And here Post had a vision of the *Winnie Mae* speeding over the track from England to Australia in the thin air above 30,000 feet and taking advantage of the powerful tailwinds that he knew existed at very high altitudes.

Shortly after his return from the 1933 around-the-world flight, Post had told the Aeronautical Chamber of Commerce about his high-altitude plans, and he had frequently referred to the great promise of high-altitude flight during his Radio City Music Hall lectures. In the July 24, 1933, number of the *Oklahoma City Times*, Post remarked further:

> The next development for long-distance flying after blind flying and blind landing will be high altitude flying, flying in the stratosphere. I think that the development of supercharged planes, that is with the cabin as well as the engines kept sufficiently supplied with oxygen in the rarified atmosphere, will come in the very near future.

No one else in 1933 was speaking words similar to these, much less making the plans that Post was. There were indeed high-altitude "records"; but they in fact were artificial flights, simply made up and down in order to get the desired lines inked in on the drum of a barograph. No one spoke seriously about long-distance point-to-point flights above 30,000 feet, or even 20,000 feet, except this one-eyed man from Oklahoma.

With respect to the *Winnie Mae*, Post knew that it was impossible to pressurize her plywood shell, and the complications attendant to building a pressurized cockpit chamber into her were so great, it was wholly impracticable. Post knew that he had to find another solution to the pressurization problem, and that was to pressurize himself. If he could achieve this, it would open the way to a new realm of flight.

Post calculated that if he could climb the *Winnie Mae* to altitudes of 30,000 to 50,000 feet, and provide himself with an adequate supply of oxygen, he could take advantage of the thinner air and make such a high, true airspeed that he could win the MacRobertson Race. Post also had the impression that extremely fast streams of air—"high winds," he called them—existed in the stratosphere, which would balance off the air-pressure differentials that prevailed over different areas of the globe at different times.[3] If he could intercept one of these powerful streams of air, he could literally ride along with it, which would serve to create a phenomenal increase in his ground speed.

What Post had here was a crude prevision of those incredibly powerful aspects of upper air's circulation which since World War II have come to be known as

71

"jetstreams." Interestingly enough, Post was by no means the first to glimpse their potential. Writing in the 1850s, the great American balloonist John Wise looked forward to ascending to great heights, where he was sure he would encounter a "great river of air" that would not only sweep him across the Atlantic, but on around the world!

In 1928, M. Luckiesh reported that in the cirrus region of the sky (20,000 to 50,000 feet), observations showed that winds sometimes obtained velocities of 100 and even 200 miles per hour; more significantly, these speeds sometimes maintained themselves for days. Luckiesh predicted that "flying records will be made in these regions before long."[4]

As early as 1920 the U.S. Army's Air Service had attempted to develop a practical means of accomplishing pressurized flight by aircraft. An oval, steel tank with a glass port was built into the cockpit of a biplane and a gear-driven supercharger was employed to pressurize the tank. A manually controlled tank-exhaust valve was added and the pilot's controls were arranged inside the tank. On June 8, 1921, the aircraft made a trial flight, but the pressure cabin, such as it was, rapidly over-pressurized to minus 7,000 feet, i.e., 7,000 feet below sea level! A further problem was that the compressor delivered an inflow of air in excess to the outflow, and the ambient temperature inside the chamber was driven up to 150° F. The pilot was extremely uncomfortable; he experienced terrible ear pains, and was barely able to land the airplane. Plans for further experiments were abandoned.[5]

The impracticability of pressurizing the *Winnie Mae* led Post to conceive the design and fabrication of a pressure suit for flight. He would have the suit tailored to his body dimensions, and with certain modifications to the *Winnie Mae*, he should be able to accomplish ground speeds in excess of 250 miles per hour. The concept of a pressure suit for aircraft was imaginative and radical, and testifies to Post's creative aeronautical genius.

In early 1934, Wiley consulted his friend Jimmy Doolittle, who had joined Shell Oil Company as director of aviation. They discussed the possibility of constructing the pressure suit, and Doolittle referred Wiley to the Los Angeles branch of the B. F. Goodrich Company.[6] Post wanted his unique approach to winning the MacRobertson Race to be a secret, so he discussed his plans with very few people, although he revealed certain features of his pressure-suit work in various magazine articles.

Post visited the Los Angeles Goodrich plant on April 6, 1934, and requested the following:

FIGURE 70.—Post's first full pressure suit and helmet. This suit was made of rubberized parachute fabric. Earphone bulges are shown on the helmet. The rectangular plastic vision plate was replaced in the later version with a circular glass window. The metal belt sealed the top half of the suit to the bottom half, when the suit was pressurized. The suit was entered at the waist. Photograph taken on roof of B. F. Goodrich plant, Los Angeles, June 1934. (Courtesy 1935 Aircraft Year Book.)

A rubber suit which will enable me to operate and live in an atmosphere of approximately twelve pounds absolute (5,500 feet altitude equivalent). I expect to fly through rarefied areas where the pressure is as low as five pounds absolute (27,000 feet). The temperature will be taken care of by heating the air from the supercharger by coiling it around the exhaust manifolds.[7]

It is noted that Post was requesting a seven-pound-per-square-inch (psi) differential pressure between his suit interior and the outer atmospheric pressure of five pounds per square inch. This means that Post, when using outside air having 20 percent oxygen, would be exposed within the suit to a 5,500-foot physiologic altitude (12 psi) while flying at a height of 27,000 feet.[8] Post intended to tap a new external engine supercharger for a source of compressed air to provide suit pressurization and ventilation.

A Wright Field report of June 21, 1934, first mentions Post's plans to use oxygen with the suit; the

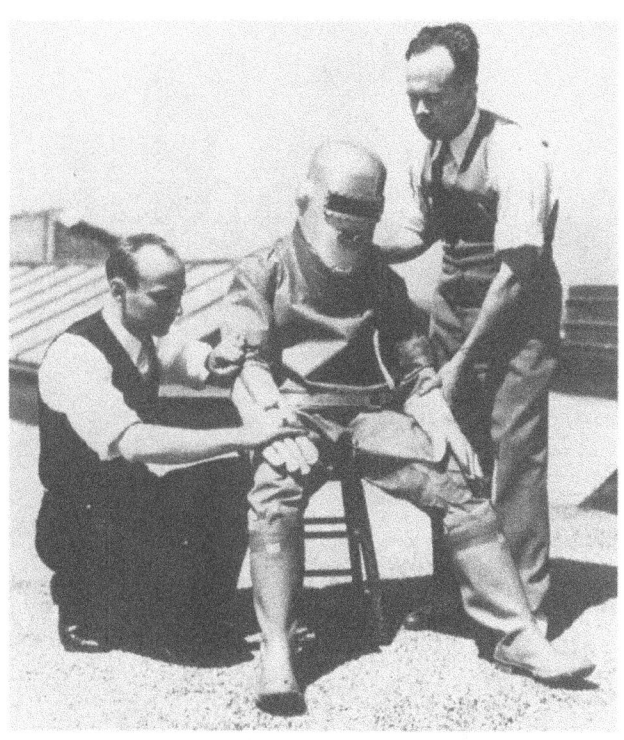

FIGURE 71.—W. R. Hucks (standing) and J. Stevens, of the B. F. Goodrich Co., in Los Angeles, scrutinize Wiley Post's first pressure suit, which they had just completed to his specifications. Photograph taken in June 1934. A laboratory assistant is in the suit and the helmet's mouth opening for food intake and speaking (during unpressurized periods) is shown with open cover. The suit was discarded when it ruptured during static tests at Dayton, Ohio. R. Colley of B. F. Goodrich kept the helmet, which is on display now at the Smithsonian Institution. (Courtesy NEA.)

pure oxygen at 6.7 pounds per square inch would provide almost three times the oxygen available to persons in a sea-level normal atmosphere (of the 14.7-psi normal atmospheric pressure, oxygen represents 2.7 psi). Post's suit specifications could handle 6.7 pounds per square inch of pure oxygen, which would provide two and one-half times the amount of oxygen necessary to maintain a physiological sea-level condition. It was necessary to have some excess suit oxygen because Post's exhalations would yield carbon dioxide and water vapor that would dilute the inside oxygen atmosphere. To preclude excess accumulations of carbon dioxide and water vapor, and to make room for the incoming oxygen supply, an outflow valve was necessary.

Wiley was pursuing the development of a pressure suit because adequate oxygen masks did not exist and, also, above 35,000 feet, oxygen masks began to have decreasing effectiveness. Above 35,000 feet any sustained flying with oxygen masks alone was totally impractical. J. B. S. Haldane, A British biologist, and oxygen was to be carried in liquid form. The first suit by Post had satisfactorily passed a pressure-differential test of five pounds per square inch at the Los Angeles Goodrich plant by inflating the suit pressure to 19.7-pounds-per-square-inch absolute (14.7 psi plus 5 psi). But a higher differential would be necessary if Post wished to exceed 29,000 feet in altitude. However, if oxygen could be added to the incoming air (or replace the incoming air entirely), much higher altitudes could be achieved without increasing the suit-differential pressure because an internally tolerable oxygen-rich atmosphere would exist.

Physiologically, Post was on the right track. This is shown by the following calculation based upon a five-pound-per-square-inch pressure differential. If one assumes suit inflation with 100 percent oxygen, then at a pressure differential of five pounds per square inch, at a 50,000-foot altitude (1.7-psi absolute outside pressure), he would need to supply a source of oxygen capable of producing an absolute inside pressure of 6.7 pounds per square inch (1.7 plus 5 equal 6.7). Calculations show that an atmosphere of

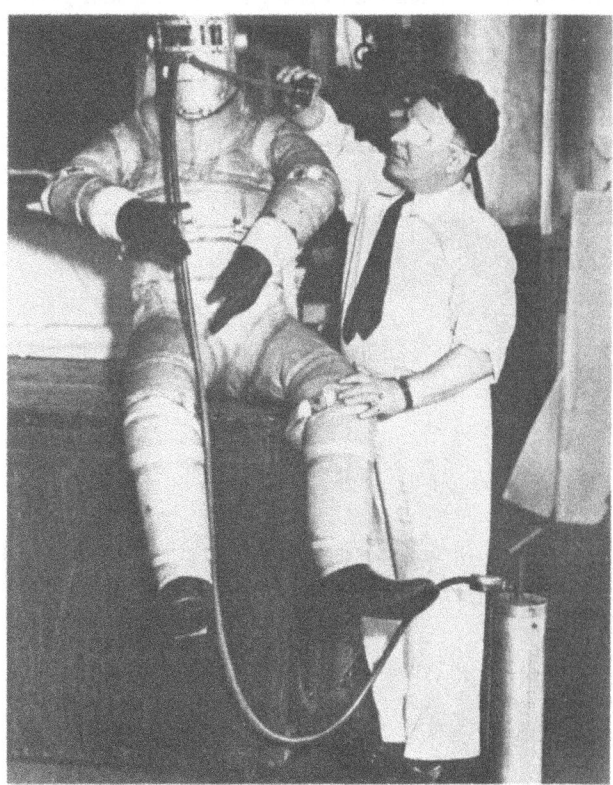

FIGURE 72.—Wiley Post's second pressure suit is shown during a static pressure test at the B. F. Goodrich Company in Akron, Ohio. This pressure suit was the first to employ flexible elbow and knee points. The suit was entered through the waist, which was sealed with two large metal plates held together with wing nuts. The oxygen was brought in just below the visor. Post had to be cut out of the suit when he became stuck in it. Photograph made in July 1934. (Courtesy Popular Mechanics Magazine.)

Sir R. H. Davis, a British expert on diving suits, had collaborated in 1933 on the construction of a modified diving suit for high-altitude use. This suit was tested by the man it was built for, the American balloonist Mark Ridge, in a pressure chamber in England in 1933. It is reported that on November 29, 1933, while protected by the suit, Ridge was able to withstand a chamber pressure as low as 17 millimeters of mercury (84,000 feet) for 30 minutes. However, no record exists that Ridge ever made a real balloon ascension in his suit. In any case, it is likely that the suit would have been too cumbersome for Wiley's airplane-piloting needs; and it is very unlikely that Post or Goodrich knew of this British effort.

The Goodrich Company in Los Angeles assigned William Hucks as project engineer, with John A. Diehl as assistant, for the construction of Post's requested pressure suit. This first suit (which we shall refer to as Suit No. 1) was made out of parachute cloth and required six yards of rubberized double-ply material. The two layers were glued together on a bias to minimize stretch. The sleeves of Suit No. 1 were carried to the neckline in a raglan cut. Pigskin gloves were used to protect the hands and the feet were sealed in rubber boots.

For this first pressure suit, an aluminum helmet (which we shall denote as Helmet No. 1), and which resembled a welder's helmet, was constructed, weigh-

FIGURE 74.—Wiley Post's second helmet. Two inlets are located on the sides of the round faceplate. One inlet was for compressed air which originally was to be obtained from the external engine supercharger. The other inlet was for oxygen derived from a liquid-oxygen source. In practice, the oxygen source alone proved the practical approach. The faceplate could be screwed out by the gloved fingers of the pressure suit for ground- and low-altitude operations. The cord was for the headset for broadcast station tuning in relation to the radio compass. (Courtesy Phillips Petroleum Company.)

FIGURE 73.—The U.S. Army Air Service's low-pressure chamber at Wright Field, used by Wiley Post's pioneering tests of his third pressure suit on August 27–28, 1934. (Courtesy U.S. Air Force.)

ing three and one-half pounds. Helmet No. 1 had a foam-rubber pad on the inside of the top for head protection, and a rectangular visor made of two layers of clear plastic. It was hoped that having two layers would reduce faceplate fogging if cockpit temperatures became too cold, because in the stratosphere the temperatures are in the region of —70° F. A bulge was located over each ear to accommodate headphones and a small door was placed over the mouth. When the suit was unpressurized, breathing, speaking, and even eating through the door were possible. Front and back helmet tie-down handles were provided at the lower edges because, when the suit was under pressure, the helmet tended to rise.

The cost of Post's first pressure suit—the world's first—was estimated at $75. As previously noted, it was tested at the Los Angeles Goodrich plant and proved to hold a five-pound-per-square-inch pressure differential, although some leakage was detected from the waist joint.

Major Charles Wilson, a physician with the U.S. Air Force, discovered a Wright Field report of June 21, 1934, by F. G. Nesbit entitled, "Test of Oxygen Pressure Flying Suit for High Altitude Flying," which describes a planned altitude-chamber test of Post's suit.[9] The report recommends that a medical officer be present during the tests (probably the dispensary medical officer, Dr. Harding). At this period and up to September 15, 1934, Lt. Col. Malcom C. Grow, a flight surgeon in the Army Medical Corps serving at Patterson Field (near to Wright Field), was in close touch with Post's tests and recognized their significance.[10]

Post visited Wright Field and dealt directly with its engineering section, whose Equipment Branch was responsible for evaluating such items as flying suits, methods of protecting aircrew against cold (—40° F.) effectiveness of goggles (antifogging), and other simi-

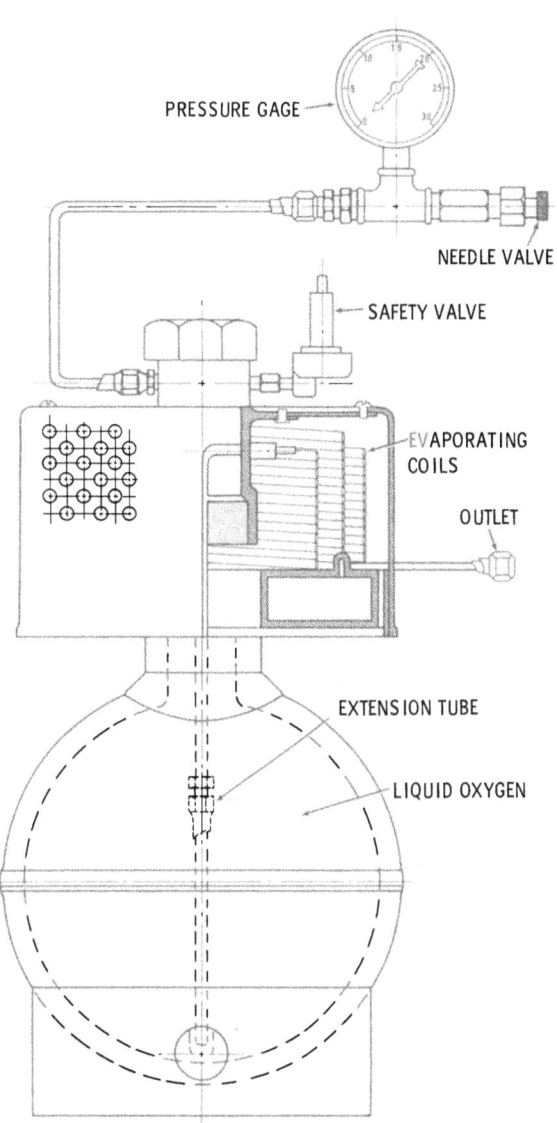

FIGURE 76.—*Schematic Drawing of the Liquid Oxygen Container Utilized by Post in 1934–1935 Stratosphere Flights.* The liquid oxygen was maintained at a temperature below —182.5°C in a double-walled vacuum metal container. A regulator valve when turned permitted a flow of gaseous oxygen through the evaporating coils that picked up heat from the surrounding air in the process. The gaseous oxygen flowed through the outlet valve to the pressure suit. A pressure gauge provided data relative to the degree to which the regulator had been opened. (After H. G. Armstrong.)

FIGURE 75.—The complete pressure-suit ensemble used by Wiley Post for inflight studies. Liquid oxygen is in the spherical tank. The liquid-to-gas conversion unit is attached to the top of the tank. The oxygen-inflow tube leads from the converter to the left side of the helmet. In Post's left hand is the outflow pressure-monitoring gauge. A second gauge on the oxygen converter gives inflow pressure information. Photograph made at Wright Field, August 27, 1934. (Courtesy U.S. Air Force.)

lar items. A low-pressure chamber was available to assist in this work, but it had been used only for such work as checking altimeters. This chamber came from the old Air Services Medical Research Laboratory in Mineola, New York, where in March 1921 a fire had destroyed much of the laboratory. Fortunately, the chamber had been saved, otherwise a new one would have had to have been procured. A new chamber

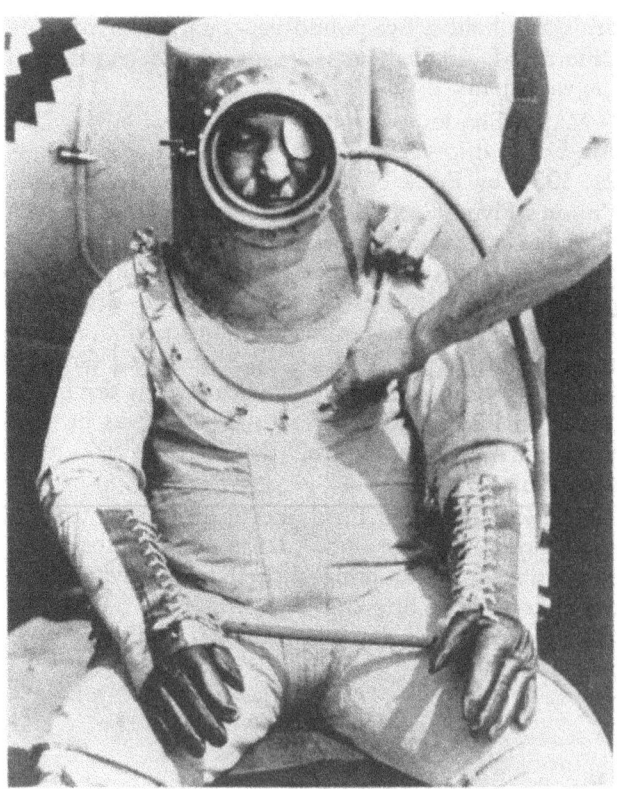

Figure 77.—Wiley Post dons the third and final version of his pressure suits. The pressure gauge held in his right hand was used to monitor the suit pressure. Just below the left inner knee is seen the outflow port to which the gauge could be attached. Note the ingenious joints at the knee and elbow portions of the suit, facilitating limb motion. Post had on his traditional "long-johns" under the suit. The suit was entered at the neck. Photograph taken at Dayton, Ohio, August 1934. The glass faceplate is screwed onto the helmet. The Pure Oil Company insignia is just forward of the door, but the edge of the *E* had been deleted from the picture at the request of a later sponsor. (Courtesy Goodrich Company.)

Figure 78.—Post's second helmet is being fitted to his third pressure suit (the successful ensemble used in his stratosphere flights). The helmet is attached with wing nuts, and its attachment and removal had to be accomplished by an assistant. The inflow-oxygen tube is shown attached to the left side of the faceplate base (the flow of oxygen served secondarily to defog the inside of the glass faceplate). The glass faceplate is off. Since Post's eye patch was on the left side, the oxygen flow did not tend to dry the cornea as would have been the case in right-side inflow. An extra valve was provided on the right side of the helmet, which originally was intended as the attachment for compressed air derived from the external engine supercharger (Post found that the liquid-oxygen source alone was more practical for his purposes). Note the edge of the Pure Oil symbol just forward of the door. This company sponsored the Chicago high-altitude flight of September 4, 1934. (Courtesy Goodrich Company.)

would have cost only a few thousand dollars, but in the straitened financial circumstances of 1934, it might have taken the Air Corps two or three years to get it into their budget.[11]

Post's physiological assistance came largely from the engineers at Wright Field, since Captain Harry G. Armstrong (an aeromedical officer), did not arrive until September 15, 1934, when he established the Aeromedical Unit of the Equipment Branch. Dr. Armstrong came to Wright Field after three years of flight-surgeon duties with the First Pursuit Group at Selfridge Field, Michigan.

After the first pressure suit—Suit No. 1—was static tested by Goodrich in Los Angeles (by attaching a compressed air line to the suit's side attachment), the suit was shipped to Wiley in Ohio. On June 23, 1934, he tried it on in his Dayton hotel room.[12] It is a good thing that the maid did not drop in to straighten up the room at this moment, or she would surely have experienced the same fright that H. E. Mertz would experience eight months later. Wiley later pressurized the empty suit at Wright Field to a differential of two pounds per square inch, at which point a piece of reinforcing tape failed. Concurrent to these tests at Wright Field, an article in *The Cleveland News*, entitled "Post Tests Flying Suit," suggests that Wiley wore this suit at least once, in an unpressurized state, in the *Winnie Mae* during July 1934.

When Suit No. 1 failed to hold pressure, Wiley began to consider the design of a new pressure suit

FIGURE 79.—The *Winnie Mae* in early September 1934, as used in the high-altitude flight-record attempts at Chicago. The sponsoring Pure Oil Company emblem is prominently displayed. The exhaust stacks are separately vented by cylinder and an "external" Bendix supercharger has been added to the top of the Pratt & Whitney Wasp engine. The separate exhaust stacks reduced back pressure, and enabled an increase in horsepower, as well as more efficient engine cooling. (Courtesy Pure Oil Company.)

that would use Helmet No. 1. He took the damaged suit to the Goodrich plant in Akron, where Russel S. Colley was assigned as Goodrich's technical representative in the effort. Colley had a rich backlog of experience in the development of aeronautical rubber products, especially Goodrich's famous "de-icers." In December 1931 he and Wesley L. Smith had used a National Air Transport mail plane in a series of tests in which they deliberately penetrated in-flight icing conditions to test the Goodrich de-icing "boots." The rubber "boots" were cemented to the leading edges of the wings and tailgroup and were alternately inflated and deflated through annular passages along their length by an air pump; the rapid pulsation of the boot served to crack off the ice formations. In late 1932, William S. "Billy" Brock flew further tests of the equipment, using the Goodrich Company's own Lockheed Vega named *Miss Silvertown*. By 1934 the Goodrich de-icers were becoming standard equipment on American airliners; they were one of the greatest contributions to flight safety during the 1930s. Colley and his colleagues had successfully beaten back the in-flight icing problem; now Post handed them an even more-novel project.

Meanwhile, time was running out. The MacRobertson Race was only three months away. Post was evidently playing his cards very close to his chest with regard to using his pressure suit in the air race. The Goodrich people at Akron were not told that he had tested the suit at Wright Field; they assumed that it had been damaged at the Goodrich plant in Los Angeles. The Los Angeles Goodrich people assumed that all of the testing was being done at Akron. For these reasons, certain details on Post's important work became confused for several decades.[13]

Post and Colley worked fast to develop a second suit for use with Helmet No. 1. Suit No. 2 had new upper and lower torso sections and a heavy-duty waist clamp that was bolted together with a series of wing nuts. This was an improvement over the metal belt used to hold the waist section on Suit No. 1.

An oxygen-hose fitting was now inserted below the helmet's visor. Newly conceived elbow and knee ring joints were incorporated to allow limb movement when the suit was inflated. This joint flexibility represented a new and major technological achievement in pressure-suit design.

Late in July 1934, Wiley tried on Suit No. 2. The hot weather, the high humidity, and the tightness of the suit, resulted in his becoming stuck in it. However, a comparison of photos of the 5-foot, 5-inch Wiley and his own-stated 1933 weight (171 pounds), show that over the previous five years he had been gaining weight, 20 pounds since 1930. This was probably a factor in his becoming stuck in the pressure suit, especially if he had continued to gain weight after his dimensions were taken for the suit. Wiley finally had to be cut out of the suit, which was absolutely ruined in the process.

Post and Colley nevertheless learned a great deal from Suit No. 2, however short its existence, and unhappy its ending. The most important information gained was with respect to features of suit behavior under static pressure. The men were encouraged, but now decided to make an entirely new suit, from the helmet down to the soles of its boots.

Concurrent to these initial suit experiments, Wiley wrote a magazine article that appeared in the October 1934 number of *Popular Mechanics*, which described Suit No. 2 and his plans for high-altitude flight.[14] The article was probably written in July 1934, and in it Post observes:

FIGURE 80.—This photograph was made in Bartlesville, Oklahoma, in the fall of 1934, where Post had proceeded from Chicago. The Phillips Petroleum Company undertook support of Post's additional stratosphere flights. Note that the stabilizer is trimmed for a nose-high, slow-speed landing. (Courtesy Phillips Petroleum Company.)

To fly at extreme altitudes you must first have oxygen and on top of that, pressure to force it into your lungs and to keep down the tendency to bleed over the entire body.

Authors' note: Post's reference to a "tendency to bleed" if exposed while unprotected to extreme altitudes, was based on a prevailing concept that the capillaries would rupture under these conditions.

"The thirteen pounds differential pressure at high altitudes, compared with sea level, effects every cell in the unprotected body."

Authors' note: Sea-level atmospheric pressure is 14.7-pounds-per-square-inch absolute, on the average. Post refers to an outside atmospheric pressure of 13 pounds per square inch less than that at sea level. He has reference, therefore, to an outside pressure of 1.7 pounds per square inch absolute, which is equivalent to an altitude of 50,000 feet.

"Blood vessels in the eye may rupture and cause permanent blindness."

Authors' note: Post appears to be referring to the development of gas bubbles in the vessels following exposures to low pressures—aeroembolism—a phenomenon known at the time.

"Heart action is affected, and other serious changes may result. Therefore, for all serious altitude flying, which we are coming to sooner or later, it is necessary to maintain pressure around the body by sealing off and pumping air into it. The same is true for certain parts of the plane itself."

Authors' note: Post found that the engine ignition system had to be either pressurized or specially sealed to prevent external electrical "arcing," and that radio equipment had to be pressurized to prevent "frequency drift." This latter phenomenon was produced, among other things, by the change in dielectric constant of the rarefied air between condenser plates.

Post also stated:

"In my opinion, to seal off the pilot's cockpit, sealing all controls like the throttle, stabilizer adjustment and retractable landing gear would involve prohibitive weight.'

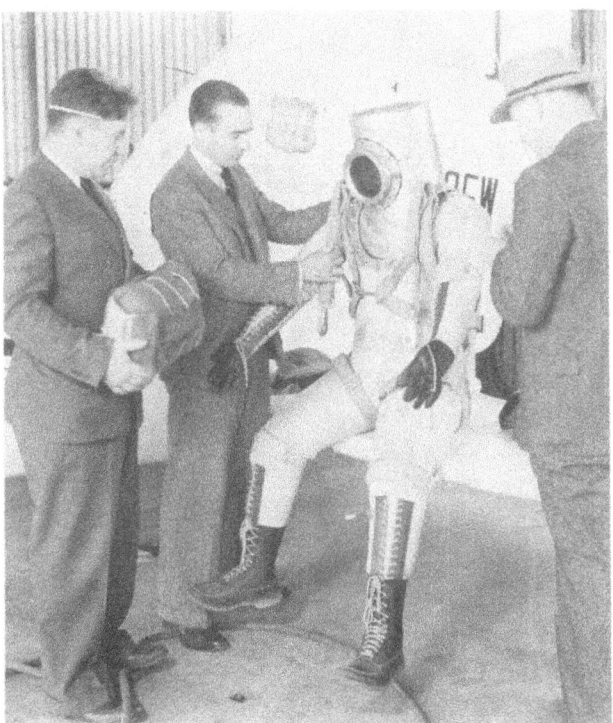

FIGURE 81.—Wiley Post is shown holding his emergency "front" parachute as Billy Parker, Aviation Director for Phillips Petroleum, adjusts parachute straps on inflated pressure suit, December 1934. The air hose used to inflate the suit is seen on the floor under Post's and Parker's feet, and plugs are seen in the oxygen intake tube by the left side of the faceplate and in the left-leg outlet on the inside of the area under the left knee of the suit. (Courtesy Phillips Petroleum.)

Authors' note: Post was referring here to his Lockheed Vega and other existing unpressurized aircraft.

"My idea is to employ a suit, something like a diver's outfit, which the pilot can wear, and which can be blown up with air or oxygen to the required pressure. Such a suit does not weigh much and is flexible enough to permit normal handling of controls."

Authors' note: Post originally planned to pressurize his first suit, including Helmet No. 1, solely by tapping the external supercharger used for the engine accessories and for boosting the air entering the carburetor. This had the disadvantage of reducing the capability of the supercharger with respect to the engine's requirements and thus reduced the maximum attainable flight altitude. This also had the disadvantage that if while flying the single-engine plane in the stratosphere, the engine quit or the supercharger failed, the suit would lose pressure and the pilot lose consciousness. The next step was to use only a minimal amount of supercharger compressed air, thus increasing the maximum attainable flight altitude and decreasing the hazard of supercharger pressure loss by enriching the air within the suit with oxygen, utilizing the Suit No. 2 with the modified Helmet No. 1. Post then decifed to use only oxygen with Suit No. 2 and Helmet No. 1. This was the next logical evolutionary development; freeing the external supercharger from servicing the presure suit so that all of the external supercharger's benefit could go to the engine, thus providing a higher engine-flight altitude capability.

A new pressure suit and a new helmet were now conceived which could be totally independent of the engine, and would utilize a source of liquid oxygen in a high-pressure spherical container initially placed between Post's legs.[51] Later, the oxygen container was to be placed behind Post, in the cabin just forward of the ADF power supply. The oxygen container was a double-walled spherical structure, with a vacuum between the two concentric double walls. This kept the liquid oxygen from overheating, and the high pressure in the container kept the oxygen in a liquid state until the regulator lowered the pressure by allowing gaseous oxygen to flow out. On the spherical container were the oxygen-evaporating coils, in which the liquid oxygen boiled off into a gas and entered a pressure-regulating valve. A short hose stretched from the regulator to the helmet to carry the gaseous oxygen. Figure 76 provides a schematic diagram of the liquid-oxygen equipment.

Liquid oxygen had a boiling point of −182.5° C. and consequently required the special equipment described above; it had the advantage over gaseous-compressed oxygen of requiring about half the weight of equipment to carry an equal amount of oxygen. Liquid oxygen expands to 790 times its liquid volume as it evaporates, and the containers have frangible caps to preclude explosions.[16] A disadvantage in the use of liquid oxygen is that it must be transferred to the aircraft oxygen container immediately prior to a flight because there is a continuous "venting," resulting in a loss of about three pounds of oxygen per 24 hours. The safety valve on the flask was set to open at 15 pounds per square inch (just above atmospheric pressure at sea level). In flight, the vaporizer worked in a semiautomatic fashion since an increased flow of oxygen occurred as altitude was increased, due to the difference in pressure inside and outside the vaporizer.

In the *Popular Mechanics* article, Post gives a three-dimensional drawing of the *Winnie Mae*, with his concept of how the second pressure suit with the first helmet would be utilized. He states his plans to use "two different methods" of maintaining pressure about the pilot:

First, for flying to about 35,000 feet altitude, the suit is inflated with clean air from the engine supercharger [the external supercharger] giving it a density about equal to that at 10,000 feet. Two lines from the supercharger carry air to the suit. One goes directly to a needle valve that can be controlled by hand. The other makes forty turns around

FIGURE 82.—Wiley Post walks slightly bent over toward the *Winnie Mae*, in preparation for a pressure-suit, airplane compatibility test. Note the criss-crossing support cords that help to keep the helmet from rising too high when the suit is inflated. The helmet faceplate is off. It was screwed on later when pressurization was necessary. Accompanying Post is Mel Mallincrodt. (Courtesy Phillips Petroleum.)

the exhaust [one stack] and then connects to a needle valve. Lines from the two needle valves merge into one that connects with the suit at the top of the helmet. From the lower end of one leg of the suit a line runs to an adjustable relief valve on the instrument panel. This valve can be set to any pressure. By adjusting the two needle valves much as you regulate the handles of a bathtub faucet, I can regulate the temperature and amount of air inside the suit. The second method of inflating the suit, used for extreme altitude flying, dispenses with the entire supercharger and employs an oxygen generator.

Post then notes that the oxygen generator will "last five hours on one filling," and that "while using the supercharger up to 35,000 feet, the oxygen is available in the event the engine stops or the supercharger fails to work."

Post also noted that the ignition "would not function properly much higher than 25,000 feet because electrical discharges would occur in the rarefied air." He also quite accurately refers to the fact that "at 50,000 feet the [air] pressure is only two pounds." He observed that ordinary gasoline boils at a pressure of seven pounds per square inch with a temperature of 100° F., and noted that a new-type gasoline with special properties would be needed to prevent boiling at 50,000 feet after the half hour climb (1,666 feet per minute) if the gasoline were at about 70° F. Post concluded the article by stating:

I believe that, in the future, all flying will be done at 50,000 feet or so when the distance is great enough to warrant climbing to that height. Transcontinental and transoceanic hauling of passengers and freight can be done in one half the present normal time, simply by use of suitable supercharging of engine, pilot, and passenger cabin. No radical changes in plane or engine are necessary, but of course, further refinements of plane and engine design and improved methods of streamlining will reduce the time even further.

S. E. Perry, Superintendent of Maintenance for Braniff Airways, Inc., remarked in 1934: "Post's plans are so revolutionary and so far advanced that it is hard even for the aeronautical engineer or aviation expert to grasp them fully." This is a very significant observation, since it helps explain the paucity of contemporary descriptions of Post's activities and also certain of the jealousies engendered in less progressive aviators.

In August of 1934, Wiley embarked on his third and more advanced pressure-suit design with Colley, a design conceived on July 30, 1934. The first and second suits had been of a double-ply, single-layer construction joined at the waist. Helmet No. 1 had

FIGURE 83.—Post prepares to climb ladder to enter *Winnie Mae*. Note the broad-banded strap which Post sat on. The strap, through its connections with criss-crossing cords to the helmet, kept the helmet from rising excessively during inflation. (Courtesy Phillips Petroleum.)

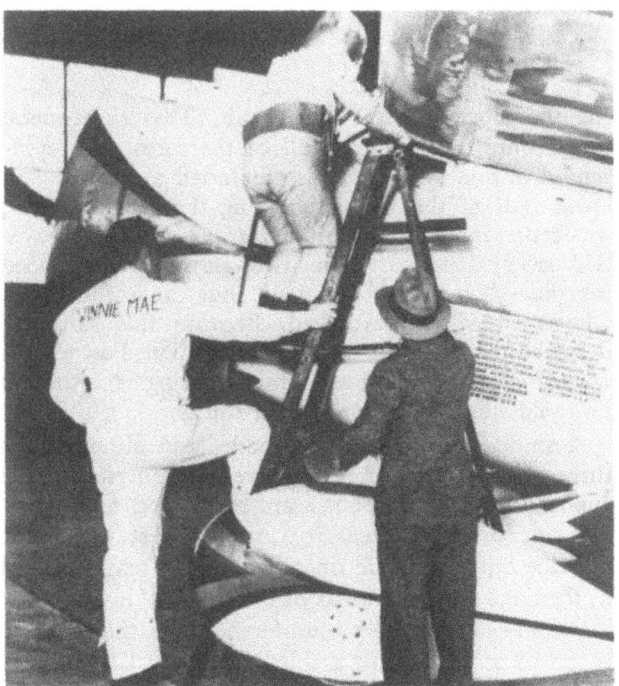

FIGURE 84.—Post ascends a shaky ladder, steadied by Mel Mallincrodt on the left, and Billy Parker on the right. Post prepared to attempt an assault on the world-altitude record at Bartlesville, Oklahoma. (Courtesy Phillips Petroleum.)

FIGURE 85.—Wiley Post eases into the cockpit with his pressure suit donned. The butterfly valve for the external supercharger is closed and may be seen just below Post's faceplate. The large grids seen in the front portions of the cowling on the left and right sides are the intercoolers that enabled the air compressed by the external supercharger to be cooled prior to entering the updraft carburetor in the lower, rear portion of the engine. The pressurized ignition harness may be seen. Billy Parker (back to view) is checking the oil filler area. (Courtesy Phillips Petroleum.)

blended into the top half of these early suits and was not detachable. Post intended for these inflated suits to adapt to the shape of his body. It was hoped that the pores of the rubberized fabric would not leak. Neither of these early suits when inflated conformed properly to Post's body. For the third suit, Colley suggested two separate layers: (1) an inner, body-contoured rubber "bag" that would contain the gaseous oxygen under pressure; (2) an outer, three-ply cloth suit, made to resist stretching and to hold the rubber suit to Post's body contours.

The third suit was designed to be entered feet-first through a large neck opening. A totally new helmet (Helmet No. 2) was designed to be bolted in place with wing nuts after Post was in the suit. The helmet seal would be made by two superimposed yokes of flat metal. Since Post could not reach the wing nuts in the back of the helmet, he would have to be helped in and out of the suit.

Suit No. 3 was planned to have a capability of holding an internal pressure of seven-pounds-per-square-inch absolute (two pounds more than the first two suits). The design was conceived on July 30, 1934.[17] It was begun by having Wiley take a comfortable sitting position, and cardboard limb and trunk forms were made from his body, which were used to

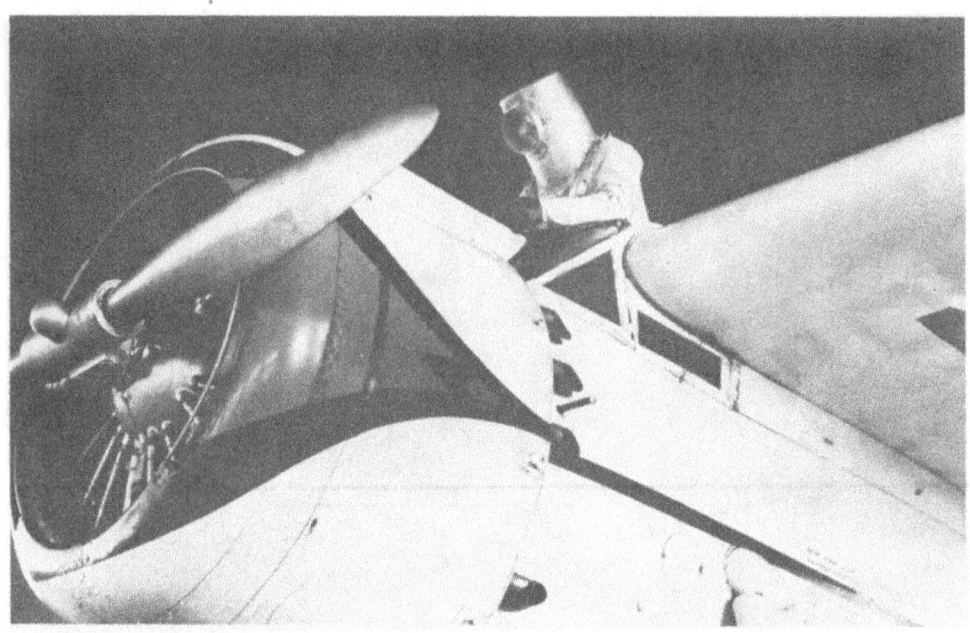

Figure 86.—Wiley Post, in his final pressure suit, smiles as he enters the top cockpit hatch of the *Winnie Mae* at Bartlesville, Oklahoma, December 1934. The *Winnie Mae* was placed within the Phillips Petrolum Hangar for this suit-cockpit compatibility test. The transparent faceplate is off the helmet and was not screwed on until climbing past approximately 17,000 feet. The fuselage landing skid is not in place at this time, but was added in January 1935 in California. The photograph was made by Frank Griggs of Bartlesville, Oklahoma. Note that the top retractable step is still out (just beneath the second exhaust stack) while the other lower step has been retracted. The top step could be retracted or extended from within the cockpit. The lower step was pushed in by foot. The oil filter cover is in place in front of the landing gear attachment. (Courtesy Phillips Petroleum Company.)

Figure 87.—A. M. Alcorn, Civil Aeronautics Administration inspector, prepares to install one of two sealed barographs in the fuselage of the *Winnie Mae* in December 1934, at Bartlesville, Oklahoma. These barographs were used in official record attempts in accordance with National Aeronautic Association procedures (note NAA initials on container). Shock cords for mounting are attached to the top of the barograph. (Courtesy Phillips Petroleum.)

cut the fabric for the outer suit. Two sheet-metal forms were then made. Half of the torso was represented in one form that also included the arms. The lower half of the torso, including the legs and feet, was represented in the other form. Liquid latex was laid over these and the two forms were spliced together. The rubber inner suit thus came into being. Gloves were then attached. Because this suit was designed primarily for the sitting position, Post always walked slightly bent over while wearing it, although he could stand straight with the suit on.

A static-pressure test was made, and although the three-ply cotton fabric suit tore along a seam, the rubber suit held. Repairs were made and reinforcing was added where necessary. Another test was made and the outer suit tore once again. The tears occured at the cross-sectional areas of the trunk—"hoop stress" locations—where the circumference was the greatest, so Post and Colley cut a third outer suit that assisted in resisting the forces, especially at the groin level, where the circumference of the body is the greatest. This modified, strenghtened ensemble proved fully successful in static testing.

Helmet No. 2 differed radically from Helmet No. 1;

FIGURE 88.—This is a photograph showing the fuselage interior of *Winnie Mae*, with the two National Aeronautic Association barographs in place. Post's official altitude-record attempts were made, using this internal arrangement. The barographs were required to match one another within a prescribed tolerance. On the far barograph the recording pointers can be seen. Also seen are the security wire and its two sealing fasteners on the right side of the picture, attaching the rearmost barograph to a longitudinal metal support of the wooden fuselage. In the altitude attempt at Bartlesville, Oklahoma, on December 7, 1934, Post reached an unofficial altitude of approximately 50,000 feet. This could not be confirmed by the Bureau of Standards because one of the two required barographs failed to function. On this flight, Post discovered 200-mile-per-hour winds and confirmed his theories about the existence of high winds in the stratosphere. Post was the first pilot to fly in the "jet stream." (Courtesy Phillips Petroleum.)

it had a larger window, which was round and made of glass. The window was left out until Post was in flight and ready to pressurize. He would then turn on the oxygen and screw the window in place. Oxygen was brought across the window from the left side (Post had the patch over his left eye) to "defog" breath moisture that might precipitate on the glass. An outlet just below the left inner knee was attached to a regulator and a pressure gauge, to allow control of the oxygen outflow from the suit, secondarily allowing control of suit pressure. This second helmet was wide enough that it accommodated earphones for ADF tuning and voice radio, and it could accommodate a throat microphone. An outlet on the right side of helmet window could be used to vent the helmet or as an additional channel for piping in compressed air or oxygen.

In August 1934, Post and Colley proceeded to Wright Field with the world's most advanced pressure suit; in fact, it was probably the world's only pressure suit! Very few people outside of the Wright Field personnel were aware of the pressure-chamber tests Post made at Wright Field; a few scattered articles were published, but Wright Field authorities would not release any detailed information. Wiley requested that the tests be kept confidential, and the data thus became classified.[18]

At this time the U.S. Army Air Corps had fallen to a low ebb, which was dramatized by its terrible experiences in flying the airmail during early 1934. The services had been reduced to several hundred operational aircraft, many made largely of wood and fabric, and most were obsolete. Appropriations for military aircraft were very small, and those for research were even less. The appearance of the progressive Wiley Post with his novel pressure equipment and Goodrich backing constituted a stimulating period for the Wright Field laboratory staff. Aeronautics records show that there were only about 15,000 civil aircraft active in the United States at that time, and most of these were slow, open-cockpit airplanes without radio-navigation equipment. In this context, Post's

Figure 89.—In late 1934 at Bartlesville, Oklahoma, the *Winnie Mae* is prepared for a stratosphere record attempt. Mel Mallincrodt stands in the cockpit and fuels the aircraft through a funnel and chamois skin. Ernie Shults stands under the wing. The *Winnie Mae's* engine has the supercharger in place (air scoop in front of cockpit window), but the wooden skid has not yet been installed under the fuselage. This skid and droppable landing gear were included later in Burbank, California. Also, the window in the door was later placed in the lower portion of the door for the transcontinental stratosphere flights. (Courtesy Phillips Petroleum.)

concept of a high-altitude pressure suit seemed like something snatched out of Buck Rogers or Flash Gordon.

Mae Post had accompanied Wiley to Wright Field, and waited anxiously in an outer room while he wore the new Suit No. 3 in the low-pressure chamber.[19] On August 27, 1934, Post made the first United States altitude-chamber tests in a flight-pressure suit, and there were many persons on the staff of the Wright Field laboratory crowding around the chamber to witness the experiments. Nesbit recorded the findings in Wright Field Report I-54-458, as noted by Wilson.[20] The reports were as follows:

8/27/34: He was placed in the chamber, sealed in, and they started the pumps to lower the pressure. At a pressure corresponding to 18,000 feet, Mr. Post screwed in the glass window in the helmet and the suit took an inflated position (2 psi) in less than thirty seconds. At an altitude of 21,000 feet, Mr. Post indicated he wish to descend. He was in the chamber 27 minutes. Tank temperature was 58° F. Failure of the oxygen generators to provide sufficient volume had caused him to half decompression to a higher altitude.

Author's note: The liquid oxygen had to be converted to gaseous oxygen in the "oxygen generators," the term used for the evaporating coils. In this process, the temperature of the system falls very low as the liquid oxygen changes to gaseous form, and it is likely that in the absence of a supply of heat, the efficiency of the oxygen liquid to gas conversion would suffer. Also, note that Post could utilize his hands through the gloves to "screw in the glass window" of his faceplate, demonstrating the practicality of the suit by allowing the hands to accomplish tasks. The faceplate edge had large notches to accommodate gloved fingers.

8/28/34: Another test was made in the altitude chamber to 23,000 feet. Mr. Post signaled to be brought down. The first test had shown the necessity of tying down the helmet. Mr. Post was in the chamber 35 minutes and being completely satisfied that the suit was O.K., proceeded to Chicago that night.

Author's note: Helmet No. 2 tended to rise as was the case with Helmet No. 1, due to the increasing internal-gas pressure in the longitudinal axis of the suit as the outside pressure fell. Helmet tie-down was effected by bandolera-type cords looped around the helmet and attached to a semirigid eight-inch wide belt upon which Post sat. Without the tie-down, the helmet rose and gave Post the sensation of "going down in the sewer."[21] *Post took the suit to Akron, Ohio, and made in the* Winnie Mae *the first flight ever made in a pressure suit.*

On September 5, 1934, Post reported that he achieved an altitude of 40,000 feet over Chicago. This was an attempt at setting a world's altitude record and was sponsored by the Pure Oil Company. This flight was in connection with the Chicago World's Fair and was listed as a feature of the Fair. The flight revealed that the pressure suit worked well,

FIGURE 90.—Wiley Post watches a serviceman named "Bevo" descend from the *Winnie Mae*, following topping of the fuel tanks with Phillips 77 aviation fuel. Ernie Shults is on the fuel truck. (Courtesy Phillips Petroleum.)

although some minor adjustments would be necessary.[22] Among the adjustments was the placing of an extension on the control stick to improve the ease of control when the suit was inflated. Post thus became the first pilot to fly in a pressure suit and the first person to utilize liquid oxygen with a pressure suit. Lauren D. Lyman, the *New York Times* aviation specialist, called the flight "an extraordinary achievement" which was primarily made possible by the engine superchargers.[23]

One of the minor changes Post made was to attach a piece of sponge rubber to the outer top of the helmet, to keep the helmet from hitting the top of the cockpit. The metal helmet top had touched the overhead cockpit structure and transmitted irritating "bumping noises" to Post.[24] Also, Post complained that the oxygen gas flowing across his face was very cold. He preferred an eye patch in these flights to a glass eye because the glass eye got cold and gave him a headache. He intended to do something at a future date concerning warming the gaseous oxygen prior to its entry into the helmet.

During the first test flight on September 5, it became manifest that the *Winnie Mae* required further modification. The time required to accomplish this put Post out of the MacRobertson Race, which started October 20th. That Post was correct in assessing the *Winnie Mae's* need of further modifications is suggested by the fact that the winner of the race proved to be one of the three sleek DeHaviland DH.88 Comets entered in the race, and new all-metal Douglas DC-2 and Boeing 247 transports took second and third place, respectively. All three winners were twin-engine aircraft.

However, the Comet's average speed over the tract from England to Australia was 171 miles per hour. Post's average speed around the world with the *Winnie Mae* in 1933 had been about 144 miles per hour, and this over a much longer track. The differential of 26 miles per hour is considerable; but after what Post would soon discover above 30,000 feet, it is to be wondered if, had all gone well with his plans, the aging *Winnie Mae* might have swept the field in the MacRobertson Race.

FIGURE 91.—Wiley Post is congratulated by Frank Phillips after Post successfully penetrated the stratosphere with the pressure suit, December 1934, Bartlesville, Oklahoma. Phillips provided basic financial support for the stratosphere flights. Phillips is dressed against the December climate. Post's pressure suit had three layers: (1) "long-john" underwear, (2) an inner (black) rubber air-pressure bladder, and (3) an outer, complex, cloth, contoured suit. Post is holding the helmet through the faceplate rim (the faceplate was not used unless at altitudes above 17,000 feet) and the helmet does not yet have the opening below the faceplate rim for the head-set wires. Note the relatively vertical stance enabled by the unpressurized suit. (Courtesy Phillips Petroleum.)

FIGURE 92.—Photo of Wiley Post made in latter 1934 at Bartlesville, Oklahoma, during his initial stratosphere flight tests, which were supported by Frank Phillips. (Courtesy Phillips Petroleum.)

From Chicago, Wiley called Billy Parker and told him that the Pure Oil Company and other sources of financing for his stratosphere experiments were extremely limited in the amount of support they could provide. Parker talked to Frank Phillips of the Phillips Petroleum Company, and the oilman agreed to fund Post's further experiments. Wiley flew the *Winnie Mae* to Bartlesville, Oklahoma, shortly thereafter.

Financing was now in hand, but much remained to be done before Post could even begin to attempt his goal—a coast-to-coast flight through the stratosphere.

FIGURE 93.—Post stands beside the itinerary of his around-the-world record flights painted on the *Winnie Mae* (1931 left, 1933 right). Note the cracks in the fuselage paint that were aggravated by the low temperatures of the stratosphere (as low as $-70°F$). (Courtesy Phillips Petroleum Company.)

FIGURE 94.—Wiley Post and his Lockheed Vega, the *Winnie Mae*. Picture made at Bartlesville, Oklahoma, late in 1934. Note that Post has picked up some weight since the time of the 1933 picture at Floyd Bennett Field. Note also that he has provided the Wasp engine with a separate exhaust stack for each cylinder, a recent modification he devised at the time to facilitate cylinder purging. (Courtesy Phillips Petroleum.)

FIGURE 95.—Mr. and Mrs. Frank Phillips extend greetings to Wiley Post in December 1934, Bartlesville, Oklahoma. Post's concepts and Phillips resources enabled the first systematic assault upon the stratosphere, utilizing powered flight. (Courtesy Phillips Petroleum.)

FIGURE 96.—The *Winnie Mae* is shown being prepared for a transcontinental stratosphere flight. This photograph was made in January 1935 at the original Lockheed hangar in Burbank. This hangar had been a "glass factory" prior to its use by Lockheed. The cowling has been removed and cleaned of paint (seen on floor behind fuselage). The aircraft is suspended by pullies from a ceiling beam by utilizing the hoist eye hooks on the upper wing. The belly-landing skid made of spruce has been glued in place and is now metal clad. Under the rear fuselage in the background on the workbench is the spherical container for the liquid oxygen. (Courtesy Phillips Petroleum.)

FIGURE 97.—Post poses by the evolving long-distance stratosphere modification of the *Winnie Mae*. The fuselage fuel tanks are seen through the door. The tubing at the wing root is a fuel line. (Courtesy Phillips Petroleum.)

FIGURE 98.—Wiley Post talks to Jimmy Gerschler, on his left, and A. Jack Grafman, on his right, with respect to adding the dropable landing gear to the *Winnie Mae*. Jimmy Gerschler was the project manager for this modification. (Courtesy Jimmy Gerschler.)

FIGURE 99.—The uncowled Wasp engine of the *Winnie Mae* reveals features added for stratosphere flight. The airscoop and its circular, external supercharger are shown atop the engine just forward of the windshield. The "intercooler" radiators that remove heat from the air derived from the external supercharger are between the propeller and the cylinders. Each cylinder is equipped with its own exhaust stack, some stacks surrounded with shrouds to provide heated air. The wooden, metal-clad landing skid is shown. The triangular, left cockpit window is partially open. A tag is shown on the circular cover for the special oil-tank filter opening just forward of the main landing gear fuselage attachment. The aircraft is being readied in California during January-February of 1935 for the forthcoming February transcontinental stratosphere attempt. (Courtesy Ernest Shults.)

FIGURE 100.—Details are shown of the right side of the Wasp engine and the external supercharger and intercooler arrangements, plus the landing ski, as utilized for the 1935 transcontinental stratosphere flights. (Courtesy Ernest Shults.)

NOTES

1. The race was referred to as the "MacRobertson" race, a contraction of the name of the Australian benefactor; an excellent history of this unique race is provided by Arthur Swinson in his *The Great Air Race, England-Australia, 1934* (London: Cassell & Co., 1968).
2. CLARENCE WINCHESTER, *Wonders of World Aviation* (London: Waverly Book Co., 1938), p. 692.
3. Billy Parker interview.
4. *Popular Aviation*, vol. 3, no. 5 (November 1933), pp. 20–22.
5. HARRY G. ARMSTRONG, *Principles and Practice of Aviation Medicine* (London: Baillier, Tindall and Cox, 1939), pp. 366–7.
6. CHARLES L. WILSON, "Wiley Post: First Test of High Altitude Pressure Suits in the United States," *Archives of Environmental Health*, vol. 10 (May 1965), pp. 805–810, and James Doolittle interview.
7. CHARLES L. WILSON, "Wiley Post."
8. This is about the average cabin pressure used in today's modern pressurized airliners, although these can go to a maximum allowable cabin altitude of 8,000 feet.
9. CHARLES L. WILSON, "Wiley Post."
10. Colonel Crow became the first Surgeon General of the U.S. Air Force in 1949. Taken from Robert J. Benford, *Doctors in the Sky* (Springfield, Illinois: Charles C. Thomas, 1955).
11. This upright cylindrical cork-lined chamber was later used as a food-storage bin for animals. During World War II, it was moved to the Air Force School of Aviation Medicine, San Antonio, Texas, and reactivated. It is presently in the Aeromedical Museum, Brooks Air Force Base, San Antonio, Texas.
12. CHARLES L. WILSON, "Wiley Post."
13. CHARLES L. WILSON, "Wiley Post."
14. WILEY POST, "Wiley Post Seeks New Record", *Popular Mechanics,* vol. 62 (October 1934) p. 492.
15. Russel S. Colley communication.
16. HARRY G. ARMSTRONG, Aviation Medicine.
17. CHARLES L. WILSON, "Wiley Post."
18. It was not until 1956 that T. W. Walker discovered the reports, leading eventually to their declassification.
19. Mrs. Wiley Post interview.
20. CHARLES L. WILSON, "Wiley Post."
21. Russell S. Colley communication.
22. *New York Times,* September 6, 1934, p. 21.
23. *New York Times,* September 9, 1934, VIII, 6.
24. Russell S. Colley communication.

5 / Stratosphere Flights, (1934-35)

Post's STRATOSPHERE flight plans were novel to aviation, because they were aimed at a program of practical cross-country flights through the stratosphere, ending at a previously determined destination; they were not simply up-and-down "altitude" flights. By definition, the stratosphere begins at the point where the air temperature no longer continues to drop with increasing altitude. The International Civil Aviation Organization Standard Atmosphere places this at 36,089 feet above mean sea level and minus 69.7° F, realizing that in actuality these values fluctuate somewhat with the seasons.

On September 16, 1932, Cyril Uwins of England had climbed to 43,976 feet in an unpressurized Vickers Vespa biplane, but later reported that the oxygen masks did not provide adequate oxygen.[1] Commendatore Renato Donati of the Italian Air Force made 18 attempts to break the world-altitude record, and on his eighteenth effort officially reached 47,352.219 feet. The previous record was 44,819 feet, established by Gustave Lemoine of France, September 28, 1933. Donati's flight was made in a modified Caproni 114 open-cockpit biplane with a supercharged British Bristol Pegasus engine. These high-altitude flights were essentially "local" that is, up and down; the slow open-cockpit aircraft were not adequate cross-country machines. In addition, they exposed the pilot to the very cold stratosphere temperatures, and because of the early stage of development of oxygen masks, very poor pilot oxygenation was possible at these high altitudes. Donati was so stressed by cold and low-oxygen levels (hypoxia), that upon his return to earth after the eighteenth flight, he had to be carried from the aircraft and hospitalized.

Meanwhile balloonists were also probing the stratosphere. In 1931 and 1932, Professor Auguste Piccard of Belgium and his assistant, Kipfer, ascended by balloon, while they were within a "sea level pressure" metal sphere (liquid oxygen was utilized to enrich the inside atmosphere) to 51,793 and 54,120 feet respectively. Settle and Fordney went similarly to 61,237 feet in 1933, and Kepner, Stevens, and Anderson to 60,616 feet in 1934. Piccard's twin brother, Professor J. Piccard and the latter's wife, went to 57,599 feet in 1934.[2] These balloonists, however, were little more than suspended objects, drifting where the elements elected to take them.

Post flew the *Winnie Mae* to Bartlesville, Oklahoma, and began preparations to challenge the world-altitude record of 47,352 feet set by Renato Donati. Working with Will D. "Billy" Parker, manager of the Aviation Department of the Phillips Petroleum Company, Post set up his equipment in Bartlesville, headquarters of the Phillips Company. Frank Phillips provided financial support for this phase of Post's work.[3] Billy Parker and his wife invited Wiley and Mae to stay with them in their Bartlesville home while the work progressed, and Wiley and Mae were pleased to accept.

Work on the *Winnie Mae* was taken over by Ernest H. Shultz, who operated approved airframe and engine-repair depot, number 727, in Bartlesville.[4] The *Winnie Mae's* Wasp engine had been modified by replacing the original internal supercharger with its 7:1 ratio with an experimental gear-driven internal supercharger of 13:1 ratio, having a nine-inch diameter impeller that gave the engine carburetion a sea-level pressure equivalent at about 20,000 feet of altitude. This supercharger (or "blower") is referred to variously as the "first-stage" supercharger or the "internal" supercharger, and compressed the fuel-air mixture that came from the carburetor. It provided a powerful suction of air through the carburetor, the suction being in direct proportion to the advancement of the throttle and the outside air density.

A new-type experimental supercharger for compressing the air prior to delivery to the carburetor was present. This was manufactured by Bendix and was referred to as an "external" supercharger, the "auxiliary" supercharger, or the "second-stage" supercharger. It was Bendix Auxiliary Super-Charger, serial number one.[5]

This additional supercharging capability enabled the Wasp engine with the internal 13:1 supercharger to achieve the "rated power" of 450 horsepower at 35,000 feet of altitude, and to climb to as high as 50,000 feet.

The external supercharger was attached to the generator pad on the engine (the generator was

Figure 101.—The external supercharger is seen from above. The airscoop deflects the air flow downward where it is compressed by the supercharger and thrown centrifugally outward, half to the right and half to the left, and carried forward to the "intercooler" radiators. The mechanism that controls the opening of the airscoop and engages the external supercharger with the engine is shown just behind the airscoop. The painted blade tips (one was red and the other green) are shown. This is the installation as it was used for the stratosphere flights of 1934–1935. (Courtesy Ernest Shults.)

removed) and was driven by the engine through a clutched mechanism that turned at one and one-half crankshaft speed. Pratt & Whitney prepared a special reinforced generator shaft and sent this to Shultz for the external supercharger drive shaft.

The external supercharger was mounted on top of the engine, just aft of the top cylinders and under the cowling. It contained two large impellers (approximately a foot in diameter) that were secured commonly to the shaft, one above the other.[6] The outlet for one impeller was directed outboard to the right and the other impeller outlet faced to the left. Pipes and hoses connected each of the above outlets to its respective "intercooler," mounted right and left just forward of the cylinders. These intercoolers allowed the cool, high-altitude airflow around them to remove the heat from the supercharger air, which resulted from the compression process itself, because hot air delivered to the carburetor results in decreased engine efficiency. The curved intercoolers were approximately 3 inches by 3 inches by 30 inches in dimensions, and followed the engine's outer margin.

They were attached to the cylinder rockerbox lugs and conformed to the inner margins of the front of the NACA cowling. Openings on the front of both sides of the cowling let air flow over the intercoolers.

The bottom outlets of the two intercoolers were piped to a common fitting, and this carried the airflow to the air box located on the bottom of the updraft carburetor for delivery upward. This supercharger could deliver air sufficient to double the mass received otherwise by each cylinder.

The multiple-disc clutch mechanism of the external supercharger was manually controlled from the cockpit. The control served to engage the auxiliary supercharger by opening a butterfly valve on an airscoop, which provided air to the external supercharger, and to secure a compressed flow of air into the carburetor air box. The forward facing airscoop that took advantage of the ram air of the slipstream was placed in the center of the external supercharger, providing the supercharger with an axial flow of air which was impelled outward by centrifugal force. A metal housing was placed over the scoop, attached to the upper cowling and running as far back as the windshield. To operate the external supercharger, Post slowed down the engine at about 17,000 feet and then engaged the supercharger.

Since the electric starter motor had been removed, the engine was started by hand-swinging the propeller. A battery was installed to operate the radio compass, as there was now no electrical system in the *Winnie Mae*. The wingtip and tail lights, and landing lights were removed to save weight and to decrease drag. The radio system did not carry a transmitter, thus alleviating the need for considerable electrical power.[7]

The Phillips Company provided high-quality fuel for the experiments. Aviation fuel was initially evaluated for combustion characteristics in terms of "Benzol equivalents," related to its specific gravity. Benzol as a fuel was used in cool-running, liquid-cooled engines, but did not function well in air-cooled engines, which often operated at relatively high temperatures. A new interstate highway known as U.S. Route 66—later popularized in song—was constructed across the United States from Chicago to Long Beach, California, and Frank Phillips of the Phillips Petroleum Company named his automobile fuel "Phillips 66," after this new highway. This fuel reached approximately 80 octane in terms of the Ethyl Corporation nomenclature. When a higher octane aviation fuel was developed, Will D. Parker suggested to Phillips that the term "77" be used for the aviation fuel, since this latter fuel had a higher specific gravity and an octane of approximatley 87.

The empty *Winnie Mae* weighed at this time 2,869 pounds, and had a gross weight limitation of 4,750 pounds. She was modified to carry 243 gallons of fuel. The difference between the gross weight and the basic weight was 1,881 pounds. Subtracting six pounds per gallon fuel weight from the 1,881 pounds, left 423 pounds for Post, his pressure suit, the oxygen supply, and any other items he wished to carry. The metal engine cowl weighed 50 pounds, the engine had a hand-inertia starter, and the wheel pants weighed 50 pounds. These items were included in the basic weight, as were the landing lights that weighed 30 pounds, the extra oil radiator which weighed 15 pounds, the 26-gallon oil tank that weighed 8 pounds, the automatic pilot, weighing 70 pounds, and three extra fuel tanks that accounted for 71 pounds. The above weights were certified by Aeronautics Branch Inspector Alcorn, and the aircraft-registered owner was the Fain and Post Drilling Co., of Oklahoma City (the landing lights were later removed).

For the planned stratosphere flights, a new and specially prepared carburetor that had a special setting for altitude performance (the carburetor had a painted yellow band on it for identification) was necessary. This was a double-barrel updraft carburetor, and the fuel-air mixture was then drawn into the 13:1 internal supercharger impeller. A special Breeze ignition manifold and harness was provided with increased space between the shielding and the ignition wire so that pressurization could be accomplished. The magnetos were also modified for pressurization, which came from a tube connection to the external gear-driven Bendix supercharger; this was one of the first of the pressurized ignition systems that later became standard. A set of cooling air-deflector baffles just coming into use was installed;[8] these tight baffles were needed to improve heat dissipation because the engine was now "uprated" with respect to its original horsepower. Special permission was obtained to pull in excess of 450 horsepower for five minutes with the modified engine. To increase the efficiency of cylinder-exhaust purging, the exhaust collector ring was eliminated and each cylinder was given a separate, short exhaust stack.

It was stated by Arthur Brisbane that at this time

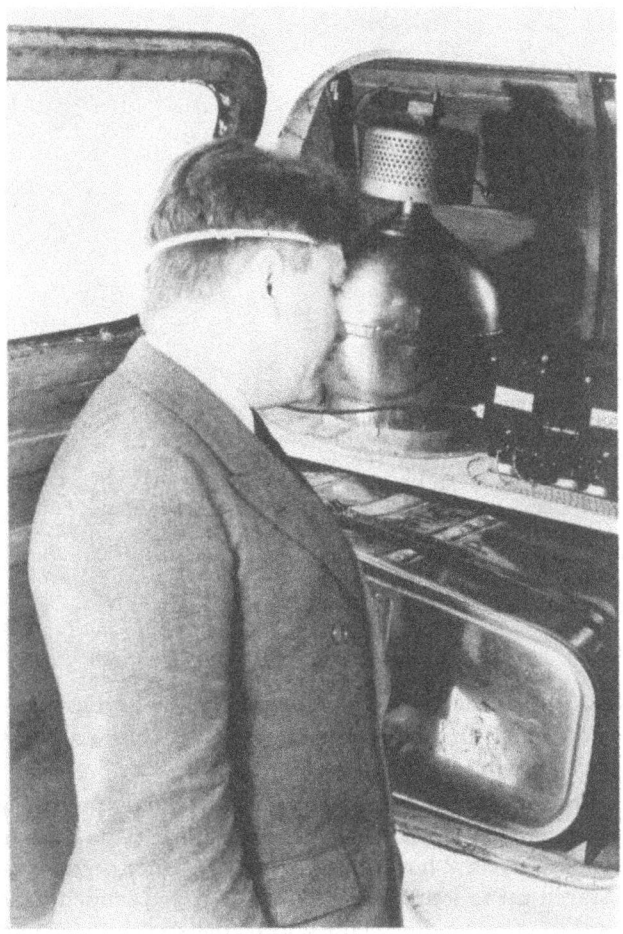

FIGURE 102.—Post views the liquid-oxygen container as stowed in the fuselage of the *Winnie Mae* in preparation for the long-distance stratosphere flights. Aft of the container is the Westport power supply for the radio compass. A fuselage fuel tank is mounted below the above equipment. (Courtesy Phillips Petroleum Co.)

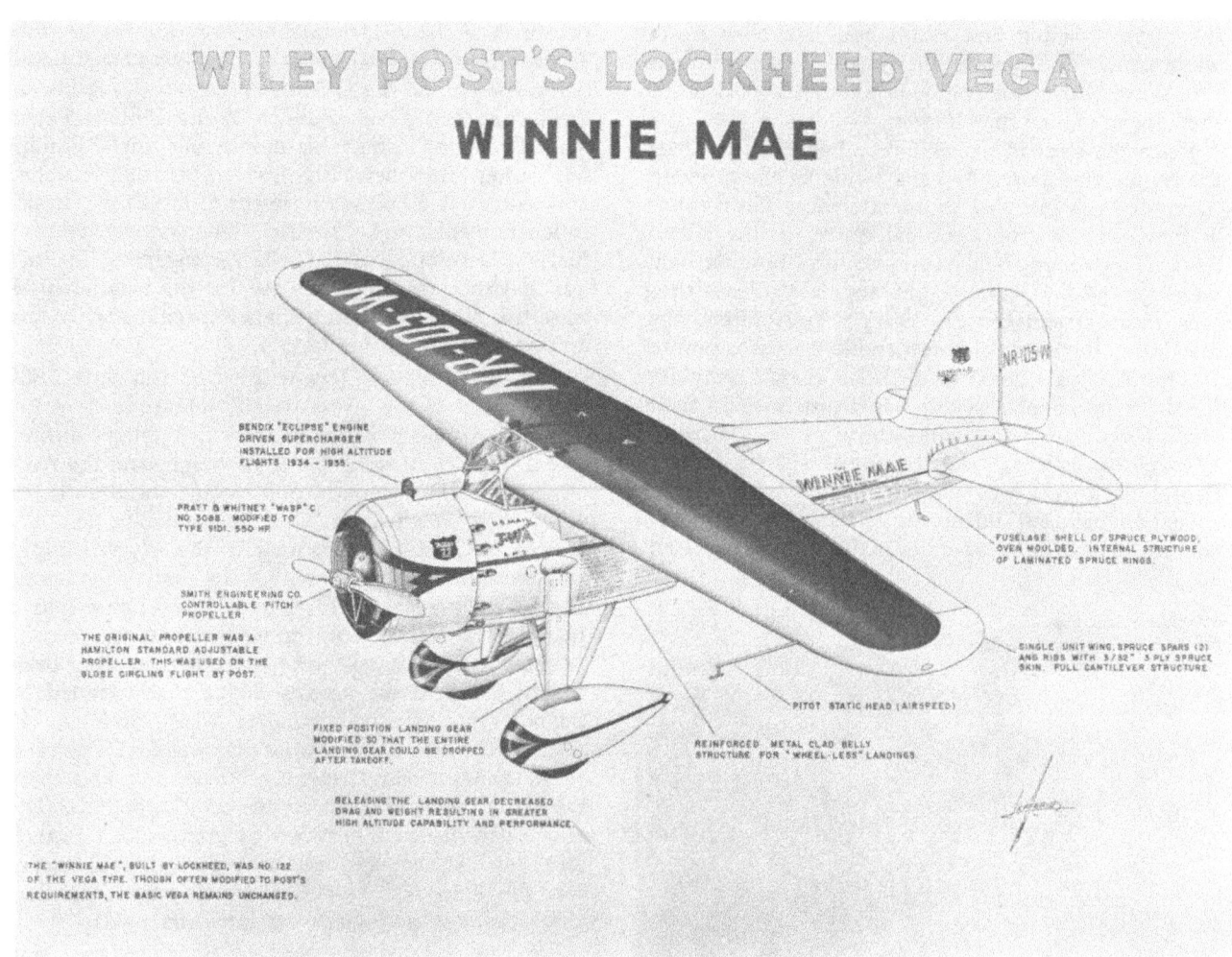

Figure 103.—This beautifully drawn diagram shows the *Winnie Mae* in the stratosphere version (except for droppable landing gear). The data on the Wasp engine actually should read as follows: "Wasp 'C', serial number 3088, modified to an 'SC', upgraded from 420 horsepower to 450 horsepower." The Department of Commerce records of the period contain the SIDI, 550-horsepower data, but this was crossed out and changed to SC and 450 horsepower shortly after review by Department personnel. Special permission by Pratt & Whitney was given in 1933, prior to the solo world flight, for Post to pull 500 horsepower with this modified engine for a few minutes with 87-octane fuel for takeoffs (at 2,200 rpm). (Courtesy Smithsonian Institution.)

Wiley and Mae cosigned a "release," absolving Frank Phillips from any claim in the event of Post's death during the stratosphere flight tests. Post is quoted: "Sure, I know it's dangerous. If I get 'popped off', that's the way I want to go, doing the things I want to do." [9]

The press referred to the upcoming flight in late November 1934 as a spectacular attempt to reach 50,000 feet. Bad weather led Post to delay the flight until December 3, when he donned his pressure suit and spent two hours in the stratosphere, flying as far east as Fort Smith, Arkansas, before turning back to Oklahoma. Due to headwings on the return flight, Post landed low on fuel at Hat Box Field, an Army post at Muskogee, 80 miles southeast of Bartlesville.[10] Post stated that he reached 48,000 feet before a faulty oxygen valve forced him to descend.[11]

Eager to continue, Post spent several days preparing for the next flight. On December 7, 1934, he took to the air for a 2-hour and 26-minute flight; because he stayed up so long, he ran out of fuel and landed dead stick. After landing, Post said of the stratosphere portion of the flight:

I headed into the wind which I estimated was blowing about 200 miles an hour. From then on I could see without difficulty Oklahoma City 110 miles away and El Reno 150 miles west of my landing field. The thermometer outside registered 70° F. below zero, yet I was comfortable. The flying suit

FIGURE 104.—The *Winnie Mae* is shown on the compass rose at Burbank. It has been placed in the cruising-flight position through the use of a dolly under the tail skid. The Trans World Airline U.S. Mail symbol is shown under the cockpit window. This references airmail contract #2. Post received sponsorship from both Phillips Petroleum and TWA for his long-distance stratosphere flight plans. (Courtesy Phillips Petroleum.)

FIGURE 105.—The *Winnie Mae* without droppable gear (but with the belly skid in place) is shown at Burbank after a test flight. The dark exhaust marks on the fuselage were not unusual following a long flight. (Courtesy Phillips Petroleum.)

FIGURE 106.—The "Wiley Post biplane," built in Oklahoma City in 1935. Post was president of the company, and 13 of these trainers were built. A modified 40-horsepower Model A Ford engine powered this side-by-side aircraft that retailed for $1,300, cruised at 60 miles-per-hour and landed at 22 miles-per-hour. Post had been the Oklahoma and Texas distributor for the Bird Aircraft Corporation since 1932. The Bird aircraft were open-cockpit biplanes manufactured in Glendale, Long Island, New York (Aero Digest, April 1932). (Courtesy Smithsonian Institution.)

worked perfectly after I had fastened the face-plate of my helmet and turned on the [external] supercharger at 20,000 feet. They hang floral offerings on good race horses. I would like to hang one on that Wasp engine of mine. It ran like a clock, and that is the same engine that won the Los Angeles-Chicago race and then flew around the world twice, not counting the regular flying I have been doing. It has gone so far I would not even estimate how many miles have passed under it. As a result of this flight I am convinced that airplanes can travel at terrific speeds above 30,000 feet by getting into the prevailing wind channel.[12]

Wiley Post thereby became the first man to ride the "jet stream" and to forecast from experience its potential benefits to air transportation.

The next morning, a story written for the North American Newspaper Alliance announced that Post had climbed to 50,000 feet, although his altimeter had broken at 35,000 feet.[13] The story offered a description of the view of the earth from nine miles high and the 200-mile per hour headwind from the west that cut his ground speed to 50 miles per hour. It also told how the 70° F. temperature peeled the paint from the *Winnie Mae's* fuselage and "chilled the engine" so badly that Post had to make a dead-stick landing.

Post, however, had only the greatest praise for his equipment and the special aviation fuel that Phillips had developed for him.

Despite the press's unofficial proclamation of a new record, it was necessary to await the official findings of the Bureau of Standards, the Government agency which calibrated Post's barographs. On December 12, the Bureau notified Post that they could not confirm that he broke the altitude record.[14] Billy Parker later revealed that one of the two required National Aeronautic Association barographs did not function properly. Although only two flights received press attention, Post made about eight high-altitude experimental flights and Parker believes Post reached close to 50,000 feet.[15]

Post now turned to the most important phase of his work: transcontinental flights in the substratosphere. Post predicted that such flight, utilizing proper equipment and taking advantage of natural phenomena, would lower the time to cross the nation to six hours. Similarly, Post forecast a 12-hour crossing between London and New York.[16]

Post and Billy Parker flew to the Lockheed

FIGURE 107.—Wiley Post, barnstormer, then executive pilot, now a scientific experimentalist, posed in 1935 in Burbank. His thoughts were of the future and of aviation progress. (Courtesy Lockheed Aircraft Company.)

Company in Burbank. At the Pacific Airmotive Hangar in Burbank, the *Winnie Mae* received an additional modification aimed at reducing air drag in flight by replacing the standard landing gear with jettisonable wheels; these were released after takeoff by a lever in the cockpit that acted as a "bomb release." The jettisonable wheels were stabilized for takeoff by metal cables running fore and aft to the fuselage from the wheel supports. Clarence L. "Kelly" Johnson and Jimmy Gerschler of Lockheed designed the system and the special cam releases for the fuselage-mounted cables.[17] Edwin O. Cooper was with Pacific Automotive at this time and was consulted by Post on various aspects of the plans.

To land the aircraft, a special landing skid was installed; it was made of a spruce timber glued to the fuselage, and the timber was faired with metal on the sides and bottom. The timber's forward end rested just inside the lower cowling, giving the rear-cowling opening an oval-shaped form. A strong V-shaped support was placed in front of the lower engine cylinders and ran to the lower front edge of the NACA cowling in order to prevent the cowling from "digging in" and pulling off the engine during skid landings.[18] Also, a smaller tail skid could be substituted for the standard tail skid. The placement of the air scoop on top of the cowling precluded scoop damage during skid landings.

On the first two occasions of Post's dead-stick skid landings, the propeller bounced around and was bent. Ernie Shults constructed a propeller-turning device that had a crank in the cockpit, which Post could use while gliding down dead-stick. The back of one blade tip was painted red and the other green. When the green tip was cranked around to the right-horizontal propeller position, the counterweight for the combined piston-connecting rods was in the lowest position, minimizing the chances of propeller change of position during the bumps of landing. If the red tip were to the right, the counterweight was high, and likely to swing around during skid landings, turning the propeller with it.

Transcontinental and Western Airlines (TWA) supplemented the Phillips Petroleum support of Post's stratosphere experiments and arranged for him to carry airmail for them, including special stamps bearing Post's picture and the inscription, "First Air Mail Stratosphere Flight."[19] On the front of each side of the fuselage, just behind the cowling, the letters TWA were placed, with the word "experimental" written across them. Above the letters was "U.S. Mail," and below, A–M–2. This latter designation referred to the contract the U.S. Post Office Department had with TWA to carry mail, contract number two. This was the beginning of a long and intensive interest in high-altitude operations by TWA. In 1935 the airline inaugurated a program of experimental high-altitude flights of its own, conducted by D. W. "Tommy" Tomlinson in a Northrop Gamma, which continued into 1936 and 1937. It is safe to say that it was Wiley Post who pointed the way. In 1940 TWA became the first airline in the world to operate an airliner with a pressurized cabin, when it put its 4-engine Boeing 307 Stratoliners into service.

In early February 1935, TWA reported that Post took the airmail pilots' oath in Kansas City, at TWA headquarters, and was a member of the flying staff of TWA. He would undertake studies of the feasibility of operating regular schedules at altitudes above 30,000 feet. Relatively few advanced radio compasses capable of keeping a course on commercial broadcast stations had been built at this time, and a new one was made for Post.[20] The National Broadcasting Company would send special weather reports each 30 minutes, that were prepared by TWA. Post could use KAAO, Denver; WOW, Omaha; WHO, Des Moines; WGN, Chicago; WTAM, Cleveland; and WJZ, New York. TWA stated that Post's flight would be nonstop.

TWA also reported that Frank Phillips, the Oklahoma oilman, was sponsoring Post's stratosphere experiments, and added that Phillips had also spon-

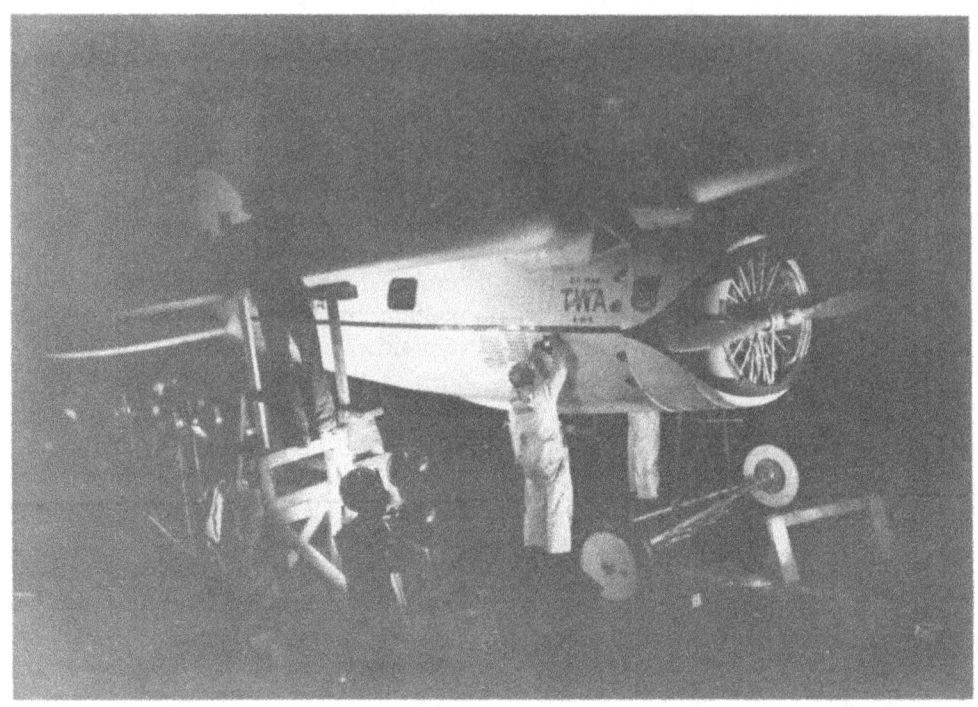

FIGURE 108.—The stratosphere version of the *Winnie Mae* is readied for a high-altitude, cross-country takeoff in the early morning hours from the Pacific Airmotive hangar, United Airport (later Hollywood-Burbank Airport), Burbank, California, February 22, 1935. The aircraft is held off the ground by wooden supports under the wings, while the droppable landing gear is readied for installation. A 200-foot ceiling due to fog covered the area. (Courtesy Lockheed Aircraft Company.)

sored Art Goebel, winner of the Dole flight from Oakland, California, to Honolulu in 1927.

During this period, Post augmented his income by taking a hero's role in a Columbia movie entitled, "Air Hawks." Ralph Bellamy played the part of the owner of a struggling young airmail company that was being threatened by a "madman sending his murder beam into the clouds" (the latter hired by a competing company). In the story, Post appears near the end of the film and flies nonstop in the stratosphere from California to New York, thus assuring the delivery of the mail on schedule and the success of Bellamy's company. Post briefly displayed his pressure suit in the film, beside a sleek Northrop Gamma. Costars were Tala Birell and Douglas Dumbrille.[21]

Post had stated in late July 1935 that he would soon attempt to fly across the nation at an altitude of more than 30,000 feet. He was approaching the culmination of a year of applied experiment and prior years of planning.[22]

In January of 1935, Wiley Post and Billy Parker went to the Joe Plosser Flight School at the Grand Central Air Terminal in Burbank, and took specific instrument training in a Kinner Fleet open-cockpit biplane. The instrument student sat in the front cockpit under a canvas hood, while the instructor occupied the rear seat. Both Post and Parker obtained their instrument ratings shortly thereafter from Inspector Reed of the Department of Commerce.

An applicant for a Bureau of Air Commerce instrument rating in 1935 had to pass a written test on meteorology, navigation, and instruments. He had to have 20 hours of instrument-flying instruction and practice, plus a license issued by the Federal Communications Commission. Ten of the 20 hours could be in a Link simulator. The flight test was conducted on instruments and consisted of straight and level flight for a given period, 180- and 360-degree turns of "moderate" bank in both directions, minimum glides, and maximum climbs and approaches to stalls, climbing turns, recovery from stall, skids, slips, and spirals, and from banks in excess of 45 degrees, and a practical demonstration of estimating arrival time, taking into account speed, wind, and drift. In addition, radio skill while flying on instruments included tuning, orientation, radio-range following, "cone of silence" location, letting down on the range by an approved instrument-approach procedure, and such other maneuvers that the inspector deemed necessary.[23]

Now, instead of the characteristic business suit attire that Post invariably wore while flying, unlike many other fliers who still donned helmets and

FIGURE 109.—The *Winnie Mae* is being hand started in the early morning hours at Burbank, California, February 22, 1935, in preparation for the start of a transcontinental stratosphere flight. Wiley Post is in his pressure suit in the cockpit. The droppable landing gear is in place, suspended by force and aft cables that Post could release after takeoff by a lever in the cockpit. This version of the *Winnie Mae* did not have an electrical system, hence the hand cranking (the radio compass was powered by dry cells). The man standing on the wheel is feeling the exhaust air as the propeller is rotated. The propeller tips were color coded so that, in preparation for the dead-stick landing, the propeller could be positioned horizontally with a specific blade on one side (by a special crank inside the cockpit) so that the crankshaft counterweight would be down, thus minimizing propeller rotation possibly induced by landing bumps. (Courtesy Lockheed Aircraft Company.)

flying suits even though they flew enclosed aircraft, Wiley readied his pressure suit. The pressure-suit helmet was provided with a small opening in the left lower front at the base of the cylindrical metal portion, through which the wires of the headphones (and to an optional throat microphone) passed. The opening was tightly sealed. The use of ADF with a pressurized radio was planned as a means of facilitating high-altitude navigation.

Post donned the pressure suit and took off, from the United Air Terminal[24] at Burbank, for New York in the early morning darkness on February 22, 1935, with 150 pounds of "U.S. Mail." Fog and a 200-foot ceiling were present and Post jettisoned the gear just before entering the clouds. The fully loaded *Winnie Mae* was headed for another dramatic flight. This one proved short lived, however, when the engine began to throw oil after 31 minutes. At first, Post thought the trouble was a leaking oil line, so he prepared for an emergency landing on Muroc Dry Lake[25] in the Mojave Desert, after a flight of only 57 miles.[26] With 300 gallons of fuel and no dump valves, Post was in a dangerous predicament, but he drew on his flying experience and skillfully glided the *Winnie Mae* to a safe landing. His descent was so silent that H. E. Mertz, who was 400 yards away, did not hear the plane land. Busy tinkering with his wind-powered "sail car" made from a Franklin auto chassis, Mertz (who ran the Muroc general store) almost collapsed from fright when Post, still clad in his altitude suit, approached and asked him for aid in unscrewing the helmet's rear wing nuts.[27]

A few days later Post announced that it was not a broken oil line that had foiled his flight, but rather a quart of emery dust that mechanics found in his engine. Someone had deliberately sabotaged the flight.

The emery dust was placed in the external super-

FIGURE 110.—The ultimate in Lockheed Vega beauty and advanced equipment is achieved in the 1935 supercharged version of the *Winnie Mae*. Post spent more flying hours in the stratosphere by June 15, 1935, than any other man. While in the jet stream during these flights, he traveled at sustained ground speeds in the vicinity of 300 miles per hour for periods longer than any other person had accomplished. Note that to reduce as many aspects of air drag as possible, not only has the landing gear been dropped, but the rudder has been decreased in size and even the tail skid has been dropped. (Courtesy Lockheed Aircraft Company.)

FIGURE 111.—The *Winnie Mae* is shown on February 16, 1935, after bellylanding at Muroc, California. Note oil-smudged fuselage due to piston-ring honing by emery dust placed by saboteur in supercharger. The airplane is tied down with heavy weights. (Courtesy George Brauer.)

FIGURE 112.—The *Winnie Mae* is raised and fitted with her landing gear in preparation for the return from Muroc, California, to Burbank. Emery dust had been added to the external supercharger by saboteurs, forcing Post to make a power-off, forced landing on the skid when the engine failed after the supercharger was "cut-in," shortly after departure from Burbank at about 17,000 feet. The flight was the initial transcontinental nonstop stratosphere attempt, February 22, 1935. The differentially painted blade tips for propeller positioning to facilitate dead-stick bellylandings are evident. (Courtesy Edwin O. Cooper.)

FIGURE 113.—A static pressure test is accomplished with Post's perfected flight-pressure suit after the Muroc forced landing, February 1935. Note the seat-belt marks above the thigh area and the outlet for the headset wire, just beneath the left, lower visor. (Courtesy Edwin O. Cooper.)

charger's air inlet the night before the flight. When Post cut in the supercharger, it sucked the dust into the engine, where it honed down the piston rings and made a general mess of everything. The engine had to be completely overhauled. Infuriated at the "dirty trick," Post and Parker said that they knew who had put the emery into the supercharger, but a formal investigation never took place. Among the intimate friends of Post, it became known that a mechanic, who was familiar with the men who worked on the *Winnie Mae* prior to the flight, was the man who had accomplished the sabotage. He had done it at the request of a disgruntled pilot, who thought that his own sources of sponsorship were being jeopardized by Post's successes.

Three weeks after the sabotage episode, Post was ready for a second transcontinental-record attempt. On March 5, 1935, he lifted the *Winnie Mae* off the runway at Burbank and pointed her nose toward New York. Flying in the substratosphere, they made excellent time. All went well until they were 100 miles east of Cleveland, where his oxygen supply became exhausted. Post turned back to Cleveland, where he brought the *Winnie Mae* down on her skid. After climbing out of the airplane and being unbuttoned from his pressure suit, Post learned that he had flown 2,035 miles in the record time of 7 hours and 19 minutes. The *Winnie Mae* had averaged a ground speed of 279 miles per hour, which was approximately

FIGURE 114.—Amelia Earhart, Wiley Post, and Roscoe Turner examine the *Winnie Mae's* Wasp engine during its overhaul, following the sabotage-forced landing at Muroc. On the engine in front of Turner is the carburetor and an associated heat-exchanger accessory, which enabled exhaust heat to warm the air entering the carburetor. On April 19, 1935, Amelia Earhart flew her Vega, Number NR 965 Y, from Burbank to Mexico City, in preparation for a record long-distance return flight to the United States. (Courtesy Lockheed Aircraft.)

100 miles per hour faster than her normal maximum air speed! At times the *Winnie Mae* had attained a ground speed of 340 miles per hour.[28] This was pretty good for a five-year-old airplane whose design was seven years old and now quite obsolescent. There is no question but that on this flight Post and the *Winnie Mae* were riding the jetstream.[29]

History never discloses its alternatives, but if Post and the *Winnie Mae* had been able to compete in the MacRobertson Race, and Post's high-altitude equipment had proved reliable, there is little doubt that they would have won the race. It would have been a terrible jolt to the world of aeronautics to see the aging Vega win against far-more-modern aircraft simply by flying at extraordinary altitudes. Even the flight from Burbank to Cleveland caused a considerable amount of excitement.

Post attracted the attention of the aviation world. One writer in the *New York Times Magazine* called the Burbank-to-Cleveland flight the "most startling development in aviation since Lindbergh spanned the Altantic."[30] Alexander Klemin, the aviation authority who wrote for the *Scientific American*, praised Post's accomplishment for its revolutionary effect on aviation. In addition to proving the practicability of Post's altitude suit and oxygen-supply system, the flight showed the safety of replacing the landing gear with a skid.[31] What is more, Post, his pressure suit, and his *Winnie Mae* had finally proved what many suspected: that the winds which prevailed from the west, at the base of the stratosphere, would increase an airplane's speed, and by a phenomenal margin.[32]

With a vote of confidence from his sponsor, Frank Phillips, Post set out again to break the transcontinental record. The third flight from Burbank, on April 14, 1935, ended when the external supercharger failed after about eight hours in the air and 1,760 miles distance, necessitating landing at Lafayette, Indiana.[33] Again, the skid worked perfectly. Post hinted that he might seek new equipment, but encouragement from Phillips led him to try a fourth time. Will Rogers, however, felt that the *Winnie Mae* deserved a place in the Smithsonian Institution. He told his newspaper readers that the five-year-old airplane was too worn out to break any more speed records. Rogers suggested that the American people

FIGURE 115.—Shown in the photo are Amelia Earhart, Wiley Post, Roscoe Turner, and Laura Ingalls (left to right). This group inspected the Wasp engine of the *Winnie Mae* in 1935 after a forced landing at Muroc. (Courtesy Lockheed Aircraft.)

help Post financially in order to allow him to continue his experiments.[34]

A fourth transcontinental attempt was nevertheless made on June 15, 1935. The *Winnie Mae* climbed out of Burbank and hurdled the Rockies at more than 35,000 feet. All seemed to be well, and she was speeding through the stratosphere over Kansas, when a piston in her hitherto reliable Wasp carried away. Post brought her down to dead-stick skid landing at Wichita, after a flight of 1,188 miles.

This incident told Post what he had long feared: his *Winnie Mae* was really getting old and her hardworking flying days were finished. Post now announced that he decided to retire the *Winnie Mae*.

On June 24, 1935, Congressman Josh Lee of Oklahoma, who represented the district in which Wiley Post's parents lived, introduced House Resolution 8622, which authorized and directed the Smithsonian Institution to purchase on behalf of the United States the *Winnie Mae*, with her original instruments that were used on her world flights, for a price not in excess of $25,000, and to place the airplane in the Institution. An additional $25,000 was authorized to carry out the provisions of the Resolution. The first step was thus taken toward providing the *Winnie Mae* with an honorable retirement.

When Wiley Post retired his *Winnie Mae*, he had achieved the goal that he had set out to accomplish; he had demonstrated the feasibility of flight through the stratosphere and the dramatic benefits to be realized therefrom.[35] Aviators agreed with Lauren D. Lyman, aviation editor of the *New York Times*, when he observed that it was Wiley Post who had moved stratospheric flight into the realm of reality.[36] Post had spent more hours in airplane flight through the stratosphere than any other man on earth; this flight time totaled about 30 hours.

Within a quarter of a century of Post's high-altitude flights, men, women, and children would be hurtling through the stratosphere at almost the speed of sound, in the comfortable pressurzied cabins of jetliners,

FIGURE 116.—Wiley Post is given best wishes by Carl Squier, General Manager of Lockheed, concerning the planned stratosphere, cross-country flights in the *Winnie Mae*. Behind them is Billy Parker's Lockheed Orion, which belonged to the Phillips Petroleum Company. (Courtesy Lockheed Aircraft.)

FIGURE 117.—Wiley Post is deplaning on March 22, 1935, after his stratosphere-flight attempt from Burbank to New York. The aircraft is a United Air Lines Boeing 247, the first modern air transport. Post was forced to land his *Winnie Mae* at Cleveland, after running low on oxygen on March 15, 1935. He proceeded to Newark, New Jersey, commercially, on March 22. (Courtesy United Air Lines.)

◀ FIGURE 118.—Following the efforts of the stratosphere flights, and prior to departing for Alaska, Post takes in a bit of relaxation at Phillips' Woolaroc Ranch near Bartlesville. (Fay Gillis Wells Scrapbook.)

FIGURE 119.—In a New York City restaurant, late June 1935, Post and Fay Gillis (now Mrs. Linton Wells) plan a flight from the west coast of the United States to Siberia in Post's recently acquired low-wing, hybrid airplane, the Orion-Explorer. (Courtesy Fay Gillis Wells.)

Figure 120.—The "Yankee Doodle," a specially constructed Lockheed Explorer, is tested on June 3, 1930, at Los Angeles, California, during preparations for a planned Paris-to-New York, nonstop flight. Arthur Goebel hoped to fly the aircraft in the east-to-west direction, to be the first to do so. This airplane, license number NR 101 W, had a gasoline capacity of 800 gallons. Goebel did not take the plane but the Pure Oil Company did, and it set a nonstop record from New York to the Canal Zone. On November 21, 1930, the airplane was damaged in an accident at the Canal Zone and the wing was salvaged by Charles Babb. This wing was used with an Orion fuselage and became the hybrid aircraft that Post and Rogers flew to Alaska. (Courtesy Pacific and Atlantic Photos.)

wholly ignorant of the frustrating labors of 1934 and 1935, unmindful of the man who met the difficulties in their rudest shapes. Yet every time a contrail runs its white chalkline across the blue, it deserves recollection that it was Wiley Post who pointed the way to putting it there.

NOTES

1. Charles L. Wilson, "Wiley Post: First Test of High Altitude Pressure Suits in the United States", *Archives of Environmental Health,* vol. 10 (May 1965), pp. 805–810.
2. Harry G. Armstrong, *Principles and Practice of Aviation Medicine* (London: Baillier, Tindall and Cox, 1939), pp. 366–367.
3. A plaque on the terminal building of the Phillips Airport commemorates the contributions Post made while flying at Bartlesville during this time.
4. Ernie Shults was in charge of aviation maintenance and overhaul for Phillips Petroleum.
5. Ernest H. Shults communication.
6. A metal plate was placed on the fire wall just aft of the external supercharger in case of rotor failure during flight, in which event the rotors of this experimental two-stage, single-speed supercharger might break loose and act as a "buzz-saw."
7. Will Parker and Ernest Shults communications.
8. Letter to Smithsonian from Harvey H. Lippincott, Pratt & Whitney, April 11, 1960.
9. Gordon Post scrapbook.
10. *The Tulsa Daily World,* December 4, 1934; *New York Times,* December 4, 1934, p. 3.
11. *New York Times,* December 4, 1934, p. 3.
12. See *The Aircraft Yearbook for 1935* (reporting notablet flights of 1934), Aeronautical Chamber of Commerce of America, New York, pages 176–178. This publication provides an illustration of Suit No. 1 with Helmet No. 1, but describes the modification of this helmet for Suit No. 2. It does not describe Suit No. 3 and Helmet No. 2, although all of the stratosphere flights were made in this latter suit. The general secrecy of details of the latter suit is illustrated by the *Yearbook's* inaccurate account on this point. The 1935 *Yearbook* is also incorrect in stating that the helmet received "air under pressure from the first engine supercharger" and also through another valve "life-sustaining oxygen." On this point, the *Yearbook* was reporting Post's concepts concerning the early planning with suit No. 2 and its Helmet No. 1. However, it deserves note that after 1931 the editing of *The Aircraft Yearbook* slipped into the ways of "public relations," and it became less and less reliable as a historical source; by the end of the 1930s it was almost worthless.
13. *New York Times,* December 8, 1934, p. 1.
14. *New York Times,* December 13, 1934, p. 26.
15. Billy Parker interview.

16. *New York Times,* December 15, 1934, p. 11.
17. Billy Parker interview.
18. *New York Times,* January 20, 1935, IX, p. 10.
19. In 1957 Transcontinental and Western Airlines reinterpreted its initials "TWA" to mean Trans World Airlines.
20. In 1930, Western Air Express (for whom Gerhard Fisher worked, a codeveloper of Post's 1933 ADF equipment) merged with Transcontinental Air Transport, which had merged with Maddox Airlines, to form Transcontinental and Western Air. Thus TWA was able to provide technical support for the automatic direction finder. For some of Gerhard Fisher's later work with ADF, for the U.S. Navy, see Richard K. Smith, *The Airships Akron & Macon: Flying Aircraft Carriers of the U.S. Navy* (Annapolis: The U.S. Naval Institute, 1965) pp. 133–134.
21. Clipping from Gordon Post's scrapbook, and movie available from Screen Gems.
22. *New York Times,* January 26, 1935, p. 19; February 10, 1935, p. 4.
23. Civil Air Regulation 20.2.
24. Later the Lockheed Air Terminal.
25. Muroc was named for the long-time Corum farm family in the area, by reversing the letter in their name.
26. *New York Times,* February 23, 1935, p. 1, 7.
27. *New York Times,* February 23, 1935, p. 1, 7.
28. *New York Times,* March 16, 1935, p. 1.
29. Schieldrop in his *Conquest of Space and Time* (1940) points out that Post made the only sustained flight at 300-mph speeds up through 1940.
30. *New York Times Magazine,* March 24, 1935, p. 3.
31. *Scientific American,* June 1935, p. 316.
32. Years later, World War II bomber pilots detected the same occurrence at about 35,000 feet. Weathermen called the winds the "jet streams." Guy Murchie, in his *Song of the Sky,* describes the phenomenon as a "Gulf Stream of the upper sky." Born when hot and cold winds meet, the jet streams gyrate around the earth, reaching speeds of more than 250 miles per hour. Murchie also notes that there are obviously two jet streams, one over the southern temperate zone and the other over the Mediterranean area, China, and the United States.
33. *New York Times,* April 15, 1935, p. 1.
34. Donald Day, *Will Rogers—A Biography* (New York: David McKay Company, 1937), pp. 34–35.
35. *New York Times,* July 1, 1935, IX, p. 7.
36. *Oklahoma City Times,* February 12, 1935.

6 / Point Barrow

SHORTLY AFTER the 1931 Post and Gatty flight, Paul Garber, curator of the aeronautics collection at the Smithsonian Institution, had been successful in getting Post to promise the *Winnie Mae* to the Smithsonian if Post ever bought another airplane. Garber later turned down a different Lockheed Vega that was offered to the Smithsonian; he wanted the *Winnie Mae* because he considered her the outstanding Vega and technical airplane of the period.[1]

As Post's stratospheric flights were nearing completion in 1935, he indicated that he would consider selling the *Winnie Mae* for $25,000. As mentioned, U.S. Representative Josh Lee of Oklahoma's Fifth District introduced a bill on June 24, 1935, calling for the purchase of the plane.[2]

Having decided that the *Winnie Mae* should be retired, Wiley proceeded to acquire another airplane. The second plane was a low-wing "hybrid," made up from parts of two previously damaged airplanes. The creation of this hybrid is a story unto itself. In May of 1933, a Lockheed Orion, Model 9E, number NC12283, Airworthiness Type Certificate 508, with a 550-horsepower Pratt & Whitney Wasp engine, was rolled out of the Lockheed factory and purchased by Transcontinental and Western Air of Kansas City.

TWA operated the Orion for two years until it was damaged in an accident. Charles H. Babb of Glendale, California, a well-known west coast airplane dealer in new and used aircraft, acquired the remains of the Orion from TWA on February 8, 1935.[3] Three days later, Post purchased the aircraft from Babb.

Babb had also purchased the wing of a Lockheed Explorer, Model 7 (Special), number NR–101W, manufactured in April of 1930, and which had no Airworthiness Type Certificate. It was a low-wing aircraft similar to the Lockheed Sirius in which Charles and Anne Lindbergh had flown the Pacific in 1931 and the Atlantic in 1933, on survey flights for Pan American Airways, but its wings were six feet longer than Lindbergh's Sirius. This Explorer was originally designed for a New York-to-Paris flight by Art Goebel in 1930, when it was named the *Yankee Doodle*, and had a fuel capacity of 800 gallons. When Goebel failed to buy the plane, the Pure Oil Company did, renamed it the *Blue Flash*, and Roy Ammel flew it nonstop from New York City to France Field in the Canal Zone, which was a first flight of its kind. While attempting takeoff from a new and unfinished field at Ancon, Canal Zone, the *Blue Flash* skidded, nosed over, and crashed on her back; Roy Ammel had to be chopped out of the wreckage with fire axes. The fuselage was a total loss, but Charlie Babb managed to salvage the wing.

The above two planes furnished parts for Post's new airplane. The Lockheed Company did not sanction this combination of parts, and did not encourage their amalgamation.[4] Post, however, was short on funds, and this was a way he could obtain a new high-powered airplane. When he applied for a restricted license, Post indicated that the plane, which carried the number NC 12283, would be rebuilt. The application to the Bureau of Aeronautics in July 23, 1935, certified that the new airplane had been rebuilt from the assembled Orion fuselage and the Lockheed "Sirius" wing, and was an Orion 9E Special. This hybrid airplane was also referred to as an Orion-Explorer.[5]

Post's hybrid carried 270 gallons of gasoline in six tanks. The propeller was a constant speed Hamilton Standard with three blades. Post had some of the *Winnie Mae's* flight instruments removed and put in this new airplane; a venturi system on each side of the fuselage created a suction to operate these. The impressive-appearing airplane was painted red with a silver stripe. Since the plane was to be used for experimental cross-country flights and special test work, the Department of Commerce affixed the "NR" restricted designation to its number (NR 12283). The aircraft had not been subjected to the Bureau of Air Commerce regulations, which governed issuance of a commercial category certificate; it was "restricted" to operations involving the pilot and two crew members, and these latter could be navigators, mechanics, observers, radio operators, etc.

Prior to Post's purchase, the Orion was certified at 3,859 pounds empty weight as a passenger aircraft, with 5,400 pounds for the gross weight.

Post's plans were not made clear to the public. There were reports that he and Mae planned to fly

FIGURE 121.—The racy, new hybrid airplane obtained by Post in the spring of 1935 was assembled from the fuselage of a damaged second-hand Lockheed Orion, and the wings of an experimental Lockheed long-distance aircraft, an Explorer. This Explorer had cracked up in the Canal Zone and had not been tested for a type certificate by the Bureau of Aeronautics of the Department of Commerce. The combination of the Explorer wing (six feet longer than that of the Sirius or Orion) with the Orion fuselage and tail produced an uncontrollable, nose-down pitching moment at low air speeds and low power settings. The substitution of improper floats for wheels aggravated an existing nose-heaviness. The Lockheed Company did not countenance this unusual airplane. Note the fixed landing gear (Orions had retractable main wheels). (Courtesy Edwin O. Cooper.)

FIGURE 122.—The front view of the Orion-Explorer with its imposing three-bladed Hamilton-Standard propeller and 550-horsepower Pratt & Whitney Wasp engine. (Courtesy Edwin O. Cooper.)

to Siberia for a six-week vacation.[6] It was also reported that Fay Gillis would accompany them.[7] In April 1935 Fay Gillis had married Linton Wells, a well-known news correspondent (Clyde Pangborn was best man), and it turned out that she had other plans. Interestingly enough Wells had covered the U.S. Army's World Flight for the Associated Press in 1924, during their passage from Japan to India, and had actually flown with them across India. In 1926 Wells had raced around the world in company with Edward Evans, using available transportation; they used aircraft across Europe and Russia as far as Omsk, and again across continental United States to make their circuit in 28 days, 14 hours, and 36 minutes.

Rumors continued to abound about Post's plans. It

FIGURE 123.—Post stands in the Pacific Airmotive Hangar, United Airport, Burbank, California, holding aerial maps of his planned flight from California to Alaska. Picture made in late July 1935. (Courtesy Edwin O. Cooper.)

was said that Post had obtained permits for himself, Mae, and Fay Gillis Wells for a six-week flight in Siberia.[8] Post supposedly wanted to study the possibilities of an airmail and passenger route between Alaska and Russia and thus bypass the hazardous flight over the Pacific.[9] It was rumored that Pan American Airways had agreed to finance the survey, but later changed its mind. Post was in any case determined to visit Alaska; he and Mae had considered moving there after Wiley completed his solo flight.[10]

A letter from the Soviet Embassy in Washington of July 5, 1935, addressed to Fay Gillis Wells reads as follows:

Dear Mrs. Wells:

I should appreciate your informing Wiley Post that permission has been granted him, Mrs. Post and yourself for the flight along the following route: Whelan or Providence Bay, Nagaevo, Yakutsk, Irkutsk, Novo-Sibirsk, Sverdlovsk, Moscow.

The Soviet Authorities are suggesting that you postpone the flight until the end of July as the necessary maps for the flight will not reach the Embassy in time for you to start in the middle of July, as Mr. Post plans. The maps have already been sent and will be forwarded to you as soon as they are received by the Embassy.

It is necessary that we cable to Moscow the exact date of your departure and the kind of radio equipment you are carrying; also the exact coloring of the different parts of

FIGURE 124.—For relaxation, Post loved to fish. He had the opportunity in the period following August 7, 1935, in Juneau, Alaska, where he and Will Rogers spent a few days prior to leaving August 12 for Dawson. (Courtesy L. E. Gray.)

the plane. Mr. Post told me in general that it is red and silver but he did not go into detail as to which parts are red and which silver. Please wire this information to me as soon as possible.

Sincerely yours,
(Signed)
B. E. Skvirsky
Counselor

Fay Gillis Wells subsequently bowed out of the proposed flight in order to accompany her reporter husband on a delayed, combined honeymoon and working trip to cover the Italo-Ethiopian war (from the Ethiopian side) for the *New York Herald Tribune*. Post then asked Will Rogers to accompany him to Alaska and Russia.

Post flew his new airplane on July 25, 1935, with Mae and Will Rogers, from Los Angeles to Albuquerque, New Mexico, and went to Waite Phillips' ranch in New Mexico's Sangre de Cristo Mountains for a brief vacation.[11] Following Rogers' meeting with Post after the 1931 flight, their mutual interest in aviation had led to a close friendship.

Just before the above flight, the press reported

that Post and Rogers were planning a flight to Russia by way of Alaska.[12] It was later revealed that Rogers was exhausted from his last movie, "Steamboat 'Round the Bend," and that Mrs. Rogers was very concerned about his health and rather arduous living habits. Rogers was also unhappy because he felt that the quality of his newspaper column was deteriorating. He told one friend that he had thought about buying a plane and keeping it in London so he could fly to the world's "hot spots" and inject a little life into his writing. He had also considered flying to Rio de Janiero and catching the German airship *Graf Zeppelin* for a flight across the South Atlantic and up the African coast. When Post came along with a new airplane and plans for a "vacation" in the wilds, Rogers was immediately interested. On several occasions he had expressed complete confidence in Wiley' flying ability.[13]

During this period, Post served as president of the Wiley Post Aircraft Corporation, Oklahoma City, Oklahoma. This company, with Johnny Burke as manager, made a small, open-cockpit, two-place side-by-side training biplane. There was one cockpit and the left seat was staggered slightly to the rear.[14] Thirteen of these aircraft were built. The aircraft had a 40-horsepower Straugham AL 1000 engine, which was a converted Model A Ford engine.[15] These aircraft were delivered for $990 f.o.b., and retailed for $1,300. Post's role was primarily that of lending his name to the company.

There was some confusion about Post's passport (whether it was to be a new passport or a renewed passport from the 1933 flight); Post had applied for a renewal at Los Angeles, but he was told that the application had been sent to the San Francisco office. At San Francisco, agent S. A. Owen of the U.S. Passport Office told the Associated Press that, "I can't tell if Post is asking for a renewal or a new passport." Reporters tried to meet Post at the Union Air Terminal in Burbank and discuss the matter, but Post "did not appear as usual where his plane is waiting." The matter was settled when Wiley flew from Los Angeles to San Francisco and visited the U.S. Immigration authorities, who issued him the passport.

When Post and Mae took off from San Francisco in the Orion-Explorer for Seattle on August 1, 1935, Rogers had not yet definitely decided whether or not to accompany them. He asked Wiley to call him from Seattle, where Edo[16] pontoons were to be installed in place of wheels on the airplane. Upon receiving Post's call from Seattle, Rogers decided to fly with him from Seattle and quickly boarded a plane in Los

FIGURE 125.—Post poses with four Alaskan ladies and a terrier in Fairbanks, Alaska, the stop immediately preceding the last flight with Will Rogers. (Courtesy Dr. John Wilson, Lockheed Aircraft Company.)

FIGURE 126.—Will Rogers poses with the same Alaskan belles as Post did, Fairbanks, Alaska, August 1935. (Courtesy John Wilson, Lockheed Aircraft.)

Figure 127.—Wiley Post stands in the cockpit of his Orion-Explorer, while Will Rogers talks with him from the wing. This photograph was made at Oklavik near Fairbanks, Alaska, just before the two departed for Dawson and shortly thereafter for their August 15, 1935, fatal accident near Point Barrow. The airplane was fully fueled at Oklavik, using a cache of Canadian Airways fuel. About 260 gallons were taken (at $1.16 per gallon). Rogers had the picture taken by a Canadian Airways worker named Hartley. (Courtesy Edwin O. Cooper.)

Angeles for Seattle.[17] The press reported that Mrs. Post planned to travel north by boat and join the two in Alaska, but a subsequent announcement revealed that she had decided to return home from Seattle. Mrs. Post later explained that she had backed out because she felt Rogers did not want her to go; he feared that the ordeal of camping out when necessary would be too hard on her.[18]

Wiley had made arrangements for pontoons to be available for the Orion-Explorer in Seattle. The ones he planned for installation by Northwest Air Services of Renton, Washington, were Edo 5300 pontoons, suitable for the high-lift, long-fuselage, high-wing aircraft, such as certain Fairchilds, commonly used by Alaskan Bush pilots.[19] He requested a set from a Pacific Alaska Airways' Fairchild, and these were being sent to the Northwest Air Service in Seattle. Joe Crosson arranged the loan of the pontoons to Post.[20] The requested floats were not in Seattle when Post and Rogers arrived; Rogers was impatient to be on the way to Alaska, and since Rogers was paying the expenses, Post looked for another set of floats.

Post found a set from a Fokker trimotor and had them installed.[21] The Fokker F-10 model weighed 7,600 pounds empty and up to 13,000 fully loaded, and thus had a set of floats much larger (and heavier) than required by the 5,400-pound Orion hybrid. When the floats were installed, Post discovered that his hybrid Orion was decidedly nose-heavy and that power had to be carried to keep the nose up for a proper water "landing." Without power, the nose-down angle became so steep and the rate of descent so fast, that a water landing was hazardous. With Rogers in the aircraft, however, in an aft location, the nose-heaviness would be counterbalanced somewhat. A larger stabilizer-elevator combination would have helped overcome this controllability problem, but there was not time to arrange such a modification. Wiley was afraid that the Department of Commerce inspector might not approve this pontoon/Orion combination, a circumstance which would delay the flight to Alaska, so he and Rogers did not procrastinate with their departure plans.

Dodging the press in Seattle, Post and Rogers loaded two cases of chili (one of Rogers' favorite foods) aboard the plane and at 9:20 a.m., August 6,

FIGURE 128.—This picture was made on August 15, 1935, 40 miles from Fairbanks, Alaska, on Lake Harding, where the Orion-Explorer was fully fueled with Stanavo (Standard Oil Aviation fuel) for the long flight to Point Barrow. (Courtesy Dr. John Wilson, Lockheed Aircraft Company.)

took off for Alaska.[22] They refused to comment on whether or not they intended to fly around the world. They landed at Juneau on the 7th to visit with friends, and their visit was prolonged several days by rain. When the weather finally cleared, they climbed back into the Lockheed and continued north;[23] they flew to Dawson in the Yukon Territory, and on August 12 took off for Fairbanks.[24] In Fairbanks, the two Oklahomans visited with Joe Crosson, the Pacific Alaska pilot, who had assisted Post at Flat, after the *Winnie Mae* had rolled out into the ditch.

Meanwhile, Rogers had developed an interest in Charlie Brower, an elderly trader and whaler who lived at Point Barrow, more than 300 miles inside the Arctic Circle. Brower was a veteran of 50 years' residency around Point Barrow and was often referred to as "King of the Arctic." Rogers wanted an interview with the old man for his newspaper column.

Post and Rogers decided to fly to Point Barrow. Joe Crosson advised against it. He at least wanted them to delay their departure until certain changes could be made in the Orion-Explorer.

Crosson was disturbed by the excessive nose-heaviness of the Lockheed hybrid. If its engine quit, especially at a low altitude, shortly after takeoff or in an approach to landing, the nose-heavy condition could lead to a crash. Crosson pointed out that in poweroff flight, i.e., a glide, the downwash over the horizontal stabilizer was diminished, which reduced the effectiveness of the elevators in counteracting the nose-heaviness. The aircraft would then pitch over, nose-down, and stabilize in an accelerating nose-down attitude.

FIGURE 129.—Refueling of the Orion-Explorer is supervised by Wiley Post at Fairbanks, Alaska, just prior to the fateful last hop. This is one of the last pictures made of Post. (Courtesy Dr. John Wilson, Lockheed Aircraft Company.)

FIGURE 130.—The Orion-Explorer rests upside down on August 15, 1935, in the small lake near Point Barrow, Alaska. The bodies of Wiley Post and Will Rogers had just been removed and a tow rope was fastened to the tie-down fitting. The relatively shallow water at the site of the accident is evident. The treeless tundra of the remote northern area is seen in the background. The large bulky floats are evident and the rear water rudder is still affixed to the left float. (Courtesy Edwin O. Cooper.)

FIGURE 131.—Another view of the Orion-Explorer which crashed at Point Barrow on August 15, 1935. The accident was instantly fatal to Post and Rogers. (Courtesy Edwin O. Cooper.)

FIGURE 132.—Charcoal drawings by Gene C. Mason capture the facial expressions of airman Wiley Post and humorist-philosopher Will Rogers. (Photograph: Dr. Michael Lategola from Gordon Post Scrapbook.)

All this made sense to Post, but Rogers was anxious to get under way. Rogers was paying most of the trip's expenses, so Post decided to take the risk.

In the face of bad weather, Post and Rogers took off from Fairbanks on August 15 after partially refueling. The Chena River at Fairbanks is tortuous and narrow and Post did not want to attempt to take off with the heavy weight of a full load of fuel. Also, Post was not too experienced in seaplanes and had not had time to become fully acquainted with the water characteristics of this one. They landed on Lake Harding (40 miles away and completely refuled with a prearranged stockpile of aviation fuel for the Point Barrow flight. They then left for Barrow, about 510 air miles away. Since the airplane was equipped with pontoons, they could land on any one of the numerous lakes if the weather closed in, and Crosson had suggested that they hug the northeast coast.[25]

The Point to which they headed is a "V" of land extending into the polar sea. Ten miles to the south is the town of Barrow, which had a population of 500 Eskimos and nine Caucasians in 1935. A small Presbyterian mission and hospital were operated there by Dr. Henry W. Griest and his wife.

Several hours after leaving Fairbanks, and getting low on fuel, Post brought the plane down on a small lagoon about 16 miles from Barrow. Post and Rogers climbed out of the airplane. Clair Okpeaha ran a sealing camp nearby, and Post asked him for directions to Barrow, while he and Rogers ate some food offered by the Eskimos.[26] In the meantime, the engine of the Orion Special cooled. Okpeaha indicated the way, and after Rogers talked some with the Eskimos, he and Post got back into the airplane and taxied out for takeoff. There was not easy means under these circumstances by which the engine could be warmed up and subjected to a proper preflight run-up.

Post pushed open the throttle and headed for takeoff. The floats frothed through the water and the plane came up on the "steps" of her floats. Then she lifted off the water, and suddenly—the engine quit.

Okpeaha saw the airplane dive straight into the shallow water, throwing spray in all directions.[27]

The impact was terrific. There was a small fire, but it immediately went out. The airplane came to rest on its back, with a broken fuselage and fractured wing. Post was killed instantly by the impact, and pinned tightly against the engine. Rogers was thrown out of the fuselage into the water.

In a state of shock, Okpeaha immediately left on foot, running for Barrow. The 16-mile trip took him five hours. In a state of exhaustion, he burst into the U.S. Department of Interior Reindeer Station at Point Barrow and gave the first news of the accident. Frank Dougherty, a United Press correspondent, got some men together, including Staff Sergeant Stanley R. Morgan of the Army Signal Corps, and proceeded immediately to the scene. They retrieved the two bodies in a whaling boat and noted that Post's gold watch had stopped at 8:18 p.m. on August 15.[28] Rogers' watch was still running. Dr. Henry Griest took two eiderdown sleeping bags from the crashed plane and carefully placed the bodies inside them.[29]

Dougherty sent the news of the Post-Rogers crash to the United Press Bureau in Seattle through the Signal Corps radio; news of the accident electrified the world. The opening paragraph of an Associated Press story was vivid: "Will Rogers, beloved humorist, and Wiley Post, master aviator, were crushed to death last night when a shiny new airplane motor faltered and bacame an engine of tragedy near the outpost of civilization." [30] The *New York Times* headlines announced that the nation was shocked by the tragedy.[31]

Mrs. Post was visiting with the "Red" Grays at Ponca City, Oklahoma. At first she refused to believe the news. Post's parents in Maysville received the news from Major Fred Scott and Editor W. E. Showen. The elder Post admitted to a long-time fear of such an outcome.[32]

Post's friend and supporter, Walter Harrison, was stunned. The day after the accident, he evaluated its impact on aviation in the following manner:[33]

It is the air's greatest tragedy because the world characters that are lost will be impressed upon the millions who

FIGURE 133.—The *Winnie Mae* in mourning at Bartlesville, Oklahoma, shortly after Post's death at Point Barrow (Courtesy Phillips Petroleum.)

115

FIGURE 134.—Mae Post and Frank Phillips view one of Wiley Post's many significant aviation awards, the Gold Medal of the Federation Aeronautique International, awarded to Post for his 1933 solo world flight. The formal award was made on October 9, 1934 in Washington, D.C., ceremonies. Only one other American had won the award at this time—Charles A. Lindbergh, for the 1927 solo Atlantic flight. (Courtesy Will D. Parker.)

read. . . . The world will forget for a season the millions of safe hours of commercial flying and check off all of the progress against the loss of Oklahoma's most famous men.

His terse description of Post is perhaps the most vivid ever written:

Post, the nerveless, taciturn, all-steel farm boy, was an enigma to most of those with whom he came in contact. He came as near to being a mechanical flying machine as any human who ever held a stick.

Aviators around the world reacted to the news of Post's death. The famous Ernst Udet of Germany proclaimed:

I consider Post the greatest flier of all time. He was a real pioneer. He ranked first both as regards positive accomplishments and fruitfulness of new ideas. He was the most advanced and courageous man aviation has thus brought forth. It was he who did more for stratosphere flying than any other man of our profession despite hard luck. He stuck to his ideas only to find them proven correct in the course of time. I do not believe the layman has an inkling of our dead American comrade's unparalleled accomplishments.[84]

Bennie Turner stated in the August 17, 1935, issue of the *Daily Oklahoman*, that "None ever knew Wiley. He was completely self-contained, so much so that few even knew he was subject to moods that could change from blue to rose in a flash." Turner also reminisced that Post had a love for hunting, guns, and cars, and of the latter once said, "I like them black, all black."

Turner further observed that Post did not like to discuss the fact that he and Mrs. Post had no children. Post was very sentimental about children and is quoted by Mr. Turner with reference to child-molesters, "I'd like to beat hell out of guys like that." [85] "He could never pass a ragged newsboy on the street without buying a paper he did not want." Once during a parade in Allentown, Pennsylvania, Post asked the police not to chase the following "kids" away from his car. "Someone should get some fun out of this," Post said.[86]

Turner also wrote other descriptive comments of Post, some possibly resulting from the shock Turner felt at losing a close friend, and some perhaps composed during periods when Turner's sadness was relieved by alcoholic beverages. He stated that Post had a little-known eccentricity that consisted of taking

FIGURE 135.—Stanley Draper, second from left, affectionately views McMurry's statue of Wiley Post during September 26, 1963, dedication program in Oklahoma City's Civic Center. (Courtesy Oklahoma City Chamber of Commerce.)

several baths a day. He also wrote that one of Post's hobbies was collecting watches and that Post loved to sit amongst these, adjusting and winding them, one by one.

Post's friends recalled that he was a "loner," traditionally on the quiet side, not talkative, and not very prone to loll about airports, "hangar flying" with other pilots. Also, they described him as "very forceful," and a person for whom those who knew him developed a great affection.

The readers of the *Maysville News* found the front page of the August 22 issue devoted to Wiley. A large picture bore the simple caption, "Wiley Post, the World's Greatest Aviator." A poem by Dorothy Willis concluded with the following stanza:

But the wings he knew have crushed and he is gone
And a million saddened hearts send up their prayer;
Now he flies a ghost ship in the Great Beyond
God grant him happy landing there.

On August 7, 1935, an AP story related that Colonel Charles Lindbergh and Joe Crosson gave behind-the-scenes aid in the aftermath of the Post-Rogers crash. Lindbergh was at North Haven, Maine, celebrating the birthday of Little Jon Lindbergh, when advised of the crash. He dropped everything to assist the widows. Through his connection with Pan American Airways, Lindbergh arranged for the Pacific-Alaskan Airways to return the bodies.

Joe Crosson, chief pilot of Pacific-Alaskan Airways, flew the bodies from Point Barrow to Fairbanks in a Fairchild seaplane. He then used a Pan American Lockheed 10 Electra to fly them to Boeing Field in Seattle, where they were covered with Floral wreaths, and William Winston flew them in a Pan American Airways Douglas DC-2 airliner to Oakland, California.

Colonel Clarence Young, Pacific coast manager of Pan American Airways, and Amon Carter of Fort Worth, were on hand to meet Crosson's airplane when it landed at Seattle. They accompanied the deceased in the Douglas DC-2, as it flew south.[37]

Will Rogers' body was removed at Los Angeles and the DC-2 with Post's remains flew to Oklahoma City, where it landed at the municipal airport.[38] Eight thousand persons were at the airport to meet the airplane carrying Post's body.

In the largest funeral Oklahoma had ever known, 20,000 persons viewed Post's casket as it lay in state in the Oklahoma State Capitol Building, Oklahoma City. Governor Marland paid tribute and General Butner from Fort Sill, President Roosevelt's personal representative, attended. An honor squadron of Post's close friends, in civil aircraft, accompanied by a flight of military airplanes, flew overhead and dropped flowers in tribute to their late colleague.

Editor Showen of Maysville viewed Post's body and thought he detected motion:

Of course it was imagination, for the immortal part of Wiley was at the moment piloting a phantom spirit ship in the ethereal realm, where there are no treacherous air pockets, no fogs and mists and sudden storms to wreck his ship and force a perilous landing.

Services were held at the First Baptist Church in Oklahoma City.[39] Pallbearers were Leslie Fain, Harry Frederickson, Joe Crosson, Bennie Turner, Ted Colbert, Billy Parker, Ernest Shults, and Red Gray. Services also had been held in Maysville, Oklahoma, at the Landmark Baptist Church, which Wiley's father had helped build.

Despite special Congressional action that allowed burial of Post in Arlington National Cemetery, his family chose a site in Oklahoma. Post was buried in Memorial Park Cemetery, Edmond, Oklahoma, a few miles north of Oklahoma City. A Distinguished Flying Cross design was placed on the gravestone.[40]

On August 29, 1935, J. Carroll Cone of the Department of Commerce, wrote to the Estate of Wiley Post and stated that the following aircraft were recorded in the name of Wiley Post, 706 West 29th Street, Oklahoma City.[41]

Model	Serial No.	Dept. No Commerce No.
Lockheed Orion Special	195	NR 12283
Curtiss-Wright CW3-L	1503	12325

The letter stated that since Mr. Post was deceased, the licenses of the two aircraft were now revoked and no authority to operate the aircraft could be granted until the new owner's recording title was filed with the Bureau of Air Commerce. The Orion Special had been destroyed and the Curtiss-Wright was in the Bartlesville Hangar, next to the *Winnie Mae*. This airplane was a small two-seat amphibian version of the Curtiss-Wright Junior, a high-wing monoplane with a 90-horsepower Lambert engine, mounted in a pusher configuration above the wing; the tandem cockpits were in front of the wing and afforded the occupant of the first seat an excellent unobstructed view. Billy Parker and Post had flown the airplane in Oklahoma and he and Post both shot coyotes from it around Bartlesville;[42] Wiley had intended to take the plane to Alaska and hunt wolves from the air.[43]

Several weeks after the accident, Eugene L. Vidal, director of the Bureau of Air Commerce, issued a report on the crash.[44] It revealed that the plane's pontoons had made the hybrid Orion decidedly nose-heavy. As previously mentioned, while in Fairbanks, Post had told Joe Crosson that Rogers had to sit at the rear of the plane to combat the imbalance. The report found no carelessness on Post's part, concerning the weather, noting that he had told Crosson that he would not fly in or above cloud banks.[45] Two months later, the official report by the accident investigators stated that:

FIGURE 136.—On September 26, 1963, the Oklahoma City Chamber of Commerce dedicated a statue of Wiley Post by Leonard McMurry, in the Civic Center of Oklahoma City. Many of Post's personal friends and relatives attended the ceremony. Shown above are Mrs. Wiley Post, center, and Mr. Will Parker, right, viewing the statue. (Courtesy Oklahoma City Chamber of Commerce.)

A study of the various changes on the airplane indicated that it was decidedly nose-heavy and must have been extremely difficult, if not impossible, to properly control without the aid of the engine. A statement made by the pilot (Post) after the change of pontoons confirms this conclusion. The exact cause of the engine failure cannot be determined. The temperature at the time was 40° F. and the failure could have been due to the engine having become cool while standing on the lagoon or to ice or water condensate forming in the carburetor. It is the opinion of the accident board that the probable cause of this accident was loss of control of the aircraft at a low altitude, after sudden engine failure, due to the extreme nose-heaviness of the aircraft.[46]

The tragedy had stirred a considerable commotion within the Bureau of Air Commerce. Because Rogers was heavily insured, various interests wanted complete information on the crash, including official copies of

FIGURE 137.—Astronaut Edwin E. Aldrin, photographed by fellow astronaut Neil A. Armstrong, Apollo 11 flight, as they make man's first walk on the moon, July 20, 1969. Their pressure suits are a direct evolutionary development of the world's first practical pressure suit that was conceived, designed, and perfected by Wiley Post. In the spring of 1935 when Post was making his stratosphere flights, astronauts Armstrong and Aldrin were four and five years of age, respectively. They were typical of the boys Post always greeted with affection and who, he knew, would build further upon the progress he made. (Courtesy National Aeronautics and Space Administration.)

the license issued for Post's plane. For some reason the original license was not on file, so the Bureau sent out certified copies.[47] There was some question as to whether the plane was duly certified after the addition of the Edo floats.[48] William S. Moore, an aeronautical inspector at Seattle, informed the chief of the General Inspection Service that the plane was not inspected after the pontoons were installed. The work was completed on the evening of August 5 and Post left for Alaska the next morning.[49]

The Department of Commerce stated its official opinion in a letter to a New York firm. J. M. Johnston, assistant secretary of commerce, noted that the aircraft's NR license permitted three persons to be aboard the airplane while it was in flight, provided that none were carried for hire. He referenced the pontoon question with this statement:

It is the belief of this Department, in view of its practice with respect to the restricted form of aircraft license here under consideration, that the substitution of pontoons for wheel type landing gear on said airplane would not constitute grounds for revocation or suspension of said license because of the purpose for which it was issued.

Congress provided a memorial to Post when it authorized the Smithsonian Institution to buy the *Winnie Mae* from Post's widow for $25,000.[50] By coincidence, the Senate had previously scheduled discussion of the bill on August 16, 1935, the day after Post's death. In such an atmosphere, the measure was passed immediately, and shortly thereafter, the Smithsonian Institution made plans to take the *Winnie Mae* to Washington, The Bureau of Air Commerce records reveal the following:

On September 3, 1935, A. M. Alcorn signed an Operation Report for the Bureau of Air Commerce on Lockheed Vega Serial No. 122, which belonged to the estate of Wiley Post. A propeller consisting of a Smith hub and Pittsburgh Screw and Bolt steel blades, was noted. The propeller was design number 450–SI, with blade numbers 2422 and 2337. The blades also were designated as B–450–S–1. It was stated on September 17, 1935, that a temporary NR license for NR 105W was considered for ferry purposes. No application was submitted.

When Paul Garber arrived at Bartlesville in November 1935 to take possession of the *Winnie Mae*, a black crepe bow was on her propeller—a meaningful reminder of the intimate relationship between the pilot and his machine.

At first Garber considered letting Billy Parker fly the *Winnie Mae* to Washington, but he feared that a mishap might destroy the priceless aircraft. In any case the *Winnie Mae's* license had expired on August 15, the day Post died. Garber dismantled the famous airplane and packed it in a railway boxcar at Bartlesville. Garber found a carpenter's clamp in the wing, apparently left there from an earlier repair.[51] He personally rode in the car as it was shuttled slowly across the country from railroad to railroad, as far as East St. Louis. Garber missed some meals because, at some stops, railroad men were uncertain how long the car would remain in place. When parts of the aircraft broke their moorings due to the jostling of the train, Garber was able to protect them from damage. Garber left at St. Louis in order that he could proceed directly to Bolling Field in Washington, D.C., and supervise the unloading of the *Winnie Mae*. The Vega was ready for public display in the Smithsonian Institution by the end of 1935.

With the money she received from the government, Mrs. Post bought a section of land in Ralls, a small town near Lubbock, Texas. The quiet life of a west Texas farm was far different from the exciting world of aviation, but in the few short years with Wiley, she garnered enough memories for a lifetime.

A memorial to Wiley Post and Will Rogers, in the form of a huge revolving airway beacon, was dedicated on the north tower of the New York side of the George Washington Bridge, which spans the Hudson to join Manhattan with Englewood, N.J. The beacon was installed by the New York Aviation Commission, with assistance from the Bureau of Air Commerce of the U.S. Department of Commerce and the New York Port Authority. On Saturday afternoon, November 30, 1935, the beacon was formally dedicated, with Mrs. Post present for the ceremonies.[52] Symbolically, this beacon, sweeping its beam through the darkness, continues to point the way for today's pilots, just as do Post's many contributions to the science of flight. Carl Squier of Lockheed has remarked, "There is a little bit of Wiley in every plane that flies."

No one sped around the world again after Post's 1933 solo until Howard Hughes flew the circuit during July 1938. Like Post, Hughes also used a Lockheed airplane, but it was a brand-new, all-metal, twin-engine Lockheed 14, nine models removed from the old *Winnie Mae*, and Hughes flew with an expert crew of five. Hughes and his crew flew over almost the same track flown by Post, but they dashed over the route in three days, 19 hours and 8 minutes, for which they received the Collier Trophy, the United States' most coveted aeronautical award.

Newsmen later asked Hughes how he thought his flight compared with that of Post. Hughes considered his answer carefully, and when he spoke, his words came slowly and with great deliberation, to be sure that everyone understood what he was saying:

Wiley Post's flight remains the most remarkable flight in history. It can never be duplicated. *He did it alone!* To make a trip of that kind is beyond comprehension. It's like pulling a rabbit out of a hat or sawing a woman in half.[53]

Twelve years after Post's death, in August 1947, William P. Odom flew around the world solo in 73 hours and 5 minutes, using a civil-modified Douglas A–26, a twin-engine attack plane, named *Reynolds Bombshell*. Of Odom's flight, the British aviation weekly *Flight* remarked, "Just what he has proved there is not clear." And *Flight* went on to observe:

The late Wiley Post took some 187 hours to do the circuit . . . but that was fourteen years ago, in a Lockheed Vega with one 450 horsepower engine. Post had far less aid from navigational facilities, and almost the only piece of equipment common to the *Winnie Mae* and the *Reynolds Bombshell* is the automatic pilot, which in both cases enabled the human pilot to take occasional short snatches of sleep. Captain Odom's engines had to run for 73 hours only, while Post's kept going for 187. Pilot strain must have been approximately proportional to the length of time taken, so if human endurance is the criterion, Post's was the greater achievement.[54]

Post's solo dash around the world thus remains not

only unique in terms of time, technology, and the annals of flight, but also in terms of human achievement—and for all times.

Post's experimental work culminated in the development of the first practical flight-pressure suit, the pioneering of pressurized flight tests, and long-distance flights through the stratosphere. When astronauts and cosmonauts step into their space suits, and test pilots, the world over, step into their pressure suits, they are stepping where Wiley Post stood first. And every airline captain who announces to his passengers that the cruising altitude of their flight will be 35,000 feet or higher, might well add that it was a one-eyed pilot, flying an obsolescent plywood airplane, who led the way to these air corridors.

Wiley Post left to the field of aviation, and the world, a legacy of achievement that in less than a decade had revolutionized aeronautics. The later high-altitude air transport and military flights, and the following man-in-space achievements, including the pressure suits used for the first walk on the moon, all have their origins in Post's pioneering work. Along with Wilbur and Orville Wright's first practical-powered airplane of December 17, 1903, and Robert H. Goddard's, March 6, 1926, first practical liquid-fuel rocket, Wiley Post's, September 5, 1934, flight-pressure suit test led to the world's first practical pressurized airplane flight in the stratosphere.

As man progresses from the earth to the moon, and onward toward the planets, it can truly be said, "There is a bit of Wiley permeating *all* the craft man flies."

NOTES

1. Paul Garber interview.
2. Josh Lee interview.
3. Department of Commerce File: record, transfer, and assignment form.
4. STEPHEN E. MILLS AND JAMES W. PHILLIPS, *Sourdough Sky* (Seattle: Superior Publishing Company, 1969).
5. The Orion-Explorer had a fixed landing gear. The 550 Wasp engine was loaned to Post by Pratt & Whitney and the buildup of the airplane was accomplished at the Union Air Terminal, Burbank. The airplane had four wing-fuel tanks of 56 gallons capacity each (2 tanks in each wing), a 30-gallon fuel tank under and to the rear of the pilot's seat, and a 16-gallon fuel tank behind the headrest on the outside of the fuselage under the headrest fairing.
6. *New York Times,* June 30, 1935, I, p. 2.
7. *New York Times,* June 30, 1935, I, p. 2.
8. *New York Times,* July 7, 1935.
9. HOMER CROY, *Our Will Rogers* (New York: Duel, Sloan and Pearce, 1953).
10. Mrs. Wiley Post interview.
11. *New York Times,* July 26, and 27, 1935.
12. *New York Times,* July 23, 1935, p. 21.
13. CROY, *Our Will Rogers,* AND DAY, *Will Rogers—A Biography.*
14. *Oklahoma City Times,* August 16, 1935.
15. *National Aeronautics,* September 1962.
16. "Edo" are the initials of Earl Dodge Osborne, the founder of the Edo Company.
17. CROY, *Our Will Rogers.*
18. Mrs. Wiley Post interview.
19. The 5,300 refers to pounds of static displacement of fresh water by one-half of one float. As a pair, the Edo J floats (5300 model) were approved for an airplane with a gross weight approximately 5,570 pounds, including water-rudder installation (Aircraft Equipment listing, FAA). There was a 10 percent safety factor on displacement by either float in that one float could support the plane if the other was punctured. The J Model 5300 floats were certified for production by Edo on May 21, 1929. The Fairchild 71, a seven-place cabin (and a sea monoplane, ATC 89, gross weigtht 5,500 pounds), was eligible to use Edo J 5300 floats. From the bouyancy standpoint, these floats were appropriate to the weight of Post's plane.
20. Archie Satterfield, *Alaska Bush Pilots in the Float Country* (Seattle: Superior Publishing Company, 1969).
21. Will D. Parker interview.
22. Orion file, 3422.
23. *New York Times,* August 8, 1935, p. 1.
24. *New York Times,* August 13, 1935, p. 19.
25. CROY, *Our Will Rogers.*
26. Okpeaha's name may be seen spelled many different ways, including Okpoeha, Oakpeha, and Oakpena.
27. *New York Herald,* August 17, 1935.
28. CROY, *Our Will Rogers.*
29. *Daily Oklahoman,* August 17, 1935 and Gordon Post scrapbook.
30. *New York Times,* August 17, 1935, p. 1.
31. *New York Times,* August 17, 1935,
32. *Oklahoma City Times,* August 16, 1935, p. 6.
33. *Oklahoma City Times,* August 16, 1935, p. 1.
34. Ernst Udet in the *Oklahoma City Times,* August 17, 1935.
35. Turner, *Daily Oklahoman,* August 17, 1935.
36. Gordon Post scrapbook.
37. Gordon Post scrapbook.
38. This airport was later named Will Rogers Field, and in 1964, Will Rogers World Airport.
39. *Daily Oklahoman,* August 22, 1935.
40. *New York Times,* August 20, 1935, p. 20.
41. The Bureau of Air Commerce records show that on August 17, 1935, the *Winnie Mae* was to be transferred to the ownership of the Smithsonian. Therefore, the *Winnie Mae* was not listed in this letter to the estate. Further details on the disposition of the *Winnie Mae* are given later in this chapter.
42. L. E. Gray interview.
43. Parker communication.
44. Bureau of Air Commerce inspector Murray Hall, stationed in Alaska, conducted the on-site accident investigation.
45. Department of Commerce News Release, September 4, 1935, Wiley Post envelope, Library of Congress.
46. *Air Commerce Bulletin,* vol. 7 (October 15, 1935), p. 94.
47. J. Carroll Cone, assistant director of Air Commerce, to Republic Investment Corporation, Hollywood, California, August 27, 1935.
48. The Department of Commerce was aware of the planned installation of Edo 5300 floats. The substitution of

the Fokker tri-motor floats and the departure from Seattle prior to inspection by the Department of Commerce was unknown to the department. Brower's burning of the aircraft remains, at the remote location, following the accident precluded a more detailed follow-up investigation of the floats.

49. Moore to Chief, General Inspection Service, August 31, 1935.

50. Other memorials followed, among them: a city park in Oklahoma City was named Wiley Post Park by city school children; a street in Los Angeles was named Wiley Post Boulevard; and, two years after the Point Barrow accident, a monument, in commemoration of Post and Rogers was built at the site of the fatal crash by Colonel Homer F. Kellems. In addition, Tulakes Airport, northwest of Oklahoma City, was renamed Wiley Post Airport, in October 1961. Mrs. Wiley Post and many old friends of Post attended the ceremonies. A life-sized bronze statue of Wiley Post by sculptor Leonard McMurry was placed in the Oklahoma City Civic Center and dedicated on September 26, 1963, by the Oklahoma City Chamber of Commerce. Mrs. Post and old friends were present for the ceremonies.

51. Paul Garber interview.

52. Gordon Post scrapbook.

53. JOHN KEATS, *Howard Hughes* (New York: Random House, 1966), p. 117.

54. "Round the World Flight Again," *Flight,* vol. 52 (August 14, 1947), p. 154.

Appendix

INFORMATION FROM POST'S PILOT RECORDS

W. H. Post

March 19, 1930 (born Nov. 22, 1898)
Age: 31
Weight: 155
Height: 5'5"
Brown hair
Brown eyes
September 15, 1930

706 W. 29th Street
Oklahoma City, Oklahoma

Department of Commerce
Aeronautics Branch
(Original lost prior to 1960)

Transport Pilot's License No. 3259 issued to Wiley Post
(cancelled November 20, 1934, reissued January 3, 1935)

Date	Interim Flight Hours Since Last Report	Total Flight Hours
9/15/31	160	3,100
3/15/32	400	3,500
9/15/32	14	3,514
3/15/33	235	2,749
9/15/33	116	3,865
3/15/34	275	4,140
9/15/34	85	4,225
6/30/35	50	4,275

POST'S THREE AIRPLANES

The three airplanes flown by Wiley Post during 1929–1935 had the following histories (information derived from FAA records and *Revolution in the Sky* by Richard S. Allen, The Stephen Greene Press, Brattleboro, Vermont, 1964).

Winnie Mae #1:

The first "Winnie Mae" was a Lockheed Vega completed on August 12, 1928, containing license number NC7954 (and NR7954). A Pratt and Whitney Wasp engine, Number 920, 420 horsepower, was installed. This airplane was about the fourth "Wasp-Vega" to come off the production line. It did not have an "approved Type Certificate." The award of an "ATC" was first made by the Aeronautics Branch of the Department of Commerce in 1927, but it took some time to get around to all of the companies (*U.S. Civil Aircraft, Vol. 1*, Joseph Juptner, Aero Publishers, Inc., Los Angeles, California, 1962).

These Vegas had a 41 foot wing span and a 102 inch chord at the wing root. The wing used a Clark Y-18 airfoil at the root and a Clark Y-9.5 airfoil at the tip. The wing had 275 square feet of area. The aircraft were 27 feet 8 inches long and stood 8 feet 6 inches high. They weighed 2,361 pounds when empty, and had a useful load of 1,672 pounds. The payload was 1,012 pounds. The gross weight was 4,033 pounds.

This early type Vega could cruise at 140 mph with a 170 mph top speed. It landed at 54 mph, and climbed at 1300 feet per minute. The ceiling was

20,000 feet. The fuel capacity was 96 gallons, with ten gallons of oil for the large nine cylinder engine. The range was 725 miles. In July of 1928, the factory price was $18,500.

The fuselage was put together by making two shell halves of laminated plywood. Each shell was shaped in a concrete tub mold. Circular wood formers were placed inside the fuselage.

The fuselage was fabric covered. The wings were made of spruce spars and spruce and plywood ribs. A plywood veneer, fabric covered, made up the outer wing. The tail was all wood.

Fuel tanks were placed in the wings, a metal propeller and wheel brakes were installed, and a starter using the inertia principle was standard.

F. C. Hall of Chickasha, Oklahoma, purchased Vega NC7954 in 1928 for $20,240, which included a special paint and lettering job. The airplane was named for Winnie Mae, Hall's daughter, and in 1929 was sold back to Lockheed. The name "Winnie Mae" was deleted.

Roscoe Turner named the airplane *Sirius* and flew it in the 1929 National Air Race. Nevada Airlines of Los Angeles bought the aircraft in 1929 and kept it until 1930. Wheel pants and a NACA cowl were used on the plane when Art Goebel flew it in the 1930 National Air Race (coming in second, behind Wiley Post in Hall's second "Winnie Mae" Vega). Goebel flew the airplane until 1936 when Laura Ingalls flew it from 1936 to 1941. Miss Ingalls had an accident in it in Albuquerque, August 11, 1941. She was unhurt, but the airplane was destroyed.

Winnie Mae #2:

In early 1930, a Vega model 5B was completed which was destined to hold license numbers NC105W and NR105W. F. C. Hall purchased this airplane from Lockheed in 1930 and again used the name "Winnie Mae". The airplane was white with purple and blue trim. It had a Pratt and Whitney engine, Number 3088, 420 horsepower. The airplane had ATC Number 227. All of Post's flying achievements between 1930 and 1935 were made in this airplane which is now on display in the Smithsonian Institution. Extensive modifications were made during its five years of flight.

Orion-Explorer:

Wiley Post and Will Rogers were killed in 1935 in an airplane that was hybrid in nature. During May of 1933, a low wing Lockheed Orion, Model 9E was completed, number NC12283 (and NR12283), with ATC Number 508. A Pratt and Whitney Wasp engine of 550 horsepower was used.

Transcontinental and Western Air of Kansas City bought the airplane in 1933 and flew it for about two years. In 1935 Charles Babb of Glendale, California, purchased the fuselage (Babb was an airplane broker). Babb also had purchased the wing to Lockheed Explorer, Model 7 (Special), number NR101W, manufactured in April of 1930 (this airplane had no ATC certificate). The Explorer was a low wing aircraft, similar to the Lockheed *Sirius* (a type used in the early 1930's by Lindbergh) but with wings about six feet longer than those of the *Sirius*. The Explorer noted above was designed especially for a non-stop Paris to New York City attempt to be made by Art Goebel. It had a gasoline capacity of 800 gallons and was named Yankee Doodle. For some reason Goebel didn't take the plane but Pure Oil Company did. The plane was renamed the Blue Flash, painted blue and white, and Roy Ammel planned to fly it to Paris or Rome from New York. It was damaged by a ground fire in Gila Bend, Arizona, in 1930, repaired at Lockheed, and then flown by Ammel non-stop to the Canal Zone from New York City (the first non-stop flight over this route). It was damaged in an accident on November 21, 1930 at Ancon, Canal Zone. The wing was salvaged and acquired by Babb.

Babb put the Orion fuselage and the Explorer wing together to form a "hybrid" airplane. The Lockheed Company did not like the idea. However, in the depression years, fast airplanes were scarce and expensive and this was one way to reincarnate one.

The hybrid airplane had a fixed landing gear, was painted red, and P and W Wasp engine S3H1 No. 5778 was installed. A three bladed variable pitch prop was used. Seaplane floats made by Edo were installed in Seattle. The float installation made the airplane nose-heavy due to forward displacement of the center of gravity.

The aircraft was damaged beyond repair in the fatal accident of Post and Rogers near Point Barrow, Alaska, on August 15, 1935.

The Explorer wingspan was 48 feet six inches (compared to the Orion and Sirius wingspan of 42 feet 9½ inches). The area of 313 square feet compared to 294.1 square feet for the Orion and 275 for the Vega. The Vega fuselage length of 27 feet six inches was the same as the Orion fuselage length as well as that of the Explorer.

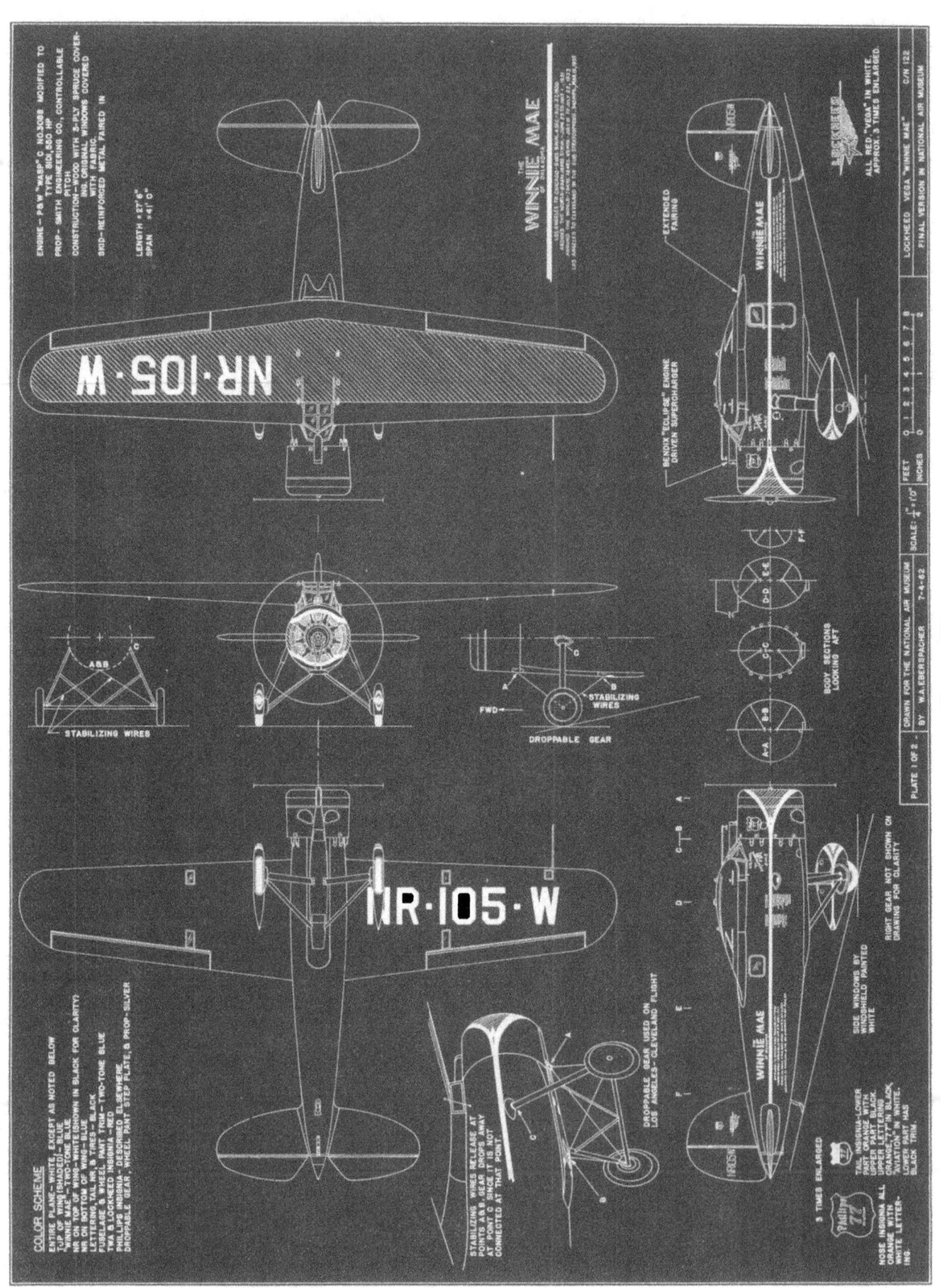

Figure 138

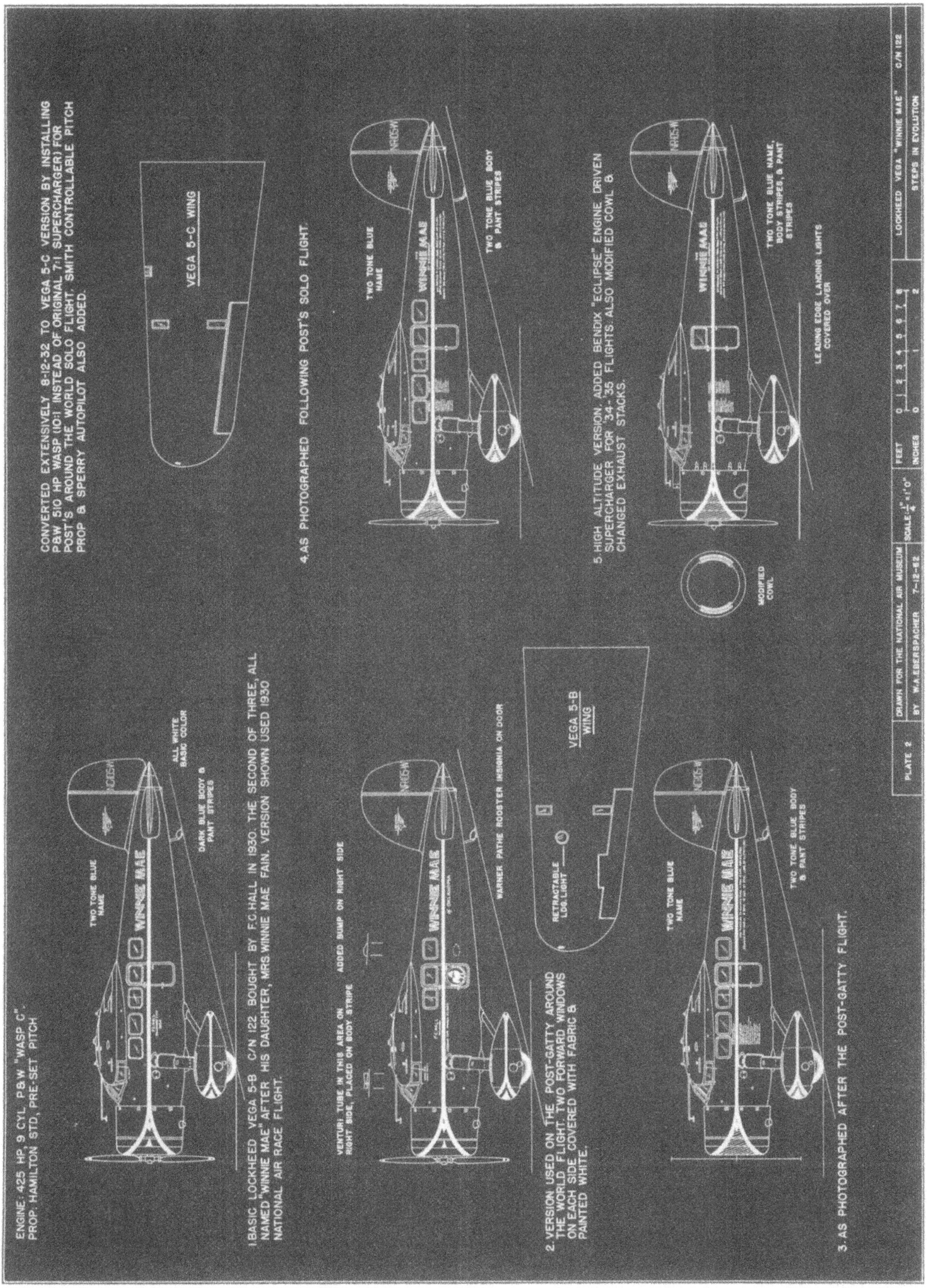

FIGURE 139

★ U.S. GOVERNMENT PRINTING OFFICE: 1971 O—443-665

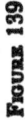

www.ingramcontent.com/pod-product-compliance
Lightning Source LLC
Chambersburg PA
CBHW080515110426
42742CB00017B/3129